The Earth on Which We Live

The Earth on Which We Live

The air that we breathe and the hidden causes of illness

Marijke Vogel, MH, MGNI

VOGEL AND VOGEL

Published by Vogel and Vogel
PO Box 3007, London NW3 2UZ
Copyright © 2001, by Marijke Vogel
ISBN 0-9540693-0-7

All rights reserved. This book is subject to the conditions that no portion of it may be reproduced or used in any form, or by any means, electronic or mechanical, including photocopying, recording or by any information storage and retrieval system without prior permission of the publishers. Neither shall it appear in any form of binding or cover other then that in which it was originally published.
It shall not be hired out or otherwise circulated without the publisher's or writer's prior written consent to include these conditions being imposed on the subsequent purchaser.

Courtesy photographs:
From the Peruvian Archives in Lima, at Prom Peru .
All photographs of the Clay eating Macaw birds.
The Cows, photograph, courtesy of the Soil Association

"Sacred Cows" photograph from a painting by Luciana Martinez de la Rosa,
with kind permission from the artist Duggie Field,
Curator of the estate of ; Luciana Martinez de la Rosa.

Drawings by: Ms Libby Lawry, on all pages: except Teela

Photographs by:
   Sebastian DuBois
   Sarah Munday
   The Writer
Front cover depicting the 5 elements. from a painting in oil on glass,
by Marijke Vogel. 1981.

Cover designed by Sebastian DuBois

Edited by Martin Noble, Oxford OX4 4ES www.copyedit.co.uk
Text design and typesetting by
John Saunders Design & Production, Reading RG8 8ER
Printed and bound in Great Britain by
Biddles Ltd. www.biddles.co.uk

This book is dedicated to the following:

To my parents and my children

To Dr Bernard Jensen (1908–2001) the most famous, most inspiring, spiritual and the longest living iridologist and nutritionist of our time. He reached the age of 93 in 2001 and still taught until 2000. We owe to him the iridology charts used by naturopaths all over the world, and his many books (over 60) on philosophy and lifestyle are an inspiration to all. I was lucky enough to receive Dr Jensen's teachings for which I will be forever grateful and he was kind enough to allow me to include his encouraging letter to me as the foreword to this book.

Contents

Preface xi

Foreword xiii

Introduction 1
    EM (effective micro-organism) technology 3

PART I THE HIDDEN FACTORS OF ILLNESS 7

1 **What went wrong?** 9
   Cows 9   Pigs 12   Chicken 13

2 **Fungus: the hidden cause of many ailments** 17
   Candida 17   Mycotoxins 18   *Candida* tips 20

3 **About teeth** 22
   TMJ 22   Mercury 24   Gums and chewing 24   Wisdom teeth 26

4 **Miscellaneous hidden factors** 27
   Childhood vaccinations 27   Meningitis C 28   'Flu injections 30
   Fluoride 30   Aspartame and saccharine 31   Sugar 33
   Monosodium glutonate (MSG) 34   Waxed fruits 34   Microwave cooking 34
   EMFs 35   Geopathic stress and gridlines 36   Feng shui 37
   Magnetic grid disruption 37   Catalytic converter 38   Tumble dryers 39

5 **Cancer** 40
   B17 and Laetrile 41   Factors involved in cancer development 44
   The breast cancer issue and pesticides 45   Cancer and candida 46
   Home therapy 46   The importance of organic foods 47
   Diet 47   Essiac 48   Most toxic foods 49   More positive approaches 49

6 **Parasites** 51
   Lack of minerals in our soil 52   How do you know if someone has
   parasites? 53   Types of parasites 53   Toxoplasmosis 58

How to get rid of them and prevent them returning 58
Herbal parasite treatment 59   More herbal treatments 60
The wild fox 61

7 **Mosquitoes and malaria** 62
Homoeopathic and herbal treatments 63   Dengue 64
Herbal treatments for Dengue: Quassia and Boneset 64

8 **Head lice** 66
Effective treatment 67

9 **Asthma** 69
Mental effects of asthma 69   Physical effects of asthma 70   Miasms 73
Specific herbs 74   The skin 74   Food for thought 76
Acidity and asthma 77   The elements 77   Yoga: the Sun Salutations 78
Kundalini yoga: Breath of Fire 80   Relaxation posture 80   Your voice 81
Kapalabathi 81   Ancient philosophy 82

10 **Depression** 83
The importance of a good mind 83   The importance of the thyroid 84
Factors that worsen the condition 85   28 rules for the body and soul 88
Health tips and general guidelines 90

PART II CLAY THERAPY 95

How the dust of the earth can help us miraculously restore our health and equilibrium

11 **We are born out of the dust (clay)** 95
Clay as a curative medium 95   Father Sebastian Kneipp 96
Animals, birds … and clay 96

12 **Back to nature** 102
Twelve things you should know about clay 103   Acidity 104
When clay is used internally 104   When clay is used externally 105

13 **The therapeutic actions of healing clay** 107

14 **Practicalities and chemical structure** 109
Storing 109   When to avoid using it 109   What should this clay look like? 109
Chemical structure 110   Radioactivity 110   Grey clay 111

15 **Trace minerals and their function** 112
The composition of fine green clay powder 112   CHONPS 113
Replenishing our Earth 116   The action of mineral elements found in clay 117
Problems with our ability to metabolise minerals 125

16 **Clay: quality and colours** 126
   The importance of quality 126   Composition of green clay 127

17 **As above, so below** 130
   Solar and lunar energy 130   Purifying the emotions 131
   Medicine and astrology 132

18 **Points to consider when using clay for the first time** 133
   The importance of particle size 133   Bentonite 134

19 **The power of clay** 135
   Enzymes in relation to clay 136   Bacteria 136

20 **How to make and apply a clay poultice** 139
   Utensils needed to prepare the poultice 142   Preparing the poultice 142

21 **How to prepare clay for drinking** 144
   Stage I 144   Stage II 144   Problems 144
   Beneficial for the intestinal flora 145   Cross-linking 145
   The importance of good water 145   BioCeramica 146

PART III A-Z GUIDE TO BETTER HEALTH 149

Abscesses 151   Acne 151   Allergies 152   Alzheimer's disease 152
Anaemia 153   Angina 153   Ankle, broken 154   Antiseptic 154
Asthma 154   Atherosclerosis 156   Arthritis 157   Baldness 158
Blood pressure, high 158   Blood pressure, low 159   Blood purifier 159
Brain health 159   Breasts 160   Breast feeding 161   Breast lumps 161
Bronchitis 162   Burns 162   Calcification 163   Canker sores 163
Catarrhal conditions 163   Cellulite 163   Chilblains 164   Chin (double or fatty) 165   Cholesterol 165   Coeliac disease 165   Congestion, leading to sluggishness 166   Constipation 166   Coughs, accompanied by a cold 167
Crohn's disease 168   Debility 168   Diarrhoea 169   Digestive problems 169
Diverticulitis, bowel pockets 170   Ear aches 170   Eczema 170   Eyes 171
Eye bags 172   Fever 172   'Flu 173   Foot care 173   Furuncle 173
Glandular fever, mononucleosis 174   Gum disease 174   Hair care: with clay 175   Halitosis 176   Hand care 177   Hangover 177   Headaches 177
Heavy metal poisoning, through amalgam fillings 178   Hypoglycemia (low blood sugar) 178   Impotence 179   Infections, viral or bacterial 180
Insect bites 180   Insomnia 182   Irritable bowel syndrome: IBS 182
Jetlag 183   Kidneys 183   Liver problems 183   Lymphatic congestion 184
ME (myalgic encephalomyelitis) 185   Menopause: the cessation of the female cycle 186   Menstruation 187   Mouth ulcers 188
Multiple sclerosis (MS) 188   Obesity: weight problems 189

Parkinsonism, a degenerative neurological disorder 190
Prostate congestion 191   Psoriasis 192   Raynaud's Disease 193
Rheumatism 193   Salmonella 194   Shingles 194   Sinus problems 195
Skin problems 195   Skin, slack 196   Sprains 196   Stones, gallbladder 197
Stones, kidneys 198   Throats, sore 198   Thyroid imbalance 198
Tonsillitis 199   Tooth abscess 200   Tumours 200   Urinary problems 200
Uticaria (hives) 201   Varicose veins 201   Verrucas 201   Whitlows 203
Wrinkles and ageing 203

Appendixes 207

1 **Cleansing** 207
2 **'How to's** 209
   A Make an infusion 209
   B Prepare an enema 209
   C Prepare mullein oil for the ears 210
   D Prepare garlic oil 210
   E Prepare ginger tea 211
   F Prepare lemon tea 211
   G Prepare a cabbage leaf poultice 212
   H Make your own barley or wheat-grass juice 212
   I Test your pH balance 212
   J Skin brushing with wood and bristle brush 212
3 **Note on high carbon foods** 214
4 **The elements** 214

Resources 215
   Suppliers, organisations and therapies 215

Recommended reading 231

Index 236

Preface

As we enter the twenty-first century, the world is changing drastically. Altered foods, new viruses, cloning, increasing chemical pollution, are but a few of the problems we face in the future. This book has been written over a period of 3 years, after much deliberating on how to deal with the problems of today and tomorrow.

It is also a response to the growing popularity of healing clay during the last 7 years, albeit only by word and mouth, I felt the need for this book to explain the miraculous way this simple substance can bring beneficial change and alleviate the symptoms in many health conditions.

I originally thought the book was just going to be about clay but, having just completed a long period of study and travel, it has considerably broadened in scope, to include all aspects of the adverse and negative conditions that affect us. We need all the help we can get.

My aim in writing this book is not to change your opinion about your diet or habits. My hopes are to give you some new ideas on how to remain naturally healthy and strong in our toxic world. I hope this book will be of help to those who suffer from long-term illness or the negative effects of drug-taking, and that some of the ideas in this book may help you to reduce or change some of the treatments on which you may have become dependent.

Remember, to take care of what you are putting into your body and your mind and always be sensible about your diet.

Note:
If you have health problems you are advised to seek the guidance of a qualified medical practitioner. This book is not in any way a substitute for any qualified medical treatment.

This statement is inserted as a caution and in some countries complies with their legal requirement. When dealing with health problems you are always recommended and advised to seek the guidance of a qualified medical professional. The author categorically states that there is no intention to advise, suggest or imply by information contained in this book that any substance or treatment referred to, will or can help prevent or alleviate any disease.

The author, her publisher and distributor accept no liability for any damages that may occur from the abuse of any information provided. This book explains what is available, what is being done and what can be done providing an alternative view on many situations and conditions.

Foreword

by the late Dr Bernard Jensen

Bernard Jensen International,
24360 Old Wagon Rd.
Escondido,
California 92027 USA

30 June 1999

Dear Marijke,

I was very happy to hear from you, and I might tell you I haven't any less feeling toward the using of clay in many of the ailments that man has. I found that the cataplasmic agent that it seem to have just helps to get the toxic material on the move and getting rid of it through one of our great elimination channels. That is the skin.

We have used a lot of clay on the internal parts of the body. This was introduced to me through the Luvos mud in Germany. I have seen many wonderful results. Here on the ranch we use Clay water along with our elimination process with wonderful bowel success.

I am glad to learn you are writing a book on clay. I do believe that it is probably one of the most universally used products when any of the natives became ill. I know Indians would go and sit in mud beside a stream to help haemorrhoidal conditions.

I know of people who have used clay for many purposes in the body. I might tell you I have had a lot of experiences with clay in my sanatorium. For instance, one lady had sprained her ankle, she couldn't walk. We packed her ankle with clay at night. The ankle was fine the next day. I have seen broken bones heal up very quickly, with the use of clay packs.

I have used it with many cases of arthritis: many patients received relief from this pain. A sterilised fine powder and diluted form of clay is a wonderful remedy for stomach ulcers. There are so many uses for clay because it has a cataplasmic agent that seems to draw out toxic materials and promotes the healing tremendously.

It gives me great pleasure to say that we should all become more acquainted with our planet, and especially clay. We can learn so much from the original natives who relied on clay for healing many ailments.

I wish you every success in your work with curative clay Marijke as well as your new book. Don't forget to get that clay out so more people can use it.

Sincere best wishes

Bernard Jensen Ph.D

Introduction

We constantly hear that in about twenty years from now nothing will ever be the same again. My daughter, who has a very clever and analytical mind, hates her science classes because her teacher tells her that in twenty years we're all going to die. The ozone layer will be depleted and we will all have to wear high-factor sun blocks. Oxygen and water will run out, and human existence will come to an end. We will not be able to drive cars any more and we will have run out of gas and other resources.

These are, of course, scientific theories which are not necessarily proven. The science teacher has a right to his opinion and if he wants he can get depressed about it, but he should understand the impact of these words on susceptible 13–14 year olds.

I agree that something will have to be done about many things. Traffic is out of hand and we only have to look at cities like Beijing and Lima to see what happens when there is really too much of it. We think we have a problem in London but compared to those cities it is nothing. At least in Europe we are taking measures to counteract the pollution. In Third World cities literally anything goes, there is absolutely no control, and that is where much of the problem (and pollution) lies.

Another really frightening factor is that we have already been subjected to genetically altered foods for quite some time and that not all shops and suppliers mention this. In Third World countries the use of genetically altered produce is even more widespread and yet hardly anybody there even knows it is happening.

I am glad to see that shops in the UK now have an obligation actually to state GM on the products that contain genetically modified foods. This gives the consumer a fair chance of avoiding it, although the writing on the package is so tiny that the fact that it is genetically modified is only discovered at home afterwards.

The problem is also that GM crops can spread their particles to other farmlands and so organic growers can be affected. There is also the danger of a disastrous diminishing of wild life and insects, which cannot survive in this artificially created environment.

The way to tackle this is *not* to buy the foods unless you know they have not been altered and they are organically grown. This is the only way you can make sure. If those foods don't sell, they will soon not be produced. Organic foods will become more widely available and as a result of competition the prices will go down.

It can't be very nice to be a young teenager and have this dismal picture as their future prospect. With all their enthusiasm for learning it does put a bit of a damper on them. It is no wonder that we see increasingly large numbers of young people hanging around the street, totally devoid of any motivation (not even bothering to go into school) and becoming involved in recreational drugs and crime. Here we have mental pollution. Which is worse and what is the original cause? Could it be what they are eating or breathing in – in other words, what they are absorbing?

It is of course a fact that the Earth on which we live is being damaged. It is very simple: we keep on reaping and do not replace any goodness. The use of chemical fertilisers and growth accelerators topped with pesticides – all of which go into our bodies and our children's bodies - has become prevalent.

People are no longer enjoying life the way they should, often lacking in zest and motivation, and are becoming dull and disinterested in what is going on. Children are being fed de-natured, de-mineralised foods and sweetened sparkling beverages, which make them lethargic or hyperactive and destructive.

There are of course other ways of dealing with life, if one can stop ignoring the numerous possibilities of how the world is going to end for a few minutes, and avoid keeping our heads in the sand/earth, as it were.

Fortunately it is not yet too late: we can and should save the Earth and thereby save ourselves. For example, on one of my study tours about four years ago I came across a substance from Japan that I know would make a huge difference to the way we grow food as well as improving the rearing of animals. I have tried it in my garden with amazing results and begged the Japanese gentleman to allow me to bring it to the UK. I was given the cold shoulder and I couldn't understand until later, when I got hold of a copy of the book written by the gentleman, Dr Teruo Higa (see Resources, p. 233).

Dr Higa was actually threatened with his life were he to attempt to promote the substance without Government approval, which may never be obtained. Just think of what is at stake here: we have these huge chemical fertiliser companies supplying several billions worth per year, as well as the manufactures of antibiotics, hormones, growth accelerators etc. which are indiscriminately given to our cows, pigs and chickens. Can you imagine the money involved here?

There are many other instances where similar situations have occurred. We only have to read the various alternative journals to discover how alternative practitioners have been prosecuted and jailed for providing patients with a cure for cancer or AIDS; or how the FDA have raided premises and taken files related to such research, with supplements confiscated and so on.

However what I'm discussing here is even beyond these cures and treatments. Alternative treatments can affect and prevent disease and works on both physical and spiritual levels; giving people joy and pleasure. Even very young children can be taught some of these ideas at nurseries.

EM (effective micro-organism) technology

The use EM (effective micro-organism) technology (which I also call 'the substance') offers the following potential advantages and benefits:

- It will help to produce quality foods that *advance* human health.
- It will be economically and spiritually beneficial to both producer and consumer.
- It is sustainable and easily practised.
- It respects and preserves nature.
- It will help to produce enough food to feed the world population.
- It helps in combating acid rain.
- It can be sprayed on to cow-dung etc. and combats disagreeable smells and so does not attract flies.
- It can be used to recycle toilet-waste, water and garbage.
- When sprinkled on to garbage it ferments and becomes compost.
- Air-filtration systems can be reduced and only used three hours a day instead of 24.
- Carpets regularly washed will have a reduced smell and attract less dirt.
- On chicken farms disease is reduced: they are sprayed with and fed with it; their waste in turn becomes good compost.
- Pigs are sprayed and fed with EM and have no smell; they are healthy and their waste matter is sold.
- Fruits, strawberries, string-beans etc. have a much better growth.
- Milk yields are increased without antibiotics.
- It can be used by mentally and physically disabled people, helping them gain confidence and making them truly useful members of society.
- Its use can easily be taught at nursery schools, making very young children understand about recycling and nature.
- It will help to reduce toxic fume emissions.
- It is a low-cost farming method that will reduce present farming costs by four-fifths (80%).
- It will help to produce safe, natural foods, with no need for anything artificial.
- It will treat polluted waters, such as lakes and ponds, reviving the flora and fauna.

This list only covers a fraction of the uses of EM. Where would the 'chemical giants' be if we started using something so natural and inexpensive that would make our vegetables, meats and fruits taste like they once did a long time ago, and make us healthy and alert as well? I don't think approval will ever be granted unless we vote for deep-thinking visionaries to run our countries.

It will take someone with a great deal of guts to take on the giants of industry, on which governments, of course, are reliant. But what is more important, if we really look ahead? Bush has children and Blair has children, they must want the best for their children's future just as I do. Why don't we ask them?

Ultimately on our Earth, everything that exists has the ability to deteriorate through oxidation, and collapse or die. The effect of anti-oxidation is to prevent oxidation of matter and living bodies. Human illness is due to an excess of oxidation of the molecules composing genes and a way of expressing malfunction. The desolation of farmland, the worsening environment, if looked at from a different standpoint, is a phenomenon of excess oxidation. Illness in animals, plants and humans, and the deterioration of matter, can also generally be understood as phenomenon of excess oxidation.

The new technology is not limited to one narrow field such as agriculture. Since EM suppresses excess oxidation, it eliminates them by generating anti-oxidants. And since it is composed of microorganisms, it has *multiple* uses. The ultimate goal of this technology is to construct a revived society, characterised by coexistence and co-prosperity.

With human population ever increasing, with a reduction of farming land and natural resources, and with increasing environmental problems, it is no wonder that many of us see our future with pessimism. People generally think that even though coexistence and symbiosis may be possible, especially for solving our problems, mutual prosperity is not. We must therefore solve our problems from the very root of society and construct a society where poverty, sickness and conflicts have no chance of developing.

Before humanity created civilisations and the human populations exploded, the Earth had developed the function to recover from entropy, take in the unlimited amount of energy from space, and continue to evolve without limits and with abundance, the results of which are; oil, coal, diverse minerals as well as plant and animal resources.

It appears that the humanity today has become detrimental to the Earth's evolution. We are building without restraint, using up and discarding an enormous amount of resources, creating an enormous amount of pollution and waste. We are becoming a *burden* to the planet, contradicting the natural evolution of our Earth. Global warming is real and a grave danger.

If these conditions of severe pollution and oxidation continues to worsen, we are heading for an environment where there will be a proliferation of harmful viruses and micro-organisms that will become stronger and stronger, making the environment further polluted and causing outbreaks of disease-carrying insects and incurable diseases which indeed *endanger all higher life forms*. And this is already taking place.

If and when the use of this technology becomes widely accepted, we will notice a change: the staggering expense of dealing with waste and water problems will be reduced. EM also has the capability of recycling plastic, rubber, paper and textiles at low costs, and high-quality recycled product have begun to be made from these.

A ceramic type of this technology can be made from such things as burnt coal ash, and blast furnace ash. In an anti-oxidant condition, carbon dioxide absorption by the micro-organisms is several tens of times faster than by terrestrial plants, and the conversion of natural resources is easier. The ability to harvest several times from the same farmland is really the same as being able to convert several times the carbon dioxide in foods and by the same proportion also cleaning the environment.

If the anti-oxidant substance is mixed into plastic bags and rice cultivated with it, this rice would remain fresh for up to five years. This technology can benefit the processing of agricultural, livestock, and fisheries products and improve various foods to maintain their freshness.

Looking at this on a global scale, with the technology naturally preserving our food supplies, it would not matter if there was a year where the harvest was poor. High-quality foods would be available all over the world, thereby solving our food problems.

The substance has begun to be used in construction and road building. Just adding 1% of powder to the cement mix, the surface active strength increases significantly and water clusters become smaller. The cement dries faster and what used to take 25–30 days is reduced to 3–4 days. The cement reinforcements will not rust and the lifespan of structures will increase several times beyond what it is now.

This application can also be used when restoring old historic buildings by high-pressure injection of the anti-oxidant substances. It can thereby also reduce termite infestation and rot.

The whole environment can only benefit from this technology and it is possible to create what the Japanese call *Iyashiro Chi* (meaning a place where everything is geared towards longevity, durability, health and so on).

At low cost, complete rust prevention technology, various mining and manufacturing commodities have begun to show the remarkable effects of the deterioration prevention of the technology. Fuel efficiency has been shown to increase by more then 50% and, due to the prevention of rust, electric lines have also been shown to increase in capacity.

Where our health is concerned, the immune system can be reinforced, and accordingly genes are able to self-restore to normal functions. For most incurable diseases treatment has been inadequate. Now there is hope: there are several reports confirming the effectiveness of the technology on combating these illnesses. There is also a form of this technology which can be used internally and acts as an internal anti-oxidant, helpful in sclerotic disease processes and the general effects of ageing.

From this short summary of the benefits of the substance, if it is applied everywhere, there is a limitless possibility of reducing the world's waste to nearly zero. See Suppliers (p. 220) for more information on where to order and obtain EM and EMX (a powerful anti-oxidant for internal use), in liquid or powder form in the US and Spain.

It is possible to obtain EM in various European countries, but at present it is not available in the UK. The good news is that large projects involving EM have recently started to take place, in countries such as The Netherlands, Spain, France, Denmark, Austria, Central America, Colombia, Ecuador, and Peru.

Natural clay

Clay is another little-known substance that can make a difference to our health albeit on a smaller scale). Part II is mainly concerned with the way a lack of minerals affects our mental and physical health. It describes the usefulness of clay and also covers the use of herbal and nutritional supplements to combat disease.

PART I The Hidden Factors of Illness

1 What went wrong

Cows

To get an idea of what has gone wrong on this planet and of some of the problems that currently affect us, we need look no further than the poor old cow.

These harmless animals that were once peaceful vegetarians have for the last two to four decades been fed substances that are not fit for them: ground up sheep-brain and fish-meal among others, even sewage according to the latest reports from one country in Europe.

They have been painted with 'organophosphate' along their spine and brain as soon as they are born or imported from abroad. This is a poison and insecticide that affects the balance and kills the brain cells of the animal slowly. In several cases the cows have grown so large through their diet, that their feet and legs cannot support their weight. They have therefore been given special wooden supports to hold them up and to keep them semi-alive while they are still able to produce large amounts of milk. Their health is in complete decline. They have no exercise, they are diseased and have tumours and mucous. And at the end of this miserable existence they are killed and eaten.

I don't think that eating the meat or drinking the milk from such an unhappy animal with such an awful life could nourish or benefit anyone. It is no wonder we now have BSE or 'mad cows disease'. It is nature's way to draw attention to this wrongdoing. It's payback time.

Humans who have eaten the tainted meats are susceptible to 'variant CJD' (Creutzfeldt-Jacob Disease) which is a fatal brain disease for which there is no cure. In 1996 one in every 50 cows was affected. The disease is thought to have originated from infected sheep's brain which since the early 1980s was routinely given to the cow as well as offal from other animals and also included their own ground-up, left-over waste and cattle parts.

The disease is associated with a protein called prion, which can be transmitted from infected sheep to cattle, from cattle to humans. It affects the brain, which turns into a sponge with holes in it. Brain scans on affected patients show lesions and plaque, which gradually worsen, affecting the balance and speech; the ability to eat normally is also reduced. Other symptoms are depression, mood swings etc.

Prion is a type of protein found normally in mammals and birds' brains. It does no harm and is neutralised by the body's enzymes. Abnormal prions, however, are quite resistant to the body' immune system. For example, they are so strong they can survive a boiling temperature's of 212 °F. When found inside the body they clump together, becoming lesions and hardened tissue, which begin to attack the nervous system. When the meat eaten is infected with abnormal prions, it is thought that they destroy the normal prions and over a period of time will destroy the nervous system.

The first case of human vCJD transmission to a new-born baby girl has just been preliminarily diagnosed, born to a mother in her twenties with vCJD in November 1999. This is a very worrying situation. Scientist already knew that the disease could be transmitted to calves and lambs, but had hoped this did not apply to human beings.

Dr Richard Lacey, a British doctor, recognised the link between the cow and the human being and tried to warn the government years before the first BSE case showed up in 1986. He believes the source is still entering the food supply even now. The average incubation period for cud is estimated to be 25–30 years, which means that we could be expecting an epidemic around 2015. Let us hope we will have found a treatment by then.

Certainly not everyone that has eaten tainted meat will be susceptible. From our naturopathic understanding it is more likely to affect those whose diet is generally compromised and who have a deficiency in their digestive processes due to excess consumption of protein and fast foods, too much sugar, fizzy drinks etc. – all highly acid-forming. Lacking the ability to digest is due to a malfunctioning and overloading of the small intestines and the pancreas which are not able to release the enzymes needed, due to the above diet.

Maybe some farmers will have learnt from this terrible experience and go back to natural farming methods. The waste from the animals that they have had to incinerate by their thousands is also a worry, and unless the waste is treated it will pollute our Earth even more. Meanwhile the cows that did not have BSE are continuing to be bred, and produce the milk we give our children, hoping that they will grow strong bones because we are told that we need calcium from this source.

Cow's milk is not meant for humans but for baby cows. I don't think the calves get it and if they are lucky only for a few short days. They will also then be fed whatever it is their mothers are eating.

Milk is an anaemia producing food. (Bernard Jensen)

Most of us don't realise that we do not need milk to get calcium. We get an abundance of calcium from our organic vegetables, grains and pulses.

1.1 'Happy cows', *courtesy of the Soil Association.*

BGH /BST: bovine growth hormone

Our nursing cows are injected with bovine growth hormones (BGH or BST, Bovine somatropin). It is injected in the cow to increase her milk production by 20%. By doing this, the problem of udder infections is increased and so is the need for antibiotics, which will end up in the milk we drink. Because BST is naturally found in cow's milk there is no scientific way to find out if it has come from synthetic, or natural sources. Additionally other foods such as pizza, baked goods, chocolate, restaurant and fast food may also contain BGH tainted dairy or meat products. We will only know that our food is BGH free if our shops display the fact in their windows. In 1994 Europe, Australia and New Zealand were not using BGH. We are not sure whether this is still the case as large quantities of the stuff have been exported from the States.

Recent studies have revealed that milk from cows injected with BST increase risk of breast and colon cancer in humans. The study summarises evidence that BGH increases insulin-like growth factors (IGF) in milk, which is a powerful stimulator and regulator of cell growth and division in humans and cows. The study states that increased levels of IGF exert their cancer-promoting effects directly on the cells lining the colon and on the cells of the breasts after absorption in the blood.

There is no federal legislation in the US, apart from Los Angeles where several district have directed their milk suppliers to be BGH free. It is not possible to know how BGH will affect the human race. Experiments on rats caused them to have enlarged feet, jaws, toes, nose and fingers.

It is obviously better, if you are uncertain whether your milk contains BGH, that you substitute organic milk, goats', rice or almond milk – or don't drink milk at all: the famous child physician, Dr Benjamin Spock stated at a meeting for Physicians for Responsible Medicine during a TV talk show in the US in 1993 that it was no longer necessary to feed your child cow's milk.

Bovine Aids (BAV) virus

A study in the US indicates that 40% of cattle is infected with BAV. In cattle Aids impairs the immune system in the same way as it does in humans. But, according to the USDA, Bovine Aids cannot infect humans only other animals.

Bovine papilloma virus

A study revealed that this could be a causative agent for cervical cancer; it is thought that the virus is transmitted through the presence of warts in milk. Many cows' udders are covered in warts and many farmers have since attempted to eradicate these diseases.

Another sad factor is that male calves are as a rule terminated within 2–3 weeks of birth. They are considered of no use as they yield very little meat, and they do not yield milk. The farmer is paid for each termination. The calves die under very miserable conditions and with unnecessary cruelty and are mostly sent abroad for this purpose.

Pigs

In 1999 reports from Holland and Belgium, told us about a very strange pig disease called 'pigs pest' that has struck large herds of pigs and piglets and which has even spread to some parts of Britain. It is highly contagious and if someone has walked

1.2 A happy pig.

on the terrain of such a diseased farm and goes on to visit the next farm the germ or virus will be on the soles of the shoes and that way carried around spreading the disease. These little pigs have had to be killed in their thousands.

The demand for hams and bacon is huge in Europe, particularly in Germany. The strangest thing is that here in Britain we have heard nothing of this awful news, whereas when BSE was first discovered it was worldwide news and the sale of British beef was prohibited abroad for quite some time.

Perhaps we are now eating contaminated hams and bacon without knowing. This is another good reason to steer well away from any meat, unless you know where it is produced and how. I don't think one country is better than any other in rearing these animals. Short cuts and savings are applied worldwide, to increase profits and to meet the demand of the public for cheap meat.

Chickens

From my childhood in Holland, I have idyllic pictures of myself and my brother and sister running around on local country farms where my father used to buy fresh eggs, fresh goat's-milk and honey, once a week. We were allowed play on the farm and help with the animals and feed the chickens, grains from big pales that had a nice smell and colour.

The chickens were friendly and were quite free to go where they pleased. Once in a rare while my parents would get a chicken from the farms and my mother would cook it in her special Dutch way. They were a special treat and delicious.

Now chickens are mass-produced and a normal part of everyday diet. There are not many chickens left that have the type of existence I remember as a small girl. Chicken is a very popular meat, often preferred and recommended by nutritionists and doctors as an alternative to red meat as it has less fat. It is less fattening and less threatening to the heart patient, and one imagines provides the sort of the protein that people want. Recent reports, however, state that one in ten chickens is infected with *salmonella* or other bugs.

1.3 The author as a child on a Dutch farm.

The sale of chicken in Britain is phenomenal. Because of the BSE scare demand has increased even more. A reported £1.65 billion per year is spent by shoppers on chicken, and poultry amounts to two-fifths of the consumption of meat in Britain. Whereas a generation ago it used to be a luxury, Marks & Spencer sells 2 million birds per week. Safeway sells 70 million birds per year, with an estimated 11–13% contaminated with *salmonella*.

The life of a chicken is very miserable indeed: from the moment they are born, they are filled with germs, bacteria and inhaled faecal dust, from competitive fighting and henpecking. They have gout caused by mycotoxins in their food, which is very painful. They are riddled with cancer, hormones and fungus, and have been fed anything but the grains, which they need and should have.

They are one of the carriers of *salmonella*, and *E. coli* - diseases which can be fatal if not treated promptly. Three-quarters of chicken meat is full of *campylo* bacteria, and one-quarter is *salmonella* bacteria. Turkey has 34 % of *campylo* bacteria, and 23% *salmonella*.

Research by the Dutch Consumer Federation states that consumption of this meat by the human population represents a grave danger to public health. During a random test on four chicken fillets they found an abnormal amount of bacteria as well as antibiotics. Every year at least 50–100 people die from *salmonella* poisoning and about 9.5 million people become very ill from *salmonella* and other bugs.

A register of cases of *salmonella* poisoning kept in the USA until 1994, when government forced its closure due to cutbacks, registered up to 1 million Americans affected by the common strain *Salmonella enteritidis* in that year. Many people fall ill every year from the less well-known *campylo* bacteria. The symptoms are stomach cramps, diarrhoea, fever and vomiting.

In 1961 green clay was tested on 35 patients in a New York hospital suffering from the above symptoms – food poisoning, diarrhoea and mucous colitis etc. Relief was obtained in 34 of the 35 tested. The virally affected had relief in as short a time as 24 hours.

Chicken farms spend up to $6 million or more each year on bacteria killing substances, adding further toxins, but they have no success. The problem is caused by faulty production methods: the chickens are bred one on top of another and if one gets an infection the whole lot is affected.

Really and truly, if kindness to animals was given as liberally as the crap they are given, you would see a change in the animals, their behaviour and the way they taste. People have lost the ability actually to taste food. It is eaten in large, fast gulps and swallowed down with beer or cola, and nobody even really appreciates the animal that is being eaten at all. It has become a habit food which is fast and easy.

In the abattoir, the birds are put on a conveyer belt, one after another and if one has *salmonella* they are also all affected. It spreads so easily. The problem is increased by the enormous popularity of chicken as a food (it is promoted as a non-fattening form of protein in the beauty magazines). Public demand is enormous and it makes a nice income for the farmers.

They are now considering subjecting the chickens to radioactive rays as the only way to abolish the bacteria. Until this is approved and you cannot imagine life without chicken, please overcook and avoid raw eggs. Well, you know how I would feel about these radioactive rays.

I am sure you remember the terrible chicken 'flu that struck Hong Kong – the news spread across the world just after Christmas in December 1997. This 'flu first appeared in March 1997 when chickens started dying on a farm in a rural area near Yuen Long. From there it spread to other nearby farms. It was caused by the virus H5N1 and at first only affected the chicken, but by December that year through scientific research in Hong Kong and countries such as Holland, the US and Japan, they found that this same virus had also spread to humans.

Some people, including young children, died within days of catching the 'flu virus. There was a severe panic and this is when the decision was taken to destroy all the chickens in Hong Kong. The chicken farmers lost everything.

Of course we know that this 'flu pandemic began much earlier: in fact it was in 1918 that many people died all over the world. It was known as Spanish Flu and in Philadelphia alone 7,500 people died in a matter of weeks. Altogether they reckon some 600,000 people died of this 'flu in the US. In India it was as many as 15 million and worldwide deaths probably reached 40 million.

In an even more recent scandal it has emerged that what the British public buys as British chicken is in fact fowl imported from Taiwan and parts of South America. Apparently as much as 20% of chickens are flown in from Third World producers. Their premises and conditions are not checked or controlled and the standards are poor and dirty.

In Britain the life of a chicken is certainly not much better, apart from better standards of hygiene and checks on the so-called 'well-being' of the animals, as governmental control is exercised regularly. The conditions under which the animals live in these countries don't even bear thinking about. I have visited some of these establishments in Peru and it was a horrific sight with much cruelty. Because of corner-cutting measures, the price of these chickens is lower then Europe's, and hence their popularity for export.

Chickens would have a good life if they were left free to roam and were given the grains I remember from my childhood, they had a better chance of staying healthy and tasty. Lets hope the farmers realise this soon and that this mass production is stopped.

Look for organic, free-range poultry, and remember that it is always wisest to overcook rather than undercook. At present *salmonella*-induced illness costs the medical establishment a small fortune. The other bug, the *campylo* bacteria, is responsible for over half the cases of reported food poisoning.

I believe it would be simpler, again, to avoid meat, or find out he source of the product. Meanwhile you will gain a lot more from a bowl of brown rice, although I realise that this is easy to say but not so easy to follow, as rice is not nearly as interesting for most of us as eating meat.

But why not keep a couple of chickens in your back yard?

End note; as this book goes to press we are in the midst of the terrible foot and mouth crisis in Britain. It is a sad time for farmers and animals. So much has been written in the press, I do not know what to say except that it is a disaster for all of us. Vegetarian and meat eater alike.

The way the animals are butchered and burned and buried is all so wrong for our earth.

The repercussions will be felt not only by the farmers and the army drafted in to do the culling. But will effect so much more. These are negative vibrations put out into our universe.

In the 1920s when there was an outbreak of FMD in my country Holland , the animals were kept indoors and treated and cared for as if they had 'flu which really is all it is, their ulcers would be swabbed with antiseptic herbal solution and they would not produce much milk while they were ill and after about 3 weeks they would be fine, perhaps one or 2 cows would die from it but they were mostly the elderly cows.

Now many cows, sheep and goats have been slaughtered just in case, many of them were perfectly healthy. The younger animals with stronger immune systems were unlikely to be affected.

Unfortunately even some of our organic farmers were unable to escape the reinforced culling. Their hard work and goodwill has just gone to waste. It will take ages to restore their life-stock and many farmers may have to give up

From this latest crisis it must be clear that a change in production methods is essential and transportation of lifestock to other European countries must be stopped. Within weeks the first case was found in Holland followed by isolated cases in various other countries. The way the animals have been fed has already been discussed and the ground up waste that they are given from restaurant leftovers known as 'SWILL' and so on must not be allowed to continue. You cannot give them meat they are vegetarians. These peaceful animals must be respected, just look into their eyes if you have a chance.

Let us hope that this latest crisis will help to bring about positive change in the whole process of meat production.

2 Fungus: the hidden cause of many ailments

Candida

Some of the symptoms of fungal-related disorders are: undiagnosed depression, hay fever, memory loss, bloated stomach, vaginal itching, thrush, chronic diarrhoea, mouth ulcers, inability to cope, lethargy, asthma, menstrual problems. It can even prevent ovulation and thus lead to sterility in women.

We all have some 200 species of friendly bacteria living in our gut, about $3^{1}/_{2}$ lbs altogether, including *Candida*, which should constitute 10–15% of our normal intestinal flora. The balance should be maintained by the friendly bacteria, which keep the *Candida* in check by competing for food. The job of the *Candida* bacteria is to process and keep a check on sugars, starches and muco-proteins.

If an overgrowth of bad bacteria, including *Candida*, glutinous waste, mucous etc., is allowed to build up, sticky deposits will start to adhere to the bowel wall, which will cause a malabsorption of nutrients. So that even if one were to adopt a perfect diet it would not make any difference until the problem is taken care of.

Candida can invade any and every organ if allowed to go unchecked. It co-exists alongside other diseases such as herpes, eczema and athlete's foot. Someone with advanced cancer may have as much as 100% *Candida* and other parasites in the GI tract. This does then not leave any room for any beneficial bacteria. Research has shown that *Candida* is present in many degenerative illnesses, such as:

- MS
- rheumatoid arthritis
- schizophrenia
- cerebral palsy
- HIV
- ME
- allergies
- asthma
- cancer

Candida does no harm unless it gets out of control and is too abundant. This can be caused by:

- excess stress;
- antibiotics;
- certain medical drugs;
- radiation or chemotherapy;
- surgery;
- catheter feeding;
- steroids;
- underlying inherent or acquired deficiency in the immune system through continued onslaught by *Candida*;
- excess of sugar in the blood, such as with diabetics;
- contraceptive pill;
- changes of acidity in the stomach due to convenience foods disturbing the pH balance;
- poor nutrition: an excess of carbohydrate, which feeds the *Candida*, or a diet of foods rich in yeast or moulds;
- drugs and alcohol;
- living in damp accommodation where fungi and mould spores can trigger the *Candida*;
- pregnancy;
- infancy, if the mother has candida the child can pick it up during birth if mother's genital area is affected; the child could have mouth blisters or oral thrush;
- old age when the immune system can decline;
- deficiency of immuno-globin A;
- tap water laden with pesticides or high levels of chlorine;
- being run down;
- extreme emotional shock.

Candida produces a type of alcohol (acetaldehyde) and other poisons, which can lead the sufferer to appear to be drunk, lethargic or mentally slow.

Mycotoxins

Recent findings have shown there are several hundred mycotoxins (from the Greek word *myke* which means fungus) coming from foods and responsible for a whole host of illness, including candida. More are being discovered daily.

A newspaper article in the *Independent* (1998) concerned a fungus that eats meat (your flesh). Another describes the effect of intensive salmon fishing, the fish ending up with fungus all over their skin. You can imagine if you eat this fish it might have a similar effect on you.

Mycotoxins first came to the attention of scientists in 1961, when an epidemic of unusual liver cancer struck Africa, affecting a sizeable 15% of the population. Investigators found a connection between sufferers and their ingestion of mouldy peanuts infested with a fungus called aflatoxin. It was found that when this same food was given to animals, it caused the same liver cancer.

Since then scientists have discovered the existence of several hundred more mycotoxins. *The Chemical Dictionary* (Thieme Verlag, Stuttgart), has the following to say about aflatoxins:

> From the culture of certain moulds arise isolated metabolic by-products, which as Mycotoxins are the strongest natural poisons and carcinogenic. The fungus *Aspergillus flavus*, which infests peanuts and cereals like maize, rice and bread, produces eight aflatoxins.

Yeast moulds thrive in moist environments; the other type of yeast mould, called dermatophytes, likes a drier environment. Both these mycoses can only survive in an acid medium. As soon as the pH level drops the chance of their developing increases. (read more about pH in Part II).

Intestinal mycosis is quite rife. Add to this the foods that encourage yeast growth – sugar, fruit juices, ice cream, lemonade etc. – and it is not surprising that mycosis is epidemic. In Germany at least 7000 people die of mycosis-related illnesses each year.

Today, these fungi can be found in all the organs and the brain. When the lungs are affected by mycosis, diagnosis is invariably unspecified pneumonia or bronchitis. When chronic, the survival rate for this condition is low; the condition is not helped by the antibiotics, which are prescribed for the problem, as they will help the yeast to grow. Unless the problem is addressed mycosis could become a type of plague. It is essential for orthodox medicine to face up to these conditions. Some skin specialists may work with this problem but it concerns a much wider field.

When the cause of the fungal-related disorder is established it is important to avoid those foods that exacerbate the condition. Until the condition is improved, these foods can than be introduced again slowly, provided the main culprits are omitted indefinitely. The known offenders are:

- peanuts;
- mushrooms;
- maize and oats (mould has been found in 55–60% maize, 40% oats, mostly caused by wrong storage and lack of hygiene in the harvesting);
- foods that are made with wheat and yeast;
- some beans, alcohol and certain cheeses.

Avoid the following for up to four weeks:

- all products containing yeast;
- all refined foods;
- stimulants;
- orange juice;
- sugar;
- cheese;
- vinegar;
- pickles;
- alcohol;
- mushrooms;
- yeasted bread;
- peanuts;
- all nuts unless self-hulled and fresh (not too many as the oil in nuts is too rich);
- pasta.

If you have felt any benefit you may consider omitting these for a longer time and slowly re-introduce what you cannot do without.

Candida tips

- Eat lots of garlic with raw or steamed vegetables or take garlic oil capsules.
- Low animal fats but have some white fish if meat is desired.
- Drink Lapacho tea (Brazil).
- Vegetable juices, celery and parsley.
- Linseed oil capsules or freshly ground seeds: 2 teaspoons daily or 3 capsules.
- Psyllium husks: 2–3 tablespoons daily in water or diluted juice, between meals for up to 10 day periods.
- Supplement with acidophilus and bifidobacterium, at least 1 billion viable organisms per daily dose. Only use the higher quality product, which needs refrigeration and has a use-by date, otherwise it will not be of the standard needed to bring results and you are wasting time and money.
- Use live goat's yoghurt, which contains acidophilus.
- Drink green clay twice daily: 1 teaspoon in a glass of water (for periods of 6 weeks).
- Take Mycropyl from Biocare.
- Oxypro drops from Biocare.
- Take Can 1 or Can 2 from Nutriscene for 2–3 months.
- Aloe vera juice.
- High-fibre diet, millet, oat bran, brown rice, buckwheat, spelt, corn.
- Cooked egg yolks.
- Nuts and seeds soaked overnight.
- Sprouted seeds.
- Brassica vegetables, such as cabbage, kale, turnips, broccoli, cauliflower, radishes, mustard, preferably steamed.
- Vitamin C 2–3g daily (at least 1g is used up, without any trouble by anyone living in a big city).
- Selenium, zinc, magnesium.
- Essential fatty acids, high GLA.
- Pancreatic enzymes.
- Deepwater fish. (Ie, orange roughy)
- L Arginine.
- Green clay is very effective (see Part II).
- Grapefruit seed extract, which is also effective against intestinal parasites.
- Kolorex, a new very effective product, in capsules for candida, as well as a Kolorex cream for fungal conditions such as athlete's foot (actually clears long-standing conditions). Available from Noma (practitioners only) or the Nutri Centre (see Resources, p. 227).
- Infectoclear (a combination of grapefruit seed extract, Propolis, low-odour organic garlic, wormwood, cloves and cayenne) is a highly recommended product, available from Regenerative Nutrition (see Resources, p. 228).

Fungus: the hidden cause of many ailments

- Zell-oxygen (resources)
- It is OK to eat fruits providing they are not overripe.
- Take only milk that is lactose free, such as Rice-dream or sheep's milk.
- Herbs that will benefit Candida are:

  From South America:
  - Lapacho or Pau d'Arco from Brazil, in capsules or powder.
  - Una de Gato, from Peru in capsules, powder or tea bags.

  followed by:
  - *Berberis vulgaris*;
  - echinacea;
  - garlic;
  - cranberry (powder available without sugar from 'Biocare');
  - golden seal;
  - liquorice;
  - sage, rich in anti-candida compounds – drink sage tea or use as a douche;
  - poke root;
  - oregano;
  - olive leaf extract – this is one of the latest well-researched herbs effective for the condition; available in capsules (enquire from Tigon Ltd. or the Nutri Centre; see Resources, pp. 227, 229).

> **Note**
> The above are suggestions which may be helpful in candida treatment, you may wish to try one or two of the remedies to see what works best for you, in conjunction with the necessary dietary adjustments.

3 About teeth

TMJ

When we have a problem with our teeth various organs of the body can be affected. Regular check ups are therefore a necessity.

However, a little-known syndrome that can affect our health is TMJ (Temporal Mandular disorder). This can be a hidden illness: it is a problem of the jaw being out of line and is a disorder which is very difficult to diagnose. Once it has been diagnosed, though, a dentist can create a special appliance which has to be worn for a while, often with good results. A visit to a cranial osteopath is also a good idea as spinal misalignment can also be a cause.

One way to find out whether you have this problem – which can be the cause of severe to excruciating headaches, stomach problems, digestive upset, through a lack of enzymes, parasites etc. as well as Candida – is as follows:

1. Put your front teeth together. The line of the top two front teeth should be in line with the bottom two front teeth (don't worry if it's only slightly out of line).
2. Put your finger in your ears and open your mouth widely, then close and open your mouth several times. If you hear a lot of creaking and crackling you may have the problem.
3. See a good dentist if you suspect this could be a problem.

I know a person who has been suffering for over two years from excruciating headaches, and despite my advice on various remedies and treatments, no cure could be found for the poor fellow. The osteopaths and acupuncturist and herbalist put it down to his stressful executive lifestyle. He spent a fortune on weekly sessions with them and was about to go to a neurologist for a brain scan when I had dinner with him and suggested he might be suffering from TMJ.

'What on earth does that mean?' he said.

I explained it to him and also how it could come about and even get worse. It is caused by various types of trauma to the head, from falling on the head, to being punched, or playing rugby or other rough sports which could involve the use of the head. It could also occur when receiving general anaesthetics. Here the mouth is wrenched open and various tubes are stuffed down the throat. If there is already a weakness this can then be made worse. There are only so many traumas the jaw will take and when it has reached its limit this will show itself in different forms.

He followed up on my advice and my suggestion was confirmed by the results of the Vega machine and the skilled person behind it. He has now consulted a dentist who specialises in this field and is well on the way to a recovery.

Note, according to Peter Bartlett, a well-known osteopath, based in London's Hale Clinic, the major link is in the vagus nerve, situated in the neck. Problems could be due to injury in the neck, bad posture or a curved spine. If this nerve is pinched anywhere it will effect everything. Sorting out this problem first, with osteopathic manipulation or McTimoney chiropractic treatment, is recommended.

A TMJ disorder influences the chemistry, the fight/flight response etc. Physical therapy, corrective exercises, e.g. Pilates, yoga, Alexander technique, are essential in the recovery. Often seen are:

- defensive posturing;
- rounded shoulders;
- not opening up to the world, which will make sufferers sicker;
- injury, perhaps to the neck or head;
- spine distorted beyond belief without any particular symptoms;
- air-sickness, associated with acidosis;
- pH imbalance;
- infections – physical cause of acidosis.

Other suggested remedies are:

- considering where and how patients sleep and adjusting sleeping arrangements;
- homoeopathic treatments;
- paying attention to living environment – maybe an ionizer could be installed.

Care must be taken of the low bearing joints, voluntary (controlled) and involuntary action of grinding the teeth at night. There may also be lymph system problems and dental work must be carried out with a lot of awareness.

When the dentist fits the appliance it is important for the patient to be standing with both feet on the ground as, due to the 'short leg syndrome' (one leg shorter then the other, quite common), the fitting can be incorrectly measured when the patient is lying down in the dentist chair. This is due to an imbalance in the pelvis, which changes the position of the jaw. The body needs to re-adapt.

A helpful herb is Ginkgo Biloba extract (up to 6 capsules daily). This herb has received more and more recognition as an aid to the circulation to the head and to help with concentration and memory. The pain will to be much less taking these. Aim at about 120mg standardised extract daily.

Mercury

Talking about dentists, it is a good idea for those of you with mercury fillings to get an opinion on how your mercury levels are affecting your health as mercury is another cause of hidden illness. It is now easier to find mercury free dentistry in Britain.

Mercury poisoning can affect the immune system, causing chronic fatigue syndrome in certain individuals, and also depression and conditions such as MS and arthritis. There are now dentists that do their own mercury testing or you can consult your nearest Vega practitioner (see Resources, p. 229).

Mercury (amalgam) fillings can be a major cause of poison accumulating in the tissues. It is a strong poison before it is put into your teeth. Old mercury fillings give off a vapour and accumulate in various organs in the body, including the colon. If and when you decide to have these fillings removed and replaced with the white fillings, it is helpful to go on a course of clay drinking for 3–6 months afterwards. This will help chelate any residue out of the system. You can use:

- superfine green; very fine green or superfine white clay – 1 teaspoon twice daily in water; or
- apple pectin powder – 1 teaspoon twice daily in diluted apple juice, for 10 days per month.

> **Note**
> Make certain, before your fillings are removed, that the dentist takes all necessary precautions to protect you; that you are given special eye glasses; and that a dam is used over the tooth to stop particles of amalgam running down your throat, which will eventually lodge in your colon and cause havoc.

Gums and chewing

When there is gum weakness, from extensive dental work, there is a chance that parasites will be found in the saliva. They feed on dead tissue and will affect your enzyme production and therefore your nutrient assimilation. You may try the parasite programme (see Chapter 6, pp. 59–60) but it is important to rinse the mouth with the appropriate diluted anthelmintic herbs as well. (The only way you can check whether you have these parasites is through humoral pathology checking – see Resources, p. 218.)

Another cause of pain in the head, which will often go undiagnosed, is that after tooth extraction, such as the removal of wisdom teeth, there is a chance that the tooth breaks off during the procedure, and that not all fragments are removed. This will lead to small pieces of tooth or root remaining in the jaw, which could cause infection as well as pressure. I came across this fact during my studies abroad.

Now a little case history: my mother was very unlucky with her teeth. She had slightly crooked front teeth and at the age of 18 she consulted her dentist (she was a pretty girl and was upset by the crookedness of her teeth, like any young person would). The dentist said the best cure would be to pull them out and wear frontal dentures. With no one to advise her to do otherwise, or help her think this through, she went ahead.

Further visits to the same dentist led her to believe she was better off without any of her own teeth, and the dentist proceeded to pull out all her teeth at great expense to my poor grandfather. She was then fitted with a complete set of dentures, having had all her perfectly healthy teeth removed – she was not yet even 20. From that day onwards her entire digestive system was affected. She always had pains in the mouth, as well as ulcers and started to get weekly debilitating migraine attacks.

Many years later (and remembering the times during my childhood when I would see my mother lying in a dark room with violent recurring headaches, after which she would have violent diarrhoea and vomiting of black bile), I suggested she should check out her dentures and have them refitted. She reluctantly did this, but afterwards was able to chew for the first time in ages.

I then suggested that she ask her dentist to check the possibility of any fragments left in her jaw after the removal of all her teeth, even after all those years, and he agreed. After X-rays to the entire jaw area at least twenty fragments were discovered in various stages of inflammation, which were also causing pressure.

She had one side of her jaw opened up at a time, and the whole procedure lasted several weeks. Afterwards she was much better, had more energy and vitality, and nowadays has hardly any headaches at all. It is more than a shame that she spent more than half her life in such unnecessary pain, having the quality of her life so adversely affected through irresponsible dental treatment when she was so young.

Ill-fitting dentures will interfere with the ability to chew. Chewing becomes painful, so soft foods are often substituted as they can be easily swallowed and need no chewing at all, thereby inhibiting the production of ptyalin, the important enzyme produced in the salivary glands, which starts the digestion of carbohydrates and turns them into simple sugars.

Saliva production is increased with chewing. Chewing stimulates the parotid gland (located on each side of the jaw behind the ear) to release parotin hormones, which not only help the digestion but also encourage the thymus to produce T cells to protect our immune system, two very important considerations.

Chewing is a very important part of the digestion. Macrobiotic dietary recommendation states that each mouthful should be chewed at least 50 times. Some people, following macrobiotic principals, believe it is good to chew 100 and even 200 times. Chewing is also an ancient Chinese technique for rejuvenation: saliva is healing and contains anti-bacterial substances and transforms food into energy.

Notes:
1. The above gives some indication as to the possible causes of headaches, however sometimes the headaches can be stress related and be quite close to home. I know of several instances when the problem turned out to be your wife or husband. But that is another matter.
2. Sudden headaches can be relieved by the drinking of a glass of red clay, 1 teaspoon to a glass of water. Also try 2 capsules of St John's wort or feverfew herb.

Other aspects related to headaches are food allergies, parasites and stress. You can check this by using applied kinesiology or Vega testing.

Wisdom teeth

One of my sons seemed to be growing into a giant at the age of 12. He suffered from migraine headaches at least 2–3 days a week, keeping him away from school, and was unable to stand up without feeling dizzy. Furthermore after every attack he seemed to have grown 1 cm. When he reached 6 ft 2in, at 12 $1/2$ I got really worried.

After ruling out dietary involvement, I took him to quite a few experts. Vega testing revealed the problem: his wisdom teeth were causing pressure on the pituitary gland, releasing excess growth hormone in his bloodstream. I had the teeth surgically removed, the growth slowed down and also the headaches disappeared.

4 Miscellaneous hidden factors

Childhood vaccinations

Research in the US has shown that the vaccines MMR can in some cases be responsible for autism in infants and a host of other ailments.

My son who at the age of 14 received the BCG shot became terribly and inexplicably ill within a few weeks of having the vaccination. He definitely suffered from inflammation affecting the membranes of the brain. It could have been vital meningitis which is not life-threatening. He had a very high raging fever that left him in a delirious state for three days with headaches and pains in the neck, but through using the Father Kneipp methods of cold-water washing we managed to reduce the fever slowly. We applied a thick, cold clay poultice to his head, neck and chest, each time leaving it there for one hour.

We were staying in Florida and I did not fancy the idea of taking him to the hospital. After three days he came out of his delirious state but was unable to walk for a week. Yet through nutrition and mineral therapy, clay and liquid tracelytes he recovered.

When he was two years old he had the vaccination for measles, and within three days he had similar symptoms and suffered the measles virus for two weeks.

Father Kneipp, famous for his water therapies and founder of hydrotherapy in Germany, was also well known as a herbalist, using herbs in his concoctions and clay packs, compresses and hot and cold baths. He maintained that water treatments managed to get the same results as drugs in acute conditions while avoiding the toxic side effects of drugs. Body temperature can be favourably reduced so as to be below the point of danger. The water cure stimulates the radiation from the heat through the skin. For more about Kneipp, see Chapter 11, p. 96 and Further reading.

Recent research has indicated that some instances of SID (sudden infant death syndrome) have occurred soon after the first childhood vaccinations. Further research will perhaps shed more light on this matter, which continues to puzzle the public at large and has brought anguish and self-doubt to many

4.1 A child with fever.

parents. Robert Sachs's *Rebirth into Pure Land* may help such parents in their loss (see Further reading).

Meningitis C

Vaccinations to prevent Meningitis C are now offered to babies and young people at colleges and universities. These groups are believed to be at highest risk. The germ is passed through mouth contact and recently several young people have died at universities from the disease, which has understandably caused quite a panic.

The bacteria, which can be spread by kissing or coughing, are normally found to be present in the throat and nose of one out of ten people, and usually don't cause any problem. This fairly new vaccine was given to the high-risk group from the early autumn of 1999. It is up to the individual concerned whether to vaccinate or not or to go for the homoeopathic form of treatment, the Meningitis C Nosode, from Homoeopathic Pharmacies.

Then there is Meningitis B for which there is no vaccination. If suspected, immediate treatment with antibiotics will save lives and should be administered even before tests have confirmed the infection. As with every other illness, maintaining a strong healthy immune system can act as a preventative.

When the immune system is compromised we are open to all viruses and bacteria. About four years ago I lost a friend to meningitis. Her name was Luciana Martinez de la Rosa. She was a very talented painter, dividing her time between London's Soho and the vibrant atmosphere of Manhattan, New York. She travelled worldwide to create her beautiful colourful paintings.

Some years before she was struck down, she started to have immune system problems. She had problems with her digestion, thyroid dysfunction and candida; she needed emergency surgery in Sardinia to remove a badly fitted coil. All sorts of things began to affect her health. She suffered quite a lot of real turmoil like so many supremely talented artists before her. She had begun to be depressed about life in general and was eventually prescribed various strong anti-depressants, including Prozac, and took them on and off for three years before she died.

(These so called 'happy drugs' play havoc with the immune system, expose users to many viruses and bacteria, and also causes constipation. Prozac lowers the defence system, even though your spirits may temporarily be up, and contributes to mood swings. When trials were recently conducted with the drug on perfectly normal people, they began to display signs of mania and hyperactivity, some even becoming violent, aggressive and suicidal.)

Luciana probably contracted the Meningitis C virus when she was very low, travelling on the subway which she frequently used, Meningitis can be transmitted through coughing. Her symptoms were similar to 'flu or food poisoning: she felt unwell for two days after which she expected to get better. She was staying with a friend who looked after her and on the evening of the second day the friend took her to hospital. Within two hours of her arrival she was on a life-support machine in intensive care. The doctors did not immediately know what the problem was and gave her a 50/50 chance to survive. She was kept on life-support for five days but after septicaemia set in she could not be saved.

4.2 I liked all of Luciana's paintings, particularly those of cows. This one was painted in India where cows are sacred and religiously respected, secured against any violation or interference. Recent reports have highlighted the secret and cruel slaughtering of these cows for their leather, sold cheaply to the US. Several animal right organisations are working on the cause. Here is the painting of the peaceful cows, reproduced as a tribute to Luciana.

Meningitis must be caught early on for there to be to be a chance to survive. Group C causes more deaths then Group B. For information on the signs and symptoms, you can call the Association for Meningitis who have a helpful information leaflet (see Resources, p. 225).

Signs to look for when you suspect meningitis
- fever and being unable to look at any light;
- strong headaches;
- aching and stiffness of the neck;
- vomiting;
- can be very similar to 'flu symptoms.

To be sure it is not just 'flu
- Do the glass test, which is probably the most effective.
- If there is any sign of a pinprick type of skin-rash or purple, bruiselike spots, (which spread quite quickly) take a normal glass and press firmly against the skin on the affected area.
- As you press, the normal rash should fade away.
- If this does not happen you must immediately call a doctor or get to the hospital.

'Flu injections

Injections for the prevention of 'flu in the elderly and those with lung conditions are offered routinely and free of charge for those at high risk at the beginning of autumn. Basically one receives the bacteria of an animal such as a sheep to prevent something that usually happens anyway when we are run down. The strain of 'flu can be different from the strain given in the vaccination; it is not uncommon to find that those who received the vaccination still get the 'flu. The vaccines tend to settle in the colon, which has a general weakening effect on the immune system.

There was a flu epidemic in early 1999 and there is one right now at the turn of the century. It is difficult to know exactly which strain is going to hit the public, which is why the jabs are not really very effective. I find that taking a combination of the herbs echinacea, elderberry flowers and peppermint as infusions, and strong doses of olive leaf extract capsules, take care of 'flu effectively. See listing in Part III (p. 173) for more details on effective 'flu treatment.

Fluoride

Fluoride, which is added to our drinking water and most toothpaste, is often recommended by dentists to help the strength of the teeth and prevent cavities. It is also given to young children in the form of drops. What dentists fail to tell you, however, is that this is very harmful for your child.

In 1984 my young son was given pink fluoride drops shortly after his first visit to the dentist when he was only one year and a few months old. At that time I had no idea that he was so allergic to artificial colours and additives. He was very hyperactive, a difficult and very sensitive child, and I believe that the drops helped to exacerbate the condition which did not improve until I cut out all that was artificial in his diet and only gave him whole food and organic produce.

Recent research actually indicates that fluoride acts as a poison and can cause hyperactivity in children, ME, and a host of other non-specific illnesses. *Fluoride weakens the immune system.* It can have a *devastating* effect on every organ in the body. It is linked with thyroid disease, stomach and bowel disorders, and various behavioural disorders and can cause genetic damage.

Recent studies have suggested that fluorine in the blood blocks the action of acetylcholine, which is an enzyme facilitating neuro-transmitter. This can give rise to memory loss and lack of concentration. Fluoride is best avoided by filtering your drinking water and avoiding toothpaste and other dental products that contain it.

It is worth checking your local water authority to find out what is in your water. The water supplied by Thames Water, for instance, does not have fluoride added. What you'll find here is the naturally occurring fluoride at 0.186ppm. Where fluoride is added to the water supply, as in parts of Florida, it comes from the manufacturers of phosphate fertilisers and aluminium smelting factories. This is industrial waste and the fluoride is toxic.

Fluoride is also found in certain anti-depressants and asthma drugs. Some symptoms should clear once the fluoride intake is stopped; help this along by drinking green clay to neutralise.

The only time when fluoride is helpful is when it comes from our food supply. We can find it naturally occurring in goat's milk and cheese, egg yolks, seaweeds and avocados.

Aspartame and saccharine

Aspartame

Aspartame, an artificial sweetener, is broken down into three chemicals, when ingested:

- aspartic acid (breaks down sensitive neurons slowly);
- phenylanine (decreases seratonin, causes sleep problems and depression);
- methanol (a poison that is transformed in the liver into formaldehyde, a neuro-toxin and carcinogenic).

Here is another terrible fad which is worth millions. People take the artificial sweetener in the hope of staving off getting fat. It is obvious it does not work if you look at all the mostly overweight and misinformed people taking it. Research has shown that it is actually carcinogenic; it slows you down, and is really bad for the brain. Continual use can give rise to the following problems:

- symptoms of hyperthyroidism: before starting on thyroid therapy, watch what happens when you start to cut out the sweetener – you may not need it;
- changes in the brain's chemistry: it affects dopamine levels, depletes seratonin, which can cause manic depression, panic attacks, violence and rage;
- seizures: if you already suffer from Parkinsonism, make up your own mind about it;
- escalation of Alzheimer's disease.

Aspartame and MS

The cause of MS is not known. It is thought to be due to changes in the nervous system, caused by some substances which dissolve or break up the fatty matter of the nerve sheaths, ending in sclerotic patches in parts of the brain, causing temporary partial paralysis and problems with the vision.

Studies have shown that aspartame is one of the contributing causes of MS. Its intake gives MS type symptoms. This is strangely on the increase, as is lupus (a skin disease). This is not surprising: just read the labels on many sweet products – they all have the additive. If you are taking in aspartame on a daily basis, you may be suffering from:

- breathing problems;
- dizziness;
- headaches, fuzzy head;
- blurred speech;
- palpitations;
- visionary disturbances;
- unexplained weight loss;
- premature ageing;

Aspartame is also found in canned fizzy drinks, such as Diet Coke. You may find an improvement once you avoid these and cut them out of your life. Read the labels. Aspartame is added to thousands of products, including most chewing gums.

A neuro-surgeon in the US said, that tests on removed brain tumours revealed high levels of aspartame.

One day I was in a basic sort of supermarket just outside London. The girl in front of me at the cash desk had bought a few basics, which included some organic kiwis and organic lemons. This shows that even the basic shop now stock organics, which is good, and that the girl was somewhat informed by the recent highly promoted benefits of organic produce. However, it was all ruined by the fact that she was purchasing two very large jars of sweetener – white powder, containing aspartame. On the one hand she wanted to be healthy and eat organic fruits; on the other hand she liked sugar and had read somewhere that sugar can make you fat so she wanted to use the supposedly non-fattening alternative.

As it happened, her total bill amount was higher then she had budgeted, so she had to put a couple of items back. She chose to return one the aspartame jars. It did not register on the till, so she returned the second jar. It turned out that the special offer of the week was two jars for the price of one. In all this commotion I was patiently waiting and picked up the jar to examine the exact ingredients.

'Oh, it is so good, and such a bargain,' she said to me. 'Why don't *you* get them if you can afford them!' She did not realise she was better off without them. But she'll be back. You see, you can be poisoned twice for one price.

All products that claim to be 'sugar free' probably have the added artificial sweetener. My advice is to avoid them for health's sake.

Saccharine

Saccharine is also best avoided for similar reasons. It has been found to cause cancer in animals. The National Academy of Sciences stated in 1978 that saccharine is a potential cancer-causing agent in humans.

Sugar

The population in the States takes up to 25% of calories as sugar. Sugar is totally denatured: first it is heated up – all the trace elements, vitamins and minerals as well as chlorophyll are destroyed – and after this process it is mixed with acid chalk, carbonic gas, sulphur dioxide and natrium bicarbonite. Then the mixture is cooked and cooled down several times, after which it goes through a crystallising and centrifugal process.

By this time the lifeless substance is treated with strontium hydroxide; then in the refinery it is cleaned by being passed over chalk carbon acid. The dark colour is then removed by adding sulphuric acid and filtered with bone charcoal, and finished by being coloured with indathrene blue or the highly toxic ultramarine. Now it has actually become a poison, with a chemical structure of $C_{12}H_{22}O_{11}$, and an atomic density of 98.4–99.5%.

This research was undertaken by Professor David Schweitzer who is becoming very well known in England for his research in discovering the 'language of the blood' through his expertise with the Darkfield microscope. He worked for many years as a medical missionary in Africa and several years in the Far East and is highly knowledgeable on both physical and spiritual sciences. Professor Schweitzer gives regular lectures and seminars which are a must for anyone who wants to learn more about staying healthy longer. He is now refining his research on photographing 'thought forms' and how they are able to change water clusters and blood. These discoveries have enabled him to monitor stored frequencies in homoeopathic remedies and the impact of positive and negative thoughts on the fluids of the body.

The HLB (Humoral Pathological Blood) test using the Darkfield microscope, was developed by Haitan, Legarde and Bradford in the 1930s and Oswald developed the test further in the 1980s. From there Dr Schweitzer has developed the ability to identify fungus in the blood through his testing methods. He states that 'many foods and drugs encourage the development of yeast. Sugar being one of the main offenders. Once the yeast fungus start to grow they can spread to all the organs including the brain.' (see Chapter 2 on Candida). With this technique life-threatening diseases can be detected and save lives (see Resources, p. 218 for more details).

An increase in sugar consumption has a definite effect on the brain, slowing the person down, and leads to a reduction of intelligence and creativity, causing hyperactivity in children and attention deficit disorders. It also contributes to an increase in violence and emotional and mental disorders.

Monosodium glutomate (MSG)

Monosodium glutomate (MSG) is an amino acid that enhances the flavour of foods. It is added to most Chinese recipes and is widely used in restaurants. The effects of MSG are sometimes known as 'Chinese restaurant syndrome'.

Avoid MSG if you can: good natural food does not require enhancement. This additive can have an immediate reaction on the mucous membranes. In several cases asthma attacks have been reported after eating food containing MSG. Sinuses fill up and the throat thickens; tiredness and brain fog are other side effects, as are thirst, increase in blood pressure, and headaches and dizziness. Hopefully restaurants are reducing the use of the additive because many people who are aware of the problem are now demanding MSG-free food.

Waxed fruits

Most fruits found in the supermarket have been waxed. This is done to protect the fruits and give them a longer shelf life. Waxed fruits have been treated with a variety of fungicides, including orthophenylphenol. These fungicides are found on most oranges and can cause a number of diseases including immune deficiencies, mental disorders, heart disease and cancer. You can now get unwaxed fruits – look out for them.

Microwave cooking

Microwave ovens are mostly used to cook convenience foods for busy – and maybe lazy – people. If you care about your health and that of your children, microwaving should be avoided as at least 90% of valuable nutrients from the food are lost in the process, and there is a carcinogenic effect from the foods thus consumed on a regular basis.

Foods heated in microwaves produces free radicals and are a source of EMFs (see next section). Many mothers routinely heat cow's milk in the microwave for their babies and small children, and often inside the baby bottle or cup (the plastic residue will be in the milk too, by the way).

There is not enough information to warn the public of the contrary effects of this radiation and you certainly won't get it from the salesperson. German and Russian microwaves studies at the Institute of Radio Technology observed that foods heated this way have a cancer-causing effect, destroying nutritional value, and biological effects from the direct exposure of the microwaves emissions to humans.

EMFs

EMFs (electromagnetic frequencies) have had a lot of press recently, particularly with the use of mobile telephones presenting a supposed risk of brain cancer. The hidden agenda is that mobile phone energy is life-threatening – according to people working in the mobile phone sales field who will not use the phones themselves and say, 'It will be at least four years until these phones are safe.' Also the radio waves received from the latest digital telephones can contribute to a lowering of the immune system.

If you can't do without, some protection can be obtained with the special earpieces you can buy in the shops, or the use of certain magnets or harmonisers.

Avoid sleeping in a room with electrical equipment: if you have any in your bedroom, switch them off at night. *Your TV or computer could make you ill.*

Children who watch too much TV are in constant contact with electromagnetic radiation, and there is a lot of brainwashing going on as well. You can protect them by placing a harmoniser on the TV set which helps cut that radiation. Try and control the amount of TV and the type of programmes or shows your child watches or they can get distorted values and warped ideas about real life, sex and who they are, and will soon start to act like the characters of their favourite soaps.

Michael DeFries – a London-based homoeopath, well-known for his work with holographic material (which can be applied to the TV or computer and also worn as pendants) which he programmes radionically to harmonise and balance energy – has said, 'For the last 10–15 years I have been aware that subliminal messages are transferred over the TV as well as via computers and the Internet.' It must be clear to most parents of young children and teenagers that this is indeed happening.

These waves are created to manipulate and brainwash the public at large. They are used to sell anything from foods, drinks, to politicians and their ideas, celebrities etc. This type of programming deadens the mind and makes us not care, we watch the cruelty of wars and all kinds of atrocities on the screen. The mind is deadened and we just go on.

In an article entitled 'Mind virus could give us shopping bug' in the *Observer*, Tracey McVeigh (26 March 2000) reports on how information is fed to people via TV and computers. Once this has been implanted it can make you desperately want the most useless gadget or accessory –obviously a dream come true for any business wishing to increase sales. Do not let your child watch endless television and not just because of the EMFs. (See Resources for further suggestions and addresses.)

Geopathic stress and gridlines

Geopathic stress

If you are always tired or run down, have frequent colds and you've tried everything, it is worth checking out if you are suffering from geopathic stress. This is caused by the natural radiation of our earth, which only becomes harmful if it is near underground streams and your home is on top of it.

The building in which you live could be making you ill. You can get the services of a dowser/geomancer who will be able to verify if that is the problem and help correct it. In China a geomancer is always called in *before* any building work commences. This had been the case for thousands of years.

You may be sleeping above a crossing stream or gridline. Gridlines are rays that pass through underground water channels, metal or oil deposits. They are actually very harmful if you are sleeping above them.

Gridlines

Among the problems that can occur if you are unfortunate to be sleeping over a gridline are cancer, MS and cot death. Gridlines are associated with other long-term illnesses as well. If your baby cries a lot and you have tried everything, try moving his cot to another part of the room and see if that helps. Use the services of a dowser, or learn the techniques yourself.

Some say that simply placing a copper coil (obtainable from hardware stores) under the bed around the area of the waistline will help. Other suggestions are to try moving the bed to another part of the room, if the position is found to be the problem.

More help can be obtained by increasing your vitality, with the help of a vortex energiser, through which you pour your drinking water. This mitigates the harmful effect of geopathic stress and is available from Regenerative Nutrition (see Resources, p. 228). The Dulwich Health Society (see Resources, pp. 219, 220) provides information on both on geopathic stress and the effect of gridlines.

Feng shui

Feng Shui (meaning 'the flow of wind and water') also originates from China but has now become very popular in the West. The wind disperses the invisible (*qi*) energy and the water contains it. Feng shui can alter the energy in our surroundings. Its practice is meant to enhance positive energy and reduce or eliminate negative ones.

Feng shui is the art of the harmonious placement of the dwelling, its surroundings and contents. Working always with the five elements, if one element dominates – for example wood – introducing the metal element as well as a touch of the earth element will quickly balance out any disharmony. The aim is to have a strong and smooth flow of *qi* (life-force) running through your home and garden. Many books are available on this subject.

Magnetic grid disruption

Recent literature published by several organisations working on the ecological and health catastrophes relating to earth magnetic grid disturbances have found that they create the following risks:

- extreme weather conditions;
- lifeless soils;
- changes in ocean currents;
- emotional health declines;
- thinning and vanishing ozone layers;
- withering plants and unexplained forest death;
- fish and animal migration changes;
- social order in upheaval;
- more frequent earthquakes;
- climatic stability deteriorates;
- animals becoming weaker and diseased;
- amphibians and reptiles vanish;
- politics become extreme;
- time seems to go faster.

For more information on the International Earth Emergency Network, contact Crystal Hill Multi Media and World Research Information Centre (see Resources, pp. 218, 223) or contact your local feng shui network (see The Feng Shui Network International, p. 220).

Catalytic converters

Most pollution in cities like London comes from:

1. buses, taxies and lorries.
2. air traffic (a major contributory factor).
3. traffic congestion, due to continuous road works
4. traffic calming schemes that have not been properly planned.

By the end of 1999 to reduce pollution we will no longer be able to put four-star petrol in our cars. Some of us may have old cars and take care to make sure that we don't pollute, but in order to keep our older cars we must have catalytic converters fitted. By law we need to have catalytic converters in Britain some time in the year 2000. Since 1993 all cars have had the device routinely fitted. Some areas of central London will be made into 'no go' areas to cars without the device in the very near future.

However, *catalytic converters create a form of nerve gas*. This can lead to all kinds of ailments affecting the nervous system, e.g. depression, exhaustion, viral and bacterial infections. It is not only the catalytic converter that causes the problem but also the unleaded petrol that must be used in them. This contains additives such as chloride compounds, which produce phosgene when burned in the presence of platinum, which happens in a catalytic converter. Phosgene is a poison gas, the same gas that was used in the First World War to destroy the lungs of the enemy. There are also high levels of benzene present, which is a well-known carcinogenic compound that tends to build up in the fatty parts of the body. Other poisons include Sarin, the poison used in a Tokyo subway by the Aum cult, March 95, which killed 12 people and injured 1000's!

These toxic gases break down cell membranes.

Catalytic converters have been linked with the debilitating illness ALS (amyotrophic lateral sclerosis). This awful illness is the end-product of a body's inability to cope with toxic chemicals and heavy metals and prevent them from causing damage to the nerve cells. For some ways to protect us from this damage, avoid cars with the above converters, and if you can choose diesel over petrol.

Not long from now – possibly within five to ten years – I believe in the Western world we will be able to obtain cars powered by hydrogen fuel cells. This is a completely new way of driving without pollution and ecologically sound. It is not easy for many people to give up their cars completely and public transport is not always reliable or safe if travelling alone at night, therefore this system will catch on fast. In the meantime:

- take mineral supplements in easily assimilated form, anti-oxidants and clay, to protect from pollution; supplementing these minerals will help to keep toxins out of the cells; or try the new goldstone tablets (Nutri Centre).
- ensure that your sodium pump is working effectively (see Part II, pp. 113, 118).

In early 2000 in London the Minister of Transport offered a small cash sum for people with old cars to give them in for scrap, as an incentive to make us get rid of our old 'bangers', considered to be more polluting then newer models, and thus to help reduce fumes and pollution. All newer cars must have a catalytic converter and soon there will be a law implementing this by force.

But what can be done now? The public transport system is due to be overhauled but will obviously take some time. We have a compulsory road-worthiness check every year - if something is not right about your car it will not pass the MOT, so we fix the problem – we have to if we want to keep the car on the road. If the car is emitting toxic fumes your car will not pass the test. However, they have not even looked into the dangers of the catalytic converter.

Tumble dryers

Avoid them. If you can't, keep them in a shed in the garden, and never use them in kitchens as they emit carcinogenic particles in the atmosphere.

4.3 A sugarcane factory in Egypt. Note the black smoke bellowing out from the sugar burning.

5 Cancer

> **Please note**
> Cancer is a serious condition that should always be carefully looked at by specialists. The information in this chapter is for educational purposes only and none of it must be used as medical advice. However, as it is important to be aware of the alternatives available, I have included them in this chapter.

According to the latest statistics, there is now a clear chance that one out of four people will contract cancer at some point in their life. That is a sad fact which has brought fear to many. Billions are spent on cancer research, and yet most people still die. Thousands of pounds have just been injected into the National Health Service by the National Lottery Fund for improved screening methods. This is a good thing, but I personally would not go for a mammogram.

Squashing a breast between two plates presents the risk that if there were a tumour it would certainly explode during this procedure and spread to other tissues. But that is purely my opinion.

Sometimes if the cancer has not spread, the tumour can be removed surgically, in the early stages, with success. This procedure is not so easy once the disease has spread to other parts. At this point chemotherapy is usually employed to kill the cancer cells. It works but also kills a lot more besides, weakening the whole immune system considerably, and the cancer usually returns at a later stage.

There are now various other ways of testing whether a lump is benign or not. That there are many natural ways to combat cancer should come as no surprise to some of you. Most of these alternative findings are swept under the carpet and the discoveries go unnoticed and unmentioned in the press save for a few magazines. Only by really digging will you find out about the alternatives that are available.

Naturopaths do not tackle 'cancer' as such. We don't work with the disease 'name' or label. By law we are not allowed to treat this particular illness, at least not without medical supervision. We work with the body system as a whole, restoring the immune system, working on the contributory factors rather then the named disease.

On my way back from LA last week I watched a tearjerker of a movie during my flight. It was about a young black attractive lawyer, married to a white, loving husband with two teenage daughters. She took the case of a young black naval officer wrongly accused of rape. Throughout the movie she met with racism and hatred. When she won the case in the end, she collapsed and after a consultation at the hospital was found to be not with child, but with terminal liver cancer.

I know this movie was not about saving her life and sending her for treatment that was not 'chemo', but at the same time it brings home to me that when someone is diagnosed with cancer it is basically accepted that you are going to die. And sadly she did die. Once cancer has spread to the liver, *it is* very difficult to turn around.

B17 and Laetrile

The following are two alternative therapies, although there are many more. The first is a treatment that involves vitamin B17, otherwise known as laetrile which is rich in nitrolisides. It was rediscovered in 1952 by an American biochemist Ernst Krebs, but kept under wraps for various reasons. Unfortunately this treatment has received a lot of bad press, so you need to make up your own mind about it. A new book by Philip Day, which explains this in great detail, is called *Cancer: Why We Are Still Dying to Know the Truth*.

B17 comes from the kernel of apricots. The use of these kernels goes back to the writings of physicians in ancient Egypt, Arabia, Rome and Greece. Famous physicians of those days include Claudius van Galen, AD 131–200, the Oracle of Medicine, Pliny the Elder, Avicenna and Marcellus Empiricus. They used extracts of the seeds from bitter almonds, apricots and peaches to treat cancer successfully.

Ancient Egyptian papyri found from 5000 years ago describe the use of aqua amigdalorum for the treatment of some tumours of the skin. This vitamin is obtained from the kernel of the apricots, which is very bitter. As a preventative you can take 7 kernels daily to boost the immune system. To obtain the vitamin you must crack the kernel, inside which is a tiny nut. You can also take it in tablet form. Take two 100mg tabs daily (enquire from Credence for availability and further addresses of suppliers; see Resources, p 218).

Cancer is virtually unknown in the Hunza people in the valleys of the Himalayas in Pakistan, where longevity is the norm: many elders reach 100–120 years. They have a natural diet that includes plenty of vegetables and grains. They all eat an abundance of apricot kernels and foods rich in nitrilosides, found in over a hundred different plants. The Hunzas also get their acidophilus from their homemade goat's yoghurt and drink the clay water running down from the glaciers above them. Their diet contains 200 times more B17 then the average Western diet.

When someone is found to have cancer the laetrile treatment has to be a bit stronger. Just eating a few kernels is not enough. You would probably need to eat something like 30–50 seeds daily. If vomiting is induced the dosage should be lowered and gradually increased. In a clinic injections of B17 between 6–9g daily are used, for at least 21 days.

If there is organ weakness caused by intensive chemotherapy or other drug treatment, it is not always possible to get good results due to the previous treatment's invasiveness. Even if the cancer can be overcome, the patient can possibly die from complications from the damaged organs.

It is important to take Laetrile treatment together with enzymes and minerals. If possible, it is better to go ahead and try the above, before invasive treatment is employed, although there are many cases where this would be impossible. Most of the time alternative treatment is only considered when allopathic treatment has been tried, the case has been given up as hopeless and the person is told they have xx weeks left to live. By that time the person's immune system is usually extremely weak. This is *why* it is so important to be well informed of these alternatives. The addresses in the Resources section (p. 216) will give you far more information then I can in these short pages.

Sometimes it helps to combine allopathic treatment – certainly after successful surgical removal of most of the tumour or after chemotherapy – with natural therapies, rebuilding the immune system.

My husband suffered from fibromatosis, when he was 17. He discovered the tumour under his right armpit, which was the size of an orange. He was taken to the National Institute of Cancer, in Maryland USA. Here, after a 24-hour operation, the tumour, as well as his arm and shoulder blade were removed. That did seem a pretty drastic action to take, but it saved him. I was not around at that time, but I think that they did a very good job, and he is still here 27 years later. They probably needed to remove those parts of his body, as the cancer may have already spread there. He is now very healthy, has lots of energy, and looks younger then his younger brother and sisters, despite being in a highly stressful occupation. He is on a nutritional programme devised by myself and always starts his day with fruits to include fresh papaya juice, which is very beneficial for the pancreas. (Pancreatic enzymes are very important in *all* cancer therapy.) He has also been a fan of clay for quite some time.

As a child, he suffered from Hepatitis A, which weakens the liver considerably. It is interesting to note the area of the tumour was directly above the liver. He had the awful habit of using strong chemical anti-perspirants, the dangers of which you can read below (pp. 46, 152, 161, 167. Liver health is usually impaired with cancer.

B17 Laetril treatment can be obtained in several clinics in Mexico and in Germany. For further information, see Resources (p. 216). The Mexican clinic have a nearly 100% recovery rate. Due to various legal requirements, it is not possible to obtain the tablets of B17 or the kernels in Britain although apricot kernels can be ordered, through some companies such as Credence Publications (see Resources, p. 218).

More alternative treatment can be obtained in a clinic in the Dominican Republic, the Centre for Cell Specific Cancer Therapy (CSCT), where they use Magnetic Energy Therapy quite successfully (see Resources, p. 217). Here treatment is offered for a flat fee and can take between 4 and 6 weeks or longer. You will be given as many treatments as needed, most of them successful. They will also take on patients unable to meet the fees at a lower rate or completely free, depending on their situation. The treatment is organised by the directors John Armstrong and Michael Reynolds under the care of the centre's medical director Dr Ariel Antonio Perez Ubiera who uses magnetic energy from the CTCT-200 to destroy the cancer cells. They have a 50% success rate; depending on at what stage the patient arrives.

The work of French-born Professor Serge Jurasunas must also be mentioned in this chapter. Jurasunas, a cancer researcher, naturopath and iridologist, lectures worldwide and has a clinic in Portugal. He is an expert on cancer treatments and works effectively with anti-ageing protocols. He also works with the HLB blood screening test.

One of his many astounding treatments include immersing the patient in a bath, known as 'the energy sand bath' filled with ceramic clay balls, which are heated to a high temperature in order for the 'far infra red rays' to be more powerful. While the patient relaxes in comfort the heated ceramics are working to remove and absorb toxic and lipid substances from the body. Afterwards the clay balls are washed under pressure and leave sebacious and dark-coloured toxic material which has been removed from the patient.

'The importance of detoxification cannot be ignored when treating any disease,' he says.

He also uses a treatment whereby the ceramics are heated in the oven, then wrapped in cotton material and applied directly to the area of the tumour. This is known as BA ceramic ball application. These ceramics were discovered in a mine on Kyushu Island in Japan, and known as 'Tenko Seki'. They emit a 'far infra red ray', which have been shown to be very effective in the treatment of cancer. Dr Y. Niwa, a Japanese immunologist, originally investigated the stones and their 'far-infra red rays' and wrote about them in the *Japanese Journal of Inflammation* in 1996 and described them as non-toxic and powerfully anti-carcinogenic.

Professor Jurasunas also works with a formula from Germany called 'Zell-oxygen' which has been developed to reduce the effects of environmental toxins. This has been used successfully over the last 25 years on over 20,000 patients. He

5.1 Photograph of a patient immersed in a bath of heated 'Tenko Seki' ceramics. Reproduced with kind permission of Professor Serge Jurasunas.

has a high success rate, particularly with breast cancer. Here is a photograph of a patient immersed in a bath of heated 'Tenko Seki' ceramics. The bath is known as the 'ESB' (Energy Sand Bath). The energy is increased by the heat of the stones.

It is interesting to note that Professor Jurasunas has also studied with the famous Dr Jensen (who wrote the Foreword of this book) but this was 37 years ago.

Professor Jurasunas is a member of the New York Academy of Sciences, the International Society for Orthomolecular Medicine, and many more notable academic institutions. He has been appointed to teach at the New Capital University of Integrative Medicine in the USA, where he will be teaching in Iridology, HLB blood analysis and integrative medicine.[1]

For more information on the work of Professor Jurasunas see Resources, p. 219.

Factors involving cancer development

Cancer can be caused by a variety of factors, nutrition being the most important as well as a low immune system. These can be dealt with by adopting a diet of natural real foods, low fat, low protein, reduction of sugar intake and using only natural salt as it occurs in foods. Other factors are:

- stress;
- chemicals;
- pesticides;
- poisons, environmental as well as household and cosmetic toxins;
- strong smelling chemical sprays, paints and liquids, including perfumes – if you are found to have cancer, these can worsen the condition;
- excessive alcohol;
- drug abuse;
- bad diet, bad company and mental strains – maintaining mental health is an important aspect.

The breast cancer issue and pesticides

According to an article by Donna Alvarado (Alvarado, 1994), research by scientists at the American Association for the Advance of Science, has shown that the increase in breast cancer can be caused by higher levels of environmental pollution, and increased levels of exposure to pesticides found in all plant foods and fruits that are non-organic, the absorption of which could mimic the action of oestrogen.

High levels of oestrogen are a contributory factor. Changes in reproduction are another reason. Women who have children later in life have a 50% higher risk of breast cancer then those with multiple pregnancies at a younger age. Late menopause also adds to the higher risk. Hormone therapy, which is started before menopause or shortly after, has shown to increase the risk by 30–40%. Women taking these in their mid to late sixties have an increased rate of 87%

According to Dr Samuel Epstein of the University of Illinois, the increase in breast cancer is also blamed on the radiation received routinely from X rays including mammograms.

Dr Devra Lee Davis, from the World Resources Institute, advises 'to reduce the risk of breast cancer eat less meat and more fruits and vegetables, regular exercise, avoid animal fat and alcohol'.

The late Congresswoman Bella Abzug said at the 1997 World Conference on Breast Cancer:

> We must take on the nuclear industry, the Chemical Industry, the makers and users of pesticides and organochorines and the other potential resources of poison in our breasts and bodies. We should demand from our governments to legislate, regulate and discipline transnational corporations.

The controversy on mammographic screening as a general rule from the age of 40 goes on. It is up to the individual and her doctor to decide. Recent safer detection methods on offer include: heat imagining lasers and magnetic resonance imaging.

Pesticides.

One problem is that some of the pesticides which have been banned in the US and Britain, due to their known toxic elements, are taken to other countries, for example South America, where they are promoted and marketed to increase crop growth and the local farmers are unaware of the poisonous dangers and pleased to increase their income. Due to the poverty in these regions compliance is obviously high, aided by the lack of information on these matters. These foods are exported to be sold in the rest of the world; so then we just get the pesticides back again. We imagine that they are grown naturally far away, where the farmland space is huge and unspoilt. There is indeed an enormous amount of unspoilt farmland out there, but for how long? Who is in control?

Another contributing factor is constipation (see Part III, p. 166). The recently discovered dangers of using of anti-perspirants have also been found to be an involving factor. The toxins normally excreted through perspiring are merely diverted to the nearest tissues right below the underarms (breasts and lymph).

Dr David Derry from British Columbia found in 1993 that the rate of formation of fybrocystic breast lumps was greatly reduced when the patient was given iodine. Results can take from two months to two years. He reckons that most people do not obtain enough iodine from their diet and that this lack is a contributing risk factor. Liquid trace minerals in tracelytes (see Resources, p. 226) contain a most sophisticated form of organic iodine, which is ionised within the liquid crystalloid complex.

Iodine can also be found in seaweeds such as kelp.

Cancer and candida

People with cancer are always found to have candida and, of course, parasites, (see Chapter 6). Further clinical treatment can be given after successful magnetic therapy from the CSCT (Cell Specific Cancer Therapy) at the Centre for Immuno Augmentation in the Bahamas. Here they help to address the basic underlying condition and show you how to keep your immune system in optimum function (see Resources, p. 217).

The Ann Wigmore Institute (see Resources, p. 215) runs courses for people needing special diets and cleansing procedures.

Home therapy

When your system has been lowered by radiation, chemotherapy, surgery and overuse of antibiotics, you can boost your state of health by:

- eating sensibly and avoiding when possible anything that has been tampered with, particularly GM food;
- eating only fresh and organic produce.

The importance of organic food

Apart from the obvious benefit to the consumer, organic food can save your farmer's life. Poisoning from pesticides has been rising steadily by 14% since 1974. Between 1975 and 1985 that figure doubled.

Farmers are at six times greater risk of contracting cancer from exposure to pesticides then the average person. Pesticides (some carcinogenic) are also poisoning groundwater, which then acts as a pollutant in various parts of the country. It is considered that 60% of all herbicides, 90% of all fungicides, and 30% of all insecticides are carcinogenic.

By involving yourself actively in choosing organic you help the farmers and the future generation. The food you choose today will be a deciding factor in your child's future health.

The Soil Association, in Britain, has information on organic produce, genetic farming etc. see Resources (p. 229).

Diet

Include the following in your diet:

- deep-water fish: 1–2 times per week;
- millet spelt, buckwheat, lentils, mung beans, sprouted alfalfa and other seeds, porridge, brown rice, dried pulses;
- carrot juice, beet juice, barley grass juice;
- Spirulina – powder or tablets;
- Rheishi or Shiitake mushrooms which stimulate the immune system to produce more interferon and reduce the side effects of radiation; also available in tablet form;
- fruits with seeds such as plums, apricots, cherries, blueberries, papayas and mangoes.
- fresh juices: drink them as soon as prepared or the vitamin and enzyme content will be diminished or gone;
- daily soups containing the following: garlic, onions, carrots, seaweeds and celery;
- plenty of vegetables – at least six types daily;
- two different fruits daily;
- superfine green clay, for 3-6 weeks;
- pancreatic enzymes
- Zell-oxygen

Avoid the following:

- anything tinned or frozen (although some frozen vegetables are not too bad);
- anything that has added colour preservatives or additives;
- anything that has added salt or white sugar;

- anything that has been cured or pickled (apart from Umebushi plums from Japan);
- meat, particularly red meat (maybe an occasional organic chicken);
- white flour products;
- milk or non-organic cheese (small quantities of eggs or cheese can be eaten but they must be organic and have 2–3 organic eggs per week);
- saturated fats
- cooking in microwaves;
- aluminium cookware – always use stainless steel;

The consumption of living green foods, wheat grass, barley grass, spirulina and chlorella is highly recommended. It is cheap and fairly easy to grow your own wheat and barley grass (see Appendix 2, p. 212). Enzymes are important, e.g. papain from papayas, bromelain from pineapples. Certain herbs have the enzymes bromelain, such as turmeric.

Eat fish, preferably from deep waters. Bear in mind that our waters are equally polluted, and fish can retain 159,000 times as much dioxin as the water in which they swim.

Beneficial herbs are: red clover, dandelion, mistletoe, violet, garlic, sage, noni, Una de Gato (cat's claw). Take at least 2g of vitamin C daily.

Essiac

The famous Essiac herb is made up of:

- sheep sorrel – 16oz powdered herb
- slippery elm – 4oz powdered herb
- burdock root – 52oz powdered herb
- turkey rhubarb – 1oz powdered herb

Take 2–3 cups of the infusion daily. Essiac is available in the UK from the Organic Herb Co. (see Resources, p. 227) or you can make up your own.
Maintain an alkaline diet, 70% alkaline, 30% acid. Drink pure water – up to $1^{1}/2$–2 pints daily – but don't overdo it. That is a modern fad and you could overtax the kidneys. To avoid constipation, take a herbal formula containing: Cascara Sagrada. Balm of Gilead, Aloe Vera.

Always aim to maintain liver health.

Get involved actively to *prevent* ill health, by following these simple ways to maintain your health.

Most toxic foods

The first step is to insist on organic and unadulterated foods wherever possible. The *most toxic foods* to avoid unless they are organic are:

- *strawberries* - which contain the most pesticides;
- *bananas* - they use benomyl (linked to birth defects) and chlorpyrifos (a neurotoxin);
- *peaches* - recent studies by the FDA found that at least 5% were contaminated;
- *apples* - organophosphate residues.

Also the following fruits and foods are high on the contamination list:

- kiwis;
- nectarines;
- grapes;
- raisins;
- milk – hormones, antibiotics etc.
- waters have been contaminated;
- corn; contains high doses of organophosphates according to research carried out by the Environmental Working Group;
- rice – pesticides used in some areas in California were so heavy that local ground waters have been contaminated;
- grains – the FDA found large amounts of pesticides residues in at least 91% tested grains;
- baby foods – tests carried out by the EWG in 1996 found 16 pesticides in half the 'well-known brand' samples tested;

(*above researched by Nature's Path. see p. 226.*)

For a few cents or pennies more we can avoid contamination by choosing organic.

More positive approaches

Learn to dance. Free yourself. It is so easy to get uptight in our modern, hard society. Ten minutes daily is all you need. Find out about Transformational Dance classes at the end of book (see Resources, p. 218) or the famous Gabrielle Roth 5 rhythm dance, or just move your body, to your music. You don't have to be perfect. Dance that pain right out of your body and your mind! If not find a body movement class in your area.

Keep a positive attitude. It is great when you can see what you can do for yourself. Avoid getting uptight and stop trying to control everything.

Cancer personalities often feel the need to be in control, are often judgmental and discriminating, bordering on arrogance. Live and let live, loosen up, free yourself, keep that flow that makes you go. Seek and you will find, if you want to, and if you are meant to.

More information can be obtained by surfing the Web.

Some Notes re. Prof. Jurasunas were taken at the 4th International Iridology Symposium, November 2000, Regent's College, London.

6 Parasites

I have devoted a whole chapter to this subject as it is another cause of hidden illness and is well hidden because these little things are unlikely to protrude outwards unless we are talking about a few pinworms which can occasionally be seen on a small child's anus and in their stool.

Most children under five have pinworms; they are easy to catch, especially if there are animals and pets in the house. Children constantly put things in their mouth and spend a lot of time crawling on the floor where all kinds of germs and bacteria are picked up.

We are subjected daily to an onslaught of these unwanted visitors. They can be in our salad, and even if well washed they can be hidden within the leaves. They can be on meats or on the hands of people who serve our food; they can be picked up from doorknobs in toilets from people who have not washed their hands after using the bathroom; they can be found in water – and so on.

Now I'm not trying to make anyone paranoid here, because even though we are subjected to these things, we can avoid them when we have our digestive juices (enzymes and acids) in good order; they are unlikely to remain with us, and will quickly exit. When our juices are of the correct pH in the stomach, it makes a less favourable environment for them and they leave as quickly as they arrived. When our pH balance is disturbed we inadvertently welcome these keen visitors, this can be caused:

- through illness;
- long-term use of drugs;
- poor nutrition;
- heavy metal fillings, metal in crowns and root canals;
- lack of electrolytes, (essential chemical elements).

Again, when the immune system works well they are unlikely to remain in the body. Worms and parasites always live in degenerated areas of the body. They can cause havoc to the body and do a lot of damage. They can be one of the causes of anaemia and give allergy like symptoms. They can obstruct organs such as the intestines, the gallbladder, the pancreas and the liver, create pressure on the brain and cause:

- chronic fatigue
- inability to gain weight and uncontrolled appetite
- PMS
- prostatitis
- candida

and can be a reason for unexplained headaches.

Parasites take advantage of our nourishment; it is such a common problem hardly anyone escapes it. Taking a regular vermifuge herbal would be a good idea, because that would warrant some sort of control. (The original 'Yogi Tea' is a good start as it contains a mixture of vermifuge herbs and it is organic).

While serving his prison sentence in Singapore, Nick Leeson, the former Barings Bank dealer, was found to be suffering from bowel cancer; during surgery it was discovered that the bowel was totally infested with parasites.

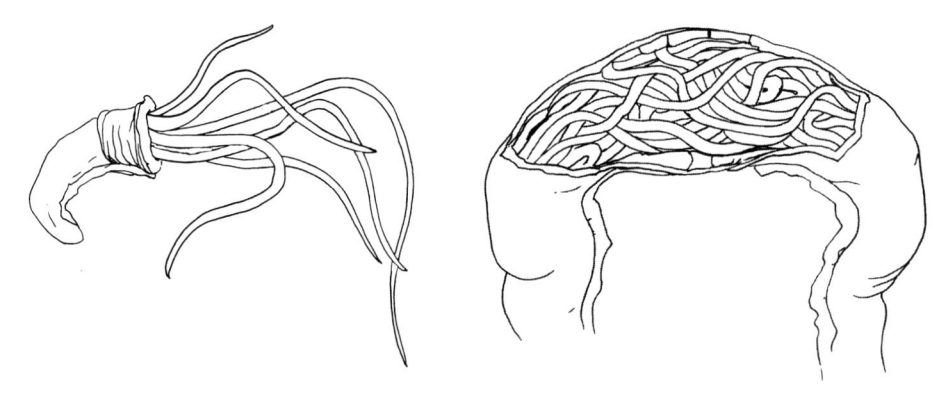

6.1 Two drawings of parasitic bowel invasion:
(left) vermiform appendix of the large intestine; (right) ascarides in the large bowel.

Lack of minerals in our soil

Our soils and drinking water have become dangerously depleted of trace minerals in the past 50 years or so – intensive farming methods have seen to that. This has caused faults in our digestive process. Electrolytes in minerals as found in a glass of clay water enhance the production of digestive juices. They assist the body in maintaining proper pH in the transverse colon, which encourage production of good friendly bacteria.

We cannot break down the valuable minerals in our food if we do not produce enough hydrochloric acid. The production of HCl declines with age, but if we take minerals this will normalise gastric secretion due to the balancing effect. We may also need to take a short course of enzyme therapy.

6.2 Dwarf tapeworm: hymenolepiasis nana.

Tapeworms love starches, milk, and sugar. Removing a tapeworm only works if the head comes out as well – they have a tendency to break into bits that can then continue to grow again. An old-fashioned remedy to get the tapeworm out is to put the patient in a bath of warm milk even adding a little sugar, the worm will soon come.

Personally, I prefer the parasite programme, followed by a skilled colonic irrigation at the end of it.

How do you know if someone has parasites?

It is difficult to diagnose but here are some guidelines.

1. excessive nose-picking;
2. grinding of teeth;
3. scratching of the anus;
4. itching of the anus;
5. spots on the bottom;
6. failure to put on weight;
7. blue rings around the eyes;
8. itchy eyes;
9. falling hair;
10. belching, bloating;
11. continual unexplained cough;
12. tiredness all the time;
13. lack of energy;
14. anaemia;
15. erratic sleeping pattern;
16. bad breath;
17. blisters in mouth;
18. poorly textured skin;
19. dry skin and hair;
20. bladder infections;
21. certain heart conditions;
22. constipation;
23. diarrhoea;
24. abdominal pain;
25. asthma;
26. allergies;
27. aching joints;
28. skin problems;
29. perspiration more noticeable on one side of the body;
30. granulomas;
31. immune dysfunction;
32. snoring;
33. restlessness;
34. nervousness;
35. observation of the iris by a qualified iridologist;
36. by Vega testing or dark field microscopy;
37. cancer (see Hulda Clark's book in Resources, p. 232).

Types of parasites

What types of parasites and cysts are there and what do they look like? How big are they, where do they come from and where do they live? If you really want to know!

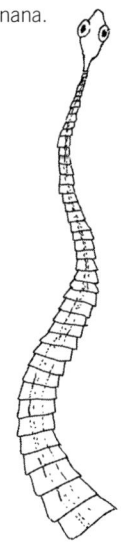

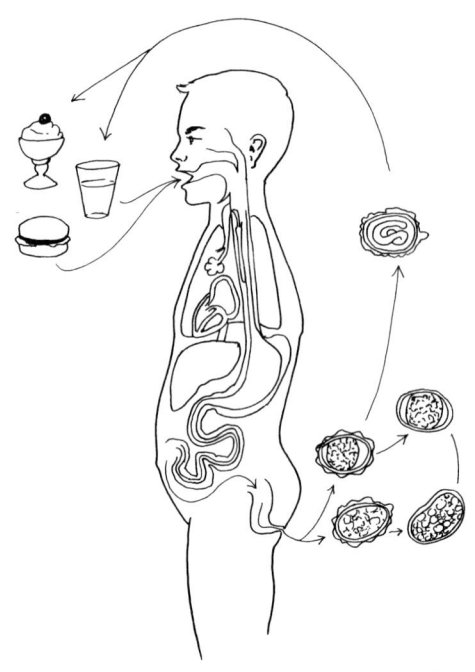

There are the common ones, pinworms, roundworms, tapeworms, flukes, amoebas, giardia intestinalis, giardia lamblia, entamoeba coli, endolimax nana, blastocystis hominus, entamoeba histolytica, nematodes. Some of these may cause no apparent symptoms or the symptoms are not generally associated with parasitic invasion, even though it will affect the quality of life. Symptoms are often merely seen as a simple case of arthritis, thrush, fatigue, indigestion and a state of general unwellness.

Larvae can also be picked up through the soles of our feet when walking barefoot in the meadows, woods or sand.

6.3 Drawing showing one of the pathways of the parasites entering the body. Larvae can also be picked up through the soles of our feet when walking barefoot in the meadows, woods or sand.

Amoeba: a water parasite – live in the intestines, liver and the eyes; found mainly in the drinking water of under developed countries.

Ascarides (various types of roundworm): adult worms 20–30cm long; from the ingestion of eggs found in food and water, ova, larvae find their way to the duodenum, portal veins, lungs, bronchi, small and large intestines and skin; common in tropical climates but can be found worldwide; can create a deficiency in calcium.

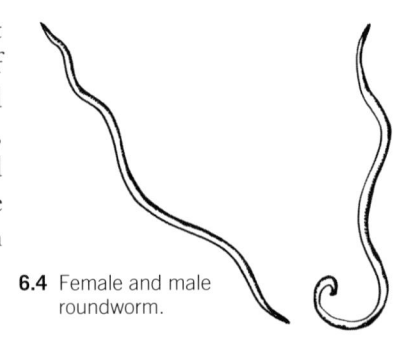

6.4 Female and male roundworm.

Fluke (*trematodes*): adults are 20–75mm long; like to live in the liver, lungs and the blood and can be found anywhere in the body. They come mainly from the Far East and originate from snails and fish; larvae in snails become cysts on plants. When ingested the larvae emerge from the cysts in the duodenum and fix to the mucosal wall of the small intestines; from there they go to the liver and biliary ducts where they like to be based. Blood flukes, found in under developed countries and other parasites, attack blood, create blood clots, and can cause strokes. Fish flukes, from undercooked fish or raw fish (sushi), can cause skin problems and intestinal troubles. Lung flukes can cause shortness of breath and anaemia. Liver flukes come from water plants that grow in polluted waters. They create all kinds of liver problems. Infestation occurs through ingestion of raw water plants and raw fish from food handlers in restaurants who do not wash their hands after using the washroom facilities. They take a bit longer to get rid of and can also stretch, become long and thin and mould themselves on and around the blood cells.

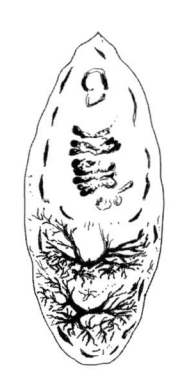

6.5 Average shape of a Fluke parasite (they can also stretch, become long and thin and mould themselves on and around the blood cells).

Tapeworm (*cestodes*): from pork, beef and fish, are very hungry and make a lot of toxins in the body.

Pork tapeworm (*Taeniasis solium*): 2–3m long, 1mm diameter; from undercooked, infested pork. Infestation also from ingestion of mature eggs passing from an infested person. Anus to mouth, e.g. food handlers that do not wash their hands after using the bathroom.

6.6 Detail of scolex (anchors to the mucosa of the intestinal wall) of a pork tapeworm.

Beef tapeworm (*Taeniasis saginata*): adult worm 4–10m long, 1–2mm diameter, reaching a diameter of 12mm. Cattle when grazing can ingest the eggs. Uncooked or undercooked infested beef can cause embryos to settle into the small intestine of man where it develops. The adult worm attaches itself to the intestinal mucosa from the top end of the worm, which is called the *scolex*; it has four suckers on a long neck, which leads to a number of segmented bits called proglottids (see Figure 6.8, p.56). Some of these segments detach themselves and are expelled in the stools. On the ground they rupture and the eggs are released. There is usually only one of these worms present in man. The symptoms are mild; in some cases, though, the appetite may increase or strangely diminish, and there can be nausea, indigestion, diarrhoea alternated by constipation, pruritis ani, nervous disorders, headaches, dizziness and irritability as well as change of character. In severe rare cases intestinal obstruction can occur.

6.7 Detail of scolex of a beef tapeworm (*Taeniasis saginata*).

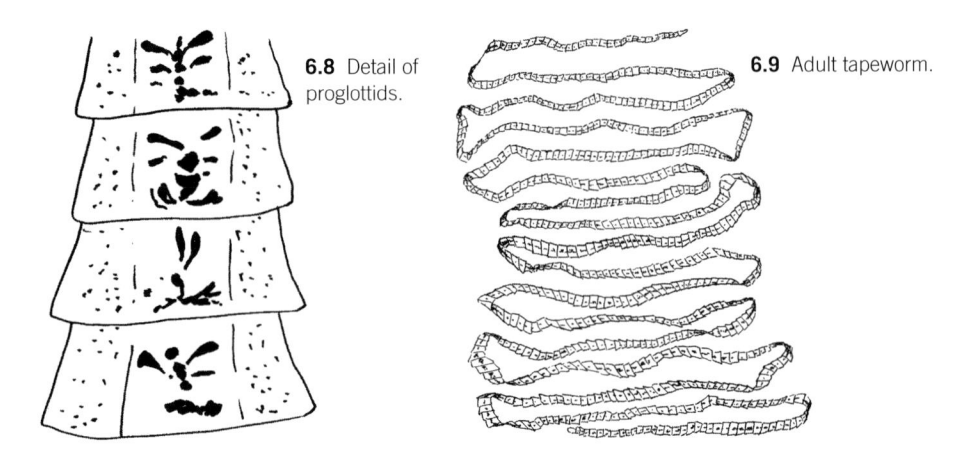

6.8 Detail of proglottids.

6.9 Adult tapeworm.

Fish tapeworm (*Diphyllobothrium latum*): adults can be 3–10m long and take 3–4 weeks to develop. From raw or poorly cooked fish. Come from adult freshwater fish caught in lakes and rivers in Europe. Siberia, Japan, North and South America. Inhabits the intestines of fish-consuming animals and humans. Symptoms similar to the above tapeworms. Like to live in the colon, robbers of everything including Vitamin B12 and folic acid, and can cause a blood sugar imbalance.

Dwarf tapeworm (*Hymenolepisis nana*): the most common tapeworm, of similar appearance as the above but much smaller in size (5–45mm long, 0.5–1mm diameter). From food and water. There can be a large number of them, up to several hundreds.

6.10 Detail of scolex of a dwarf tapeworm.

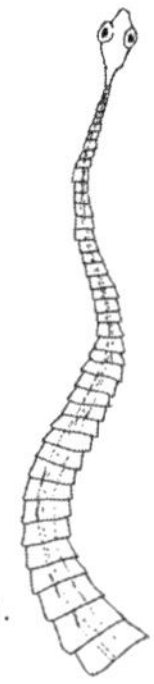

6.11 Adult dwarf tapeworm.

Whipworm (*Trichuriasis*): male 30–45 mm long, female 35–50mm long. Like to be in the cecum and appendix. They enter via contaminated food supplies from infected soil, e.g. from uncooked vegetables or indirectly from water and hands and from flies, insects and pets. More common in warm climates. As the eggs are swallowed they develop in the intestines. The symptoms, usually mild, can be mistaken for those of allergies (from parasite toxins) and types of mild inflammation. Can affect the nervous system. They can give symptoms similar to appendicitis.

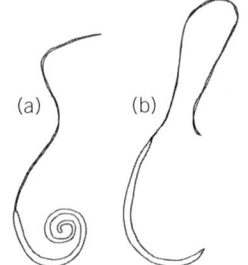

6.12 Human whipworm: (a) male; (b) female.

Only when the infestation is intense will diarrhoea, abdominal pain, distension and anaemia manifest.

Pinworm (*Oxyuris vermicularis*): male 2–5mm long, 0.3–0.5 mm diameter; female 9–11mm, 0.3–0.5 mm diameter. A very common parasite found worldwide. They like to be in the colon, the small and large intestines, cecum and appendix. Arrive from food and water. Symptoms, mild response; catarrhal inflammation of the intestinal mucosa, slight allergy, rash and joint pains. Heavier infestation may cause acute appendicitis, vulvitis, vaginitis, pruritis, leucorrhoea, lack of appetite, insomnia, restlessness, irritability, emotional instability.

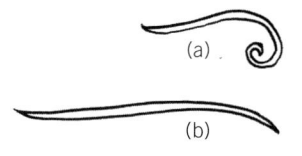

6.13 Pinworms: (a) male; (b) female.

Threadworm (*Anguillulu intestinalis*): lives in the small intestines, quite common in warm climates. They are expelled in the faeces and the larvae develop in the earth under suitable conditions. The larvae can enter the body via the soles of the feet from where they travel to the lungs; from there they ascend to the pharynx and are swallowed to end up in the small intestines where they develop; they can cause dysentery-like symptoms and diarrhoea. Sometimes the larvae remain in the lungs, particularly where there is bronchial congestion where they can then develop and cause some problems. On the whole the general condition is not so remarkable, apart from the anaemia often seen with parasitic invasions; some symptoms can be an irritating itch anywhere on the body. When the condition becomes chronic and recurring it should be dealt with.

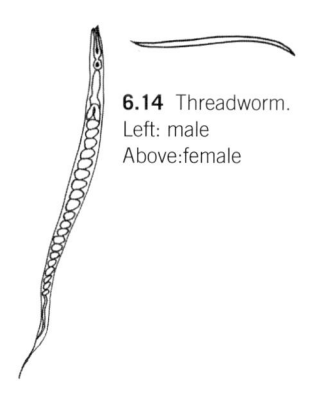

6.14 Threadworm. Left: male Above: female

Round or hookworm (*Necator americanus*): male 7–9mm long, diameter 0.3; female 9–11mm, 0.4 diameter; warm moist tropical climates. Found in the small intestines. The eggs enter through the skin, carried by the blood to the heart and

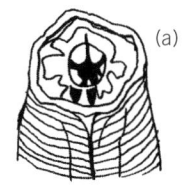

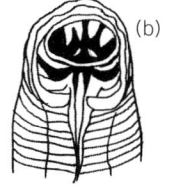

6.15 Detail of the mouth of a round or hookworm: (a) (*Necator americanus*); (b) *Ancylostoma duodenale*.

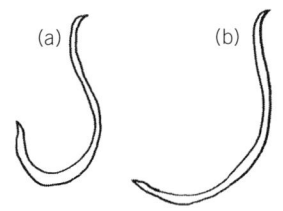

6.16 (a) male; (b) female round or hook worm.

lungs, from where they travel to the duodenum and small intestines. Here they develop into adult male and female worms. Symptoms are: from the larvae's penetration through the skin a rash may develop. In the intestines, cramps, diarrhoea, hyper-peristalsis. A mild infestation may develop into mild anaemia condition due to the sucking of blood by the mature worm, from the intestinal mucosa. Heavy infestation can induce severe anaemia, headaches, nausea, and pulmonary and circulatory disturbances. Also causes a calcium deficiency.

Toxoplasmosis

This is a disease that can be caused by an infection from a protozea (parasite), which you can get from eating undercooked meat. It is also found in the faeces of cats or from contaminated soil, attacks the foetus and lowers blood sugar levels. (Pregnant women must never change a cat litter tray, and avoid eating under cooked meat).

How to get rid of them and prevent them returning

The best way is to follow a detox and nutritional programmes, and take precautions against a recurrence. Every day we take in new toxins and parasites are part of that.

Maintain a good and strong immune and digestive system. Avoid constipation: moving the bowel regularly gives them less chance to hold on. Drink water as pure as possible, rinse your mouth with a mixture of black walnut tincture from time to time. Parasites can start to multiply in degenerated areas of your gums particularly where there is amalgam or other types of metal. Always wash your hands before handling foods.

Be careful where you shop and eat. Make sure the person handling your groceries observes hygienic standards. If you eat out a lot (even in really expensive restaurants) you have more chances of picking up parasites. Add pumpkin seeds to the diet, roasted. Have loads of garlic – including garlic juice – and onions. Avoid sugar (but don't substitute artificial sweeteners – see Chapter 4, p. 31). Boil figs before consumption, as parasitic eggs could be in them. Take:

- acidophilus;
- emulsified Vitamin A to heal the holes made by the worms;
- flaxseed oil supplements (1–5g daily) when treating the removal of worms;
- aloe vera juice;
- minerals;
- grapefruit seed extract;
- digestive enzymes (for a while).

Drink clay. Parasites can sometimes be noticed in the stools of recent clay-drinkers.

Beware of hot tubs (chlorinated) – plenty of parasites there, they also have recently been found to cause Legionnaire's disease. Legionnaire's is a type of pneumonia, caused by inhalation of water droplets. Aches and pains are rapidly followed by high temperature, coughs and breathing problems after incubation of up to 10 days. At a health exhibition in Holland last year where a jacuzzi was being demonstrated, eight people were struck down with the problem, which was discovered to be caused by the instrument.

For small children there is an over the counter remedy called 'Ovex' which will get rid of pin worms, the most common ones for them. Repeat the dose after three weeks to take care of any hatched eggs. Check with your pharmacist for details, dosage and from what age the medicine can be given. If you prefer to use a herbal remedy for your child with pin or roundworms you could try infusion of tansy flowers – a cup twice daily for a few days. Prepare 1 pint of boiling water and pour over 1oz of the herb. Steep for 10–15 minutes and keep refrigerated.

A useful herb to treat roundworms is wormseed levant (*Artemisia cina*) or use the recipe in the next chapter on the Quassia herb. Take 1 teaspoon in a little water 2–3 times daily, as well as a laxative herb in the evening.

You can try the Zapper, a device you wear around your wrists, for 1 hour daily, which is supposed to zap the creatures. This was created by Hulda Clark, author of *A Cure for all Cancers* (see Resources, p. 232).

Herbal parasite treatment

You can take a homoeopathic form of turpentine under the guidance of a homoeopath or you can go on the intensive herbal parasite programme, which I would always use at first. (This is not ideal for small children, however; you should also avoid taking it when pregnant.)

The herbal Parasite Intensive recommendation is as follows:

- 3 capsules of cloves three times daily (breakfast, lunch, dinner);
- 30 drops of black or green walnut tincture three times daily;
- 10–14 capsules of wormwood combination 2 hours before bedtime; *taken with a glass of water*, for period of five days.

While on this programme, be sure to avoid sugar and minimise starches. Increase your intake of garlic. Eat a mainly vegetable diet and drink plenty of water. Also take amino acids, which protect the liver, considering the high level of herbs taken:

- *L. arginine* – 500mg in the morning
  > (1 capsule);
- *L. ornithine* – 500 mg in the evening as follows:
   o 1 capsule on the first night;

- ○ 2 capsules on the second night;
- ○ 3 capsules on the third night;
- ○ 3 or 4 capsules on the fourth night;
- ○ 4 capsules on the fifth night.

The aminos help to protect the liver as you are taking quite a high dosage of herbs. They also neutralise the alcohols (acetate, ammonia, pyruvate and carbon dioxide) produced by the parasites, which could keep you awake.

> In short, *L. ornithine* helps you to sleep, while protecting the liver,
> and the *L. arginine* helps you to wake up, while protecting the liver.

You can take the vitamin and mineral supplements you are already on, such as your Bs and Cs. On the fourth day of this programme you may feel a little weak and have some cramps: try to take it easy on that day – maybe plan this to be a weekend day. This is the day where the mass *exodus* usually takes place. Continue on with day 5.

You should feel pretty good and a lot lighter physically and mentally afterwards, feeling a renewed energy, clear skin and healthy hair. Friends will comment, without knowing exactly what it is, on how well you look. Repeat the above one-day per week for one month. Continue with two capsules of *L. ornithine* and one capsule of *L. arginine* for several weeks (optional). Do one of these five-day intensives at least twice a year or more.

Rinse your mouth for two minutes with 2ml of wormwood tincture, diluted in a little water, twice daily before meals while on the intensive, and continue at regular intervals. This is a powerful programme and even if you are put off by having to take so many capsules, it is in my opinion the best thing to do. Or you can do it slowly and take less remedy over a much longer period - eventually it should work.

More herbal treatments

For another effective way to destroy the worms and rebuild the system (also suitable for children), try:

- 1 tablespoon of psyllium husks, three times daily; (*for seven to 10 days periods*)
- 1 teaspoon of very fine green clay twice daily in a glass of water. (*for periods of three weeks*)

It may be advisable to follow both of the above under the guidance of a qualified naturopathic practitioner. Some practitioners prefer to use a lower dosage of the herbs over a stretched-out period, which in the case of flukes is necessary.

When travelling abroad protect yourself from these unwanted visitors by taking two wormwood capsules and one clove capsule daily; every evening rinse your mouth with black walnut tincture as above.

If you have digestive problems, you are more likely to be a target for parasites, as a good supply of digestive juices renders them harmless and allows them to pass straight through. If that is the case try digestive enzymes from your clinic or health shop, and use them for a couple of months. Once your own production has increased you can use digestive enzymes now and then.

The following herbs are powerful vermifuges, anthelmintics and antiparasitic.

- black walnut;
- cloves;
- garlic;
- capsicum;
- male fern;
- sage;
- sassafras;
- tansy;
- thyme;
- oregano;
- pomegranate;
- papaya;
- pumpkin seeds;
- mullein;
- butternut bark;
- wood betony;
- wormwood;
- quassia;
- cranberry juice, from powder, not the sweetened kind, for a short while (from Biocare – see Resources, p. 216).

Important note:
It can take from three to six months to get rid of the blood fluke worms, if you have them. You'll need to continue to take the same herbs as in the intensive programme for a longer period of time, at a lower dosage, following the intensive. You may need to seek the guidance of a professional. Fluke worms can be observed through Humoral Pathology testing, using the Dark Field Microscope or use Applied Kinesiology.

The wild fox

Recent scare reports from Holland focus on the wild fox as, apparently, when the animal sneezes, particles containing the tapeworm's eggs are spread in the atmosphere and the person inhaling these particles will catch the worm this way. And within 15 years the poor affected person will die due to the liver becoming filled up with the worms.

All wild animals, dogs and cats, zoo animals and 90% of humans have parasites. This is nothing new. Maybe it is a way of justifying fox hunting.

Once again I must emphasise the fact that if our immune system is working well, many ailments including worms don't have a chance.

Thank God for creating plants.

6.17 One of the many rare orchids found in the Peruvian Amazon.

7 Mosquitoes and malaria

The bite from a mosquito can be deadly, as we heard in summer '99, when five or six people died after being bitten by mosquitoes in New York of all places. After that, *nasty* insecticides were sprayed by helicopter all around the suburbs of New York, excluding Manhattan. Yes, it seems that mosquitoes are getting more annoyingly active, even in regions where they have been harmless for ages.

In London where there always have been mosquitoes, they never used to bite. This last summer was different. It is maybe a different strain, and they bite now and leave huge swellings that take days to go down, and are very itchy. Well, we can put it down to one or two of the many changes we are encountering in our fast food, fast everything, changing world.

In the last 15 years mosquito-borne diseases have killed 50 million people all over the world. That is ten times more then the number of people killed by AIDS, and it is very worrying. Scientists are desperately trying to find new vaccines for the ever-increasing resistant strains. Somewhere on our earth someone dies of a mosquito bite every 20 seconds and according to the World Health Organisation, it is estimated that 2,000 million people in over 100 countries, are exposed to malaria. Most of these cases are in the developing countries, Africa being the most affected. Latin America has approximately 2 million cases per year.

For centuries the Peruvian Indians used the bark of the cinchona tree to curb the parasite bite. The bitter alkaloid from the bark is called quinine. This is quite toxic and poisonous in large doses and affects the heart, kidneys and liver and also weakens the central nervous system. It has in modern times been replaced by chloroquine. Quinine is still used sometimes under supervision for

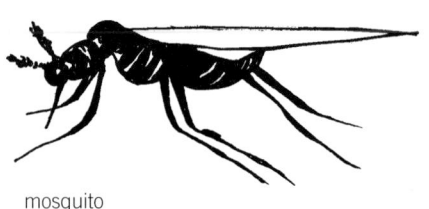

7.1 One drawing of the carrier mosquito and the mosquito parasite (*Wuchereria bancrofti*): in the tropics we can expect to get any form of malaria from the insects.

mosquito   parasite

resistant cases. The minimum toxic dose is about 3–4g for adults. Children cannot take more then 1/2 g always under medical supervision.

Peruvian scientist have recently found out about various herbs from their Amazon jungle, which have given very good results to treat malaria, but until the scientists have been able to extract the exact constituent that is the effective agent in the herb and transformed it into a vaccine, we will not be able to have it available in clinics. As you know these trial can take many years.

It is interesting to note that Samuel Hahnemann (1755–1843), the father of homoeopathy, used to give quinine for Marsh fever (another name for malaria). When an excessive amount of quinine was taken, causing poisoning, the same symptoms appeared in the patient as those that are caused by malaria. He found that the correct amount of quinine was a cure for malaria. He used quinine and performed other experiments on his own body, not on animals, making himself quite ill sometimes. This demonstrates how in homoeopathy, 'like cures like'. That is how homeopathy came about. From there he experimented with several substances with similar results, taking a highly diluted substance of a similar type to the disease to treat that same disease.

However, the usual drugs given for malaria, chloroquine and mefloquine, are no longer very effective. Bill Gates, the famous Microsoft computer giant, has kindly donated $50 million to the research into a vaccine for the killer bite. The worst strain, *Plasmodium falciparum*, is found in Kenya and Ghana.

Filarial elephantiasis (*Wuchereria bancrofti*) is a parasitic infestation caused by the mosquito bite in tropical countries. It results in a thickening and swelling of the skin, mostly in the lower limbs, due to lymphatic obstruction. The skin starts to look like the skin of an elephant.

Yellow fever is characterised by jaundice, from forest mosquitoes, mainly found in Africa and South America. You can be immunised for this before travelling to the affected regions. You will not be allowed to enter some of these regions without a certificate of immunisation.

Homoeopathic and herbal treatments

You can take a homoeopathic form of malaria treatment (see Resources, pp. 222–3). When struck down by fever get your blood tested quickly to verify what the exact problem is and get the appropriate drug treatment. As a preventative, take (high dose) B complex, wormwood and cloves capsules daily. There is a highly recommended product produced by Avon Cosmetics, called SSS, found to be disliked by mosquitoes. This can be used as an oil, lotion, spray or shower gel. The scent is pleasant and is not toxic like Deet. You must reapply it several times a day when in constant contact with the insects.

Citronella

You can also try essential oil of citronella, a natural mosquito repellent and very inexpensive. To prepare a spray, take 10ml of ethyl alcohol, brandy or vodka; four drops of benzoin essential oil; and 20–30 drops of citronella essential oil; add this to 90ml distilled water in a spray bottle.

Dengue

Also getting quite common is the not easily diagnosable Dengue, from infected mosquitoes in the tropical regions. Even though most sensible people will go to their doctors to get the standard malaria treatment in the form of daily tablets or inoculations, some mosquitoes are increasingly resistant to these drugs and they do not work on the Dengue virus: this is a big problem. When struck down by Dengue there is no actual treatment apart from analgesics. It is a painful condition with excessive fevers, draining sweats, severe aching in the bones, heavy painful legs, great weight loss and lack of appetite. There are 'flu like symptoms but much stronger than a bad 'flu, which can recur. It can last for 14 days after incubation of 5–8 days.

Herbal treatments for Dengue (Quassia and Boneset)

The following two herbal treatments for Dengue are recommended.

1 *Quassia, from Suriname and Indonesia*

This herb reduces fever and gets rid of the parasites, reducing the associated headaches quickly. To prepare:

(a) Take 2 large tablespoons of the herb.
(b) Add to 1 1/2 pints of filtered water.
(c) Leave to stand for 24 hours.
(d) Bring to the boil and simmer for 20 minutes.
(e) Strain and cool down.
(f) Add to 2 oz of vegetable glycerine and bottle.
(g) Store in refrigerator.
(h) Take 1 tablespoon in a small glass of hot water 3-4 times daily.
(i) If you cannot get any glycerine take one tablespoon of the boiled herb 3-4 times a day. Keep in the refrigerator. The mixture will not last long without glycerine.
(j) If you have no vegetable glycerine, prepare the herb freshly every 48 hours.
(k) Take for up to a week or 10 days until improved.

2 Boneset (Eupatorium perfoliatum), from N. America and Canada

This powerful but little known herb is an ancient American Indian remedy for fevers that make you feel like your bones are broken. Hence its name. It will quickly dispel fevers, including those caused by the common influenza virus, and relieve the pains in the bones. At first some slight vomiting may occur. This is good. Wait until the vomiting has stopped and then continue the treatment, keeping the patient wrapped up in bed for 24 hours. Give doses of Boneset hot infusion with a little honey every 1 1/2 hours until copious perspiration is experienced. This herb will also increase bowel movement. Then continue to use 3–4 times daily until better. To prepare:

(a) Take 1oz of the herb put in teapot or 1 teaspoon per cup.
(b) Boil 1 1/2 pint of water, add to the herb and infuse for 30 minutes.
(c) Drink as hot as possible, one wineglass full 3–4 times a day.

You will be very weak once symptoms start to subside and you may have a lot of catarrh in the lungs. A good tonic to take after the fever has gone is a mixture of tincture of herbs:

- Wahoo;
- Berberis Vulgaris;
- Balm of Gilead;
- Take 20–40 drops of the tincture 3–4 times daily.

Alternatively, contact your local naturopathic practitioner.

8 Head lice

While we are on the subject of parasites, I would like to mention a treatment for head lice, as this is an all too common problem in our primary schools. I will give you the recipe to make your own natural repellent which will not cause your child to suffer the heavy chemicals which are so frequently employed in the common treatments. As the lice are also a form of parasite it is quite interesting to read the theory of Henry Lindlarh, a famous naturopath, and it is also interesting to notice how sometimes the same children get them again and again while others never seem to get them at all.

According to the late Dr Henry Lindlahr in *Philosophy of Natural Therapeutics*, written at the beginning of this century, the lice come from within (it makes sense if you think about it). He believed that suppression of any disease would lead the disorder to go more inwards and that in this case it could be due to one of the miasmic traits e.g. the *psora* (this was also recognised by Hahnemann, the father of homoeopathic medicine).

A miasm is the foundation of all chronic disease. Lindlahr asserted that continuous suppression of the psora (itch), was gradually responsible for turning the external skin condition inwards from where it would manifest during times of stress or illness outward, into the acute form of itch, lice, scabies, hives, itchy eczema, and internally in conditions such as asthma, and chronic destructive diseases. (You can read more about miasms in the next chapter on asthma.)

Lindlahr noticed while treating a seriously ill woman in her fifties that when she underwent her 'healing crisis' (which means that sometimes the problem gets worse, comes to a peak, before improvement sets in) she was suddenly besieged by an outbreak of head lice which stayed for three days and then went, after which she started to improve. She undertook a naturopathic cleansing and herbal programme and all she did to remove the lice was use a comb and water.

8.1 Drawing of a child with the equipment to treat head lice.

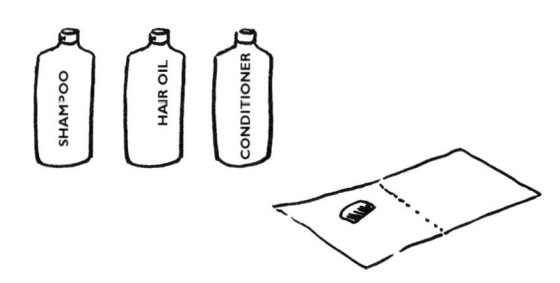

Effective treatment for head lice

There is a very effective remedy for the problem. To make your own head lice treatment, use:

- almond oil, 100 ml and the following essential oils:
- 20 drops of rose geranium oil
- 20 drops of eucalyptus oil
- 20 drops of lavender oil
- 10 drops of thyme
- 05 drops of coriander

This recipe should only be used for children aged 5 and over and kept away from the eyes

(a) Saturate the scalp with at least 30 to 40 ml of the mixture, *keeping it away from the eyes.*
(b) Then wrap the head with cling film or tinfoil.
(c) Leave on the head for at least 1–2 hours.
(d) Mix 10 ml clay shampoo (*or any natural shampoo to which you have added 1 teaspoon of green clay*) with 20 ml of water.
(e) Soap through the hair and don't add water until it starts to form foam.
(f) Then rinse off and repeat shampoo (*without adding clay*).
(g) Be sure not to put any water straight on the oily head as it will be hard to get out the oil.
(h) Use any type of conditioner if the hair is long.
(i) Comb the hair through with a normal comb.
(j) Then have the child sit at a table.
(k) Wrap a towel around her/his shoulders.
(l) Use a stainless steel nit comb.
(m) Have several white paper towels spread out near you on a table.
(n) After each comb-through with the metal comb clean the comb on the white paper-towel.
(o) You will soon see the towel filling up with wriggly black specs.

Yes, they come out easily coming as they have all passed out of the scalp. The eggs are removed at the same time. I have personally experienced this with one or two of my children and found that if it is done properly only one treatment is needed. However to be on the safe side I would repeat the procedure in 3–5 days. It is remarkably easy yet people seem to find it difficult to do and the child that is prone to them seems to have recurring attacks of the lice. It just needs a little dedication, focus and a bit of your time to do it properly.

I am planning to produce a simple video to show exactly how to do it, considering how widespread this problem is. Try it and see: your child will be so grateful.

The bonus of this treatment is also beautiful, shiny hair.

9 Asthma

In Indian Philosophy we read, 'Without breath there is no life on earth.' The Bible says, 'A man without breath is only a lifeless lump of earth, God created man from earth and breathed into his nostrils the breath of life.' It is through this respiration that Adam came to life. We can live without food for weeks, without water for several days, but if we have no air we would die in just a few minutes.

The word 'asthma' is Greek and means panting. Asthma is a laborious respiration which involves a lifting of the shoulders and severe wheezing. Its condition is characterised by periods of breathlessness, due to narrowing of the air-passages to the lungs. The narrowing can be due to spasm of the muscle wall, caused by shock or emotional upset, mucous, or swelling and inflammation of the mucous membranes from an allergic response.

I'd like to talk about this debilitating condition – lack of breath – as the illness is on the increase and affects young and old alike. The illness is little understood and few people are aware of the way the condition affects the mental side of the sufferer's health. The following shows that the problem of the asthma sufferer is not only physical but is always also mental.

Mental effects of asthma

- exhaustion;
- lack of energy;
- depression;
- stress;
- restlessness;
- lack of concentration;
- carelessness, indifferent to the extent of suffering;
- self-destructiveness – wanting things that make the condition worse;
- tiredness all the time;
- least effort wears him/her out;
- lack of confidence;
- feeling of isolation, being cut off and left out;

- feeling less worthy than other people who are 'normal';
- unable to participate in most sports events;
- poor social life, can become antisocial due to lack of breath;
- have to try harder at anything to overcome weakness;
- despair;
- do not want people to know, try to hide condition;
- do not want sympathy;
- live in hope of recovery;
- unrealistically optimistic;
- reacts to any change in the weather;
- feels better in the sun;
- feels uncomfortable during thunder storms;
- nightmares of drowning;
- insomnia;
- anxiety, fear.

There are theories that when a newborn baby cannot be breast-fed by the mother for whatever reason, and subsequently has to be bottle fed, the child can develop asthma symptoms. Later on, whenever the child drinks milk in any form, he or she may experience the same choking, gorging effect experienced from bottle feeding at a young age, when the milk from the bottle entered the baby's mouth rapidly and had to be swallowed quickly. Again, later on, when drinking milk, breathlessness may be experienced leading to panic etc. Often put down as a milk allergy, this is very common (we already discussed the effect of milk on health in an earlier chapter).

Mind and breath are closely connected: when we worry or get annoyed our breath becomes shallow. Hippocrates, the father of medicine (460–370 BC) warned the asthmatic to guard against anger. When we relax and feel good we can breathe more slowly and regularly. We can learn to regulate our breath, and thereby influence our physical and mental state.

> A gust of wind rushing through my body, I was no longer shy.
> (Kahlil Gibran, 1883–1931)

Physical effects of asthma

- lack of oxygen causes pallor;
- decrease in vitality, lack of physical strength;
- muscle waste due to lack of activity as exercise can bring on attack;
- accumulation of mucous;
- photo-phobia;
- poor posture;

- irritated throat;
- glandular enlargement, tonsils, adenoids;
- hypo-thyroid;
- shallow breathing – unable to hold the breath for long;
- recurrent cough;
- bronchial catarrh;
- unable to go for long walks, climb hills or stairs;
- dry, brittle hair and split ends;
- affects circulation;
- affects the quality of the blood, burdening all organs with wastes and toxins;
- puts a strain on the heart;
- low blood sugar;
- low immune system, frequent infection;
- affects kidneys (weakness) and adrenals, leading to adrenal exhaustion;
- affects nervous system;
- affects brain, medulla;
- tendency to hold on to toxins;
- tendency to low blood pressure;
- dizziness and sometimes fainting;
- prone to catching air borne bacteria;
- food allergies; reacts to wheat, milk and milk products, sugar; sugary things can cause cough attacks;
- often there is a problem with digestion and assimilation; fails to get enough nourishment;
- acidity;
- gynaecological disorders;
- swollen abdomen through lack of use, for abdominal breathing;
- likelihood of parasites due to lack of enzymes;
- tendency to haemorrhage and heavy periods;
- insect bites take long time to heal;
- white spots on nails;
- weak wrists and ankles;
- lungs lose their elasticity, reducing vital capacity even further with age;
- poor sleeping pattern, due to nervous hyperactivity.

These are obviously general outlines and the asthmatic may have some or all of these symptoms depending on their individual situation.

A cure as such has not been found, although a lot of medical research has been done to find one. Asthma is made worse by pollution but not caused by it, as scientist have recently proven. Research has indicated that the increase in asthma in children is just as bad in rural unpolluted parts of the country as it is in big cities, indicating the climatic and dietary involvements.

The main pollution in cities such as London comes from the buses and air-traffic. You only have to be behind a bus for a minute to realise this. As far as aircraft is concerned their pollution is invisible by the time it hits the ground, and it is therefore not often thought about or mentioned in the press. Increased pollution from too much traffic can only be changed when our public transport systems are compared to that of any other big European city, which are on the whole very efficient and cheap.

We must consider the effect of a major disturbance of the autonomic nervous system in control of the bronchial muscle. In a healthy person there is a balance between the sympathetic and parasympathetic nervous system, allowing air to flow in and out of the lungs easily. The vagus nerve in the asthmatic is in a state of hyperactivity and irritability, which in turn affects the medulla. Neural centres that control the rhythm of respiration are found in the medulla oblongata, a bulb-shaped part of the spinal cord which regulates vital life activities, blood pressure, heart rate etc. and takes care of both heart and lungs.

The nervous system is one of the most important systems to look at when treating any disease state including asthma.

The start of symptoms can sometimes be traced back to a period of time in a child's life where there may have been rejection from one or both parents for whatever reason, maybe through illness or hospitalisation of a parent, or break-up of the family unit. One parent may have had to seek work abroad and so on. To the small child this can not be explained and this terrible feeling of hurt and loss can cause tremendous suffering in this child leading to changes in the heartbeat and breathing pattern which can have lifelong repercussions affecting the spirit and the psyche.

The lungs are associated with emotion sadness. If these problems can be addressed and worked on by a trained practitioner, with the help of certain flower remedies, there can be a great improvement.

Edgar Casey has treated asthma successfully during his time of practice. He recommends various forms of healing including osteopathic manipulation, dietary considerations, climate, massage and certain minerals. To many of his patients he recommended atomidine, which seemed to bring relief in a lot of cases, taking one drop on Monday, two drops on Tuesday, and so on, and increasing it to five drops by Friday and then taking the weekend off. These are available from the EC Centre (see Resources, p. 220).

The condition can be medically controlled with the use of various medical inhalers, which can bring instant relief and alleviated by adopting a holistic lifestyle.

Naturopathically there is a lot we can do. The underlying, hidden condition manifests at certain times of year or in *certain climatic conditions* or occurs when the person is brought into contact with something that causes an allergic reaction – for example, toxic paints, such as the heavily smelling high-gloss types, favoured by many a builder: being near such fumes and smells can give an asthmatic a near attack and certainly extreme congestion in just a few minutes; they can be ill for a few days and sometimes weeks from this poison. This also can play havoc with the immune system.

There are quite a few non-toxic natural paints on the market now and I advise you to seek them out if you ever need to redecorate. Triggers also include: household dust, builder's dust, cement and plaster dust, wood dust and certain animal hairs. Avoid placing cut flowers in your bedroom, they deplete the oxygen content of the room; living plants are OK – providing you are not allergic to them, they can help to bring in more oxygen.

Sometimes asthma can be triggered after an extreme emotional upset, such as before exams, after different types of trauma, lack of sleep etc., in which case it is the stress of the situation that brings out the weakness.

Miasms

As mentioned in other chapters there could also be a miasmic involvement. A miasm 'is also known as a predisposition which is the base of all chronic diseases'. There are three main miasms or constitutions according to Hahnemann:

1 *Psora* – the itch (leprosy internalised): cannot create serious disease, only functional disorders, such as psoriasis. Psora is supposed to be the prime foundation of disease, but has to be supported by syphilis to form TB, and sycosis to give a tendency to cancer. The sycosis has to be strong to give a predisposition to cancer.
2 *Sycosis* - considered to stem from gonorrhoea. Tendency to warts, blood-disorders, overgrowth and suspicion.
3 *Syphilitic* – miasm from syphilis, ulcers, fissures, bones, soft tissues. Tendency to create a destructive energy; calcium metabolism disturbances.

Mostly we have one or more of these miasms in our constitution. Somewhere in your family's history there could have been TB. So here let us deal with the TB miasm, the fourth one, to remove the underlying cause of disease. Tuberculosis is as old as humanity, as was discovered from examining old primitive skeletons. The psora miasm is also as old, whereas the syphilitic miasm is much more recent (well, about 500 years) as this did not come about until the return to Europe, of Columbus and his crew from North America, which was then passed on from generation to generation.

To remove a predisposition is no easy task, there are layers and layers to remove. It is rather like the peeling of an onion. Ideally these layers could slowly be removed homoeopathically. This process could take a long time and needs patience. A homeopath would be able to address the situation, by examining the exact hereditary involvement, finding out about any infectious diseases in the family, what type of treatment, drugs, vaccination etc. was used. This way he or she would get a clear picture of the precise constitutional or 'like with like' remedy to prescribe.

A person with asthma will always do well to take care of the nerves, for which a good B complex formula is recommended as well as a mineral complex and a herbal nerve tonic. There is always a mineral imbalance and there are various herbs that act to tone and restore lung function and help the nervous system together. Contact a herbalist to prepare a formula to address your individual condition.

Specific herbs

Some specific herbs for asthma are:

- ephedra *
- lobelia *
- fenugreek
- golden seal
- mullein
- coltsfoot
- garlic
- ginger
- cayenne
- fennel
- liquorice
- oregano

*Some of these herbs are only available through herbalists.

Bowels must be taken care of: as you must know by now, they can contribute to any illness if they do not function as they should. Consider regular enemas. I take my own bowel formulae, which is not a laxative but tones the bowel and keeps it moving. Regular bowel movement is an important aspect of keeping the blood clean and clean blood means better oxygen for your cells.

The skin

We must not forget the skin, which is also known as our second lung. The skin must also be able to breathe in order for our health to flourish as we eliminate toxins through it.

We are used to covering up our bodies, which is no surprise in our climate. We don't perspire very much, therefore the pores have a tendency to clog up which means that toxins are not being eliminating through the skin and are subsequently recycled elsewhere in the body. An iridologist can see this clogged-up skin condition by examining 'the scurf rim' in the iris. Most asthmatics have a heavy scurf rim.

The way to try to open our pores is as follows:

- Steam baths
- Saunas
- Expose the skin to the elements when possible

- Skin brushing (dry). (See drawing under How to's)
- Epsom salt baths
- Clay poultices
- Oatmeal scrubs

Nutritionally:

- organic vegetable soups and broths, carrots, celery and parsley all prepared with Miso;
- garlic, spring onions and beetroots;
- seaweeds all types, dulse, kelp, nori etc.;
- brown rice and other grains and pulses;
- goat's milk and cheese.

Miso is a paste made from fermented barley, soya bean and other grains, and it comes from Japan. It is available in different colours, white yellow and brown. It has been cultured with a micro-organism that benefits the whole body, particularly the colon. It is helpful for the elimination of toxins, lowering cholesterol levels and is a powerful alkaliser. It is part of the daily diet for many Japanese, aiding in longevity.

To prepare Miso: take a tablespoon of the paste, and mix it with a little hot water. Experiment with the different colours and flavours. After you have prepared your soup and put it through the blender, you may add the Miso at the end, before serving. The Miso itself must never be boiled as then you will lose the valuable component in the enzymes. It is available from the macrobiotic section of your health shop.

What you should avoid

- overeating;
- mucous forming foods such as cow's cheese and milk;
- chocolate;
- shellfish;
- red meat, which takes longer to digest and adds to the toxic burden on the digestive system;
- alcohol and certain sweets, which can bring on an attack;
- foods that don't go bad as they contain many additives, e.g. bread that does not go mouldy;
- smoking.

What will help prevent asthma

- 'Rice Dream' instead of normal milk;
- small meals at regular intervals;
- plenty of water (very important for asthmatics) and herbal teas;

- plenty of vegetables and fruits, steamed or raw; but not too much citrus fruit.
- white fish, preferably deep water such as bass or deep-water cod from New Zealand;
- despite the controversy surrounding coffee, for the asthmatic one cup of real organic coffee can alleviate an attack;
- eucalyptus tea, particularly good for the lungs (also look out for eucalyptus honey, which is delicious and also helpful);
- alfalfa tablets detoxify and alkalise;
- calcium and magnesium supplements;
- drink clay often;
- use psyllium husks 3–4 or more times per year for 10 days at a time; these can be combined with clay and herbs;
- GLA fatty acids in food and capsules;
- Linseeds, 3 teaspoons daily (ground up in your coffee grinder);
- chew your food well;
- Zell-oxygen can bring about positive change and can be combined with healing clay (Resources).

Good foods will never show a side effect, unlike drugs.

Food for thought

Here are some more ideas to overcome this let down feeling.

- Avoid negative emotion, jealousy, shallowness and negative people.
- Positive thought and talk make a good body and mind, brings goodness, power and good fortune.
- Our words are our reality; don't complain a lot, only when really necessary.
- Do not gossip, criticise or talk badly about people, do not listen to those that do.
- Do not allow yourself to be contaminated by their thought and speech pattern, if you can't change them, walk away.
- Gossip is darkness, weakens your aura and attracts negativity; poisons your ear.
- Give light and blessings to those that talk and spread negativity about yourself and others.
- Don't say to yourself that you are weak – gain strength from your weakness.
- Be kind and tolerant to others; after all, it is much easier to be nice to people than not.
- Let your words be uplifting to others and not bring them down; this is the only spiritual way to be.
- Believe in what you do and try and help others.
- None of us has come on to this Earth to be perfect.
- Take care of the physical side or the mental side will suffer.
- What you fear will come upon you; you cannot live in fear.

- People are more important than material things.
- 'Marry a man without love, and what do you have? A corpse in your bed' (Bernard Jensen).
- Never take on a job that could harm another person.
- Meditate. Forgive. Let go.
- But remember, don't be a doormat either.

Acidity and asthma

The illness is associated with acidity. Mucous is acid, and asthma conditions always produces mucous. Acidity conditions lack oxygen. We need to think about alkalising in order for healing to take place. Oxygenation can only take place in an alkaline state. When we are too acid all kinds of illnesses can develop that affect out immune system. All acid states are inflammation and eventually lead to cancer.

One of the ways we get acid is through our diet, the way we react to certain foods, i.e. proteins, chemical, inhalants, toxins etc. all of which affect our pH balance. Regular detoxification and enemas as well as colonic cleansing are very important.

The elements

Everything in the universe – plant, man, fish, bird, dog, cat, cow, horse etc. – is perceived as being made up of five elements.

The five forces of energy, Ether, Air, Fire, Water, Earth, are a part of chi, yin and yang, creating an overall harmonious balance. This is 'Tao' which forms the basis of all things in the material creation and governs everything from our constitution to our taste in food, our liking for either cold or hot, raw or cooked food, salty or sweet, rain or shine etc. The key to health is to balance these elements. Whether we are dealing with mental or physical *disease*, in Asiatic cultures these elements come together in three basic principals (Tri-doshas):

- Air + Ether
- Fire + Water
- Water + Earth

These are known as Vata, Pita and Kapha. It is when these three doshas are out of balance that disharmony strikes. Vata (ectomorph) is responsible for activating the other doshas. Vata relates to movement, activity, breath and inspiration. Pita (mesomorph) is to do with the power of the inner fire, digestion, assimilation and body temperature. Kapha (endomorph) is to do with mental strength, endurance and resistance to illness. All of us have some of these three doshas in our constitutions. The dominant dosha is what determines the character type.

It is possible to correct an imbalance with certain herbs and foods. To learn more about Ayurvedic constitutions, to find out yours and to look at the best diet for each constitution, see Further reading (p. 233 and 234).

Eliminating shallow breathing is a must. This is something that is not just found in asthma – most people don't breathe properly or deeply enough. The breath is very complex; with our breath we connect body, mind, spirit and surroundings. The *in*-breath helps to nourish our cells, tissues and organs (imagine a liquid white or yellow light entering the lungs on the *in* breath), The *out* breath clears waste and toxins (imagine a dirty dark brown liquid leaving the lungs on the out breath). This you can do during a meditation of perhaps 10–20 minutes daily.

Asthmatics tend to have problems with the out-breath.

Yoga: the Sun Salutations

Yoga is very beneficial for the asthmatic as various forms of deep breathing, such as *Kapalabathi*, are practised. The daily practice of the Sun Salutations (*Surya Namaskara*), a series of 12 postures taking only a few minutes to do, is very balancing as it takes you up and down, revitalises and relaxes. This is a perfect Yin Yang exercise. The yoga movement enables you to greet the sun every day of your life and start you on your new day.

12 o'clock   Stand up straight and with your palms together in front of your chest, breathe in and out slowly a few times.

1 o'clock   Inhale as you stretch both arms behind you. Keep the head between the arms. Head back, palms facing upwards, the back arches backward.

2 o'clock   Exhale, keep the head between the arms and move forward from the waste down. Try to reach the toes and bend the knees if needed. The head, neck and shoulder should drop loosely. Head toward the knees.

3 o'clock   Bend the knees, place your hands on the ground beside the feet, stretch back the right leg, left knee remains bent, while inhaling push the head back. Hold for a few seconds.

4 o'clock   Bring the right leg back in line with the left, raise your bottom up with the body becoming a triangle shape; your chin should be touching your chest (see Figure 9.1). Hold the breath for a few seconds.

5 o'clock   Then move your feet back, lower your body until your forehead, chest and knees touch the ground. Keep your tummy elevated. Exhale as you go down.

6 o'clock	Now inhale while arching the back. Supported by the arms, with elbows slightly bent, your head goes right back and your chest is lifted of the ground; your belly and feet stay on the ground. Return to the 5 o'clock pose.
7 o'clock	Raise the hips back into a triangle (see 4 o'clock) while exhaling, heels to the ground and chin to the chest.
8 o'clock	Bring your right leg forward between the hands and raise the head, while inhaling. The left leg is stretched back and the knee touches the ground.
9 o'clock	Now bring the feet together. Keep the knees straight. Drop the torso forward from the waist. Relaxing the neck, head, shoulders and arms, let the weight fall toward the floor. Exhale.
10 o'clock	Very slowly come into an upright position as you inhale, and stretch your arms backwards. Keep the head between the arms with your palms up to the sky.
11 o'clock	Go back to the upright position while exhaling and put palms together in front of the chest. Close the eyes and remain like this for a few seconds, breathing normally.

Repeat the entire sequence two or three times. When you get stronger you can increase to 6 times, then 9 and 12 over a period suited to each individual. The postures can be done in the evening as well. Each movement should be done slowly or quickly (depending on your constitution). and held for about 5–10 seconds.

9.1 The 12 Sun Salutations postures.

Kundalini yoga: Breath of Fire

Kundalini yoga is a most profound form of yoga for the asthmatic. It involves a series of postures that nearly always use either a beautiful mantra or sound to empower or calm you. The postures involving sound are very effective for the asthmatic as the sound follows the out-breath. The special breathing exercise is called 'Breath of Fire'. This involves a rapid breathing though the nostrils, i.e. more than one inhalation per second.

- Inhale bringing the diaphragm down and out.
- Exhale bringing the diaphragm in.
- Relax the chest, so you find your abdominal area moving in and out very rapidly.

The exercise makes you feel calm and alert. Oxygen levels will increase. You can do this exercise twice or more times per day for 5–10 minutes.

9.2 The fire breath in action in Kundalini yoga.

Relaxation posture

A lot of Chakra cleansing is involved in the meditations and exercises. My teacher, Guru Dharam, uses the sounds of a gong in about the middle part of the class, while we are in the relaxation pose for about 10 minutes. The sounds fill the room and vibrate through the body and all its trillions of cells. This is a

9.3 Relaxation posture with gong in a yoga class.
9.4 Individual sound session to relieve stress and depression (see resources)

wonderful and powerful part of the session. After the classes our energy level is amazing: every cell in the body is alive. Guru Dharam also does courses in sound healing, which is of great benefit in stress release (see Resources, p. 231).

Your voice

Asthmatics' voices tend to be soft, ethereal, angel-like and unclear. Partly due to the condition and partly due to the prescribed drugs. I recommend voice classes, (to strenghten your '*channel of sound*') which involve much more then learning how to use your voice. The voice training is actually mostly to do with the breath and using imagery, whereby you drop the breath right down, through your 'channel of sound' to a point or beautiful object (say an imaginary crystal or diamond) to below the navel from which your voice should come.

On the out breath, while pushing the abdomen in, it is possible to make the 'Ahh' sound for several minutes, which is very beneficial. After a while of this practice you find your breathing much improved. There are a series of deep relaxation and breathing exercises involved, including Kapalabathi, and most of the breath exercises involve sound.

Kapalabathi

Kapalabathi is a series of fast, vigorous exhalations making a 'shee' sound followed by inhalations, which are slightly slower. It is best to sit relaxed, with the spine straight, on the floor in the yoga position using the (solar plexus) diaphragm to move the breath. This is most excellent for asthmatics (see Kundalini yoga: Breath of Fire section, above, p. 80).

Even though some of these exercises can and should be practised at home, the classes are fun and when you leave the class, relaxed and confident in your newly found voice and breathing technique, you'll want to come back for more. Try and find a class in your area by contacting your local library or check your local 'What's on' or 'Time Out' guides.

Disorders of the vocal cords, as well as the respiratory system, are exacerbated by deficient breathing techniques. Mostly the voice comes from the throat and in the asthmatic the throat is mostly raw and mucusy, and they tend to have light voices, through shallow breathing as well as from the regular use of broncho-dilators. People often ask them to repeat themselves as the voice is too light; this can be frustrating and annoying for the asthmatic. In the voice class we talk about white, grey and black sounds. Most asthmatics are speaking with a white/grey sound. After several classes you can surprise your friends with your new black sound. White sound is a mere whisper while the black sound is a power sound.

As a result of deficient breathing the asthmatic tends to catch colds more easily. They are used to breathing through the mouth due to the sinuses filling up with mucus. Mucus provides an ideal breeding ground for any passing germ or bacteria, fungus and parasites. Once the voice techniques are regularly practised, you will find not only an amazing change in the volume of your voice, but also an increased volume in the lungs.

Ancient philosophy

From the moment we are born we are given a certain number of breaths for our lifetime, according to Indian philosophy. When you breathe shallowly, you need to take more breaths per minute than you would if you breathed deeply and took longer to exhale. Therefore if you breathe shallowly you are going to run out of your given amount of breaths before your time.

If we followed the example of the ancient sages of the East who breathed slowly and lived quietly, and used their life on earth for spiritual progress, we too would be able to prolong our life and avoid sickness. These wise men realised that by regulating their breath, they maintained their vitality and strength, and avoided disease. They created special religious ceremonies consisting of the practising of deep breathing exercises and postures, with the intention that these would be practised daily by the whole population. This is known as *yoga*.

So if we now know this, it is important to repair our health any way we can. I know it is harder in the century in which we find ourselves but with a few easy-to-follow guidelines we can try. You are never too old or too ill to live life to the full. Look for help and you will find it. Above all, be positive.

> Still the breath divine does move and the breath divine is *Love*.
> (William Blake, 1757–1827)

If you are interested in looking at the karmic side of illness, there is a very good book on the subject, *Karma and Reincarnation* (see Further reading, p. 233).

10 Depression

This chapter has been written for my friend Michael, who sadly died in June 1999. Even though this is quite personal, it is I believe very relevant within the context of this book. And I wish to share this with you.

The importance of a good mind

What is in the head, or lacking therein, will affect the body. The above asthma chapter points out how the mental affects the physical. This is the case with all illnesses. *Without our spirit we have nothing at all.* Many people are selfish, stab each other in the back, materialistically orientated and shallow. They don't think about their actions or how they can hurt other people with their words. Sometimes words and malicious gossip can kill.

Lies and untruthfulness can affect the secretions needed for digestion, creating negativity in us. As we sow, we will reap.

Bernard Jensen calls it 'stinking thinking'. Your thinking can harm yourself as well as someone else. Thoughts are a substance – they are things – and your body is a temple, which follows the mind. Our thinking can destroy us, we must change our language, and words have feelings. They have vibration, their own atomic power, use it too much and it can destroy.

All disease begins from within, from the head down: your mind can make you ill. You can never be well until you rid yourself of rubbish. Bacteria survive in heat, temper and anger. Emotions affect all your important organs, particularly the thyroid. Anger affects the liver, worry affects the spleen and fear affects the kidneys. Joy affects the heart and sadness affects the lungs. It takes energy to see the perfection in people. Very few people can be bothered to use that energy.

> Pick out a new language, we see as we think, and we think as we see.
> (Dr Bernard Jensen)

If the doors of perception would be purified, we would be able to see everything, as it is, 'endless'. But we're closed in – we can only see things through the small opening of our cave.

The importance of the thyroid

The thyroid is the *master* gland of our metabolism, the gland of our emotions. Ninety percent of humanity is affected with under-active thyroid function. It is one of the most neglected organs in our body. Every emotion, conflict, argument, resentment, regret is troubling and painful to the thyroid gland. Phobias and other emotional problems can develop from a thyroid weakness, among other deficiencies. The mind is helped if we can strengthen the thyroid. Proper thyroid function is most important when we are looking to improve the health of our brain.

There are certain brain toxins that will be destroyed by thyroid hormones. These are produced by a well-functioning thyroid gland. One of the dietary ways of combating the deficiency is adding seaweed to the diet. Or taking a seaweed tincture. This will help to balance the function. To check how your thyroid is functioning, you can try the Barnes thyroid temperature test:

- For four days take your temperature under your armpit before rising in the morning; allow about 10 minutes.
- If your temperature is below 96.4 (35.8) degrees, your thyroid is under-active.
- If your temperature is above 98.2 (36.8) your thyroid is hyperactive.

A slightly hyperactive thyroid is not much to worry about, as it helps keep our weight under control and raises the energy. Only when excessively hyper will it cause discomfort. Consult a naturopathic practitioner or homoeopath for the best way to treat the hidden disorder. If the thyroid is not working efficiently it is best to work on improving its function before resorting to anti-depressants. You may need thyroxin (prescribed by your Doctor)

There is so much depression all around us. The problem of depression is reaching epidemic proportion. Only this week I read in the news about the number of Japanese executive types committing suicide over the last year. I could not believe the figure was as high as 32,863. Now that is a lot of men and I think it is very sad. Most men were in their forties or fifties, the prime time of their working life. Seventy per cent of these people died because of depression from external factors (exogenous), mainly due to the economic slump. Then there are those depressed people who suffer from hormonal or biochemical changes in the body, which can be inherited (endogenous).

Manic depression and lithium therapy

For example, manic depression is usually due to a chemical deficiency in the brain. A lack of lithium. Lithium therapy is a safe and effective medically prescribed treatment for the problem, with two 300mg tablets taken daily.

Note: seawater contains an adequate supply of lithium, in balance with nine other elements and trace elements to help stabilise moods and brain function (this could be a helpful addition).

Histamine

There could also be an excess of histamine. This can be determined by blood tests. An excess of histamine can cause mucus and allergies, make the person hyperactive, behave compulsively and become depressed. If the histamine levels get out of hand they can cause severe chronic depression and suicide.

Depressives also have low blood sugar, which makes them reach for instant pick-me-ups such as sugar, cola etc. They also tend to have mild or severe candida, which alone can create depression, as well as invite parasites. They are generally very brave and cope with their disability very well provided the emotional, nutritional and mineral side is taken care of. They desperately need security, be it emotional or financial. A good steady routine is very important. When either of these is impaired, the illness can escalate and the normally prescribed dosage of their medicine has to be increased. They can become more fearful of everything and can't imagine getting or feeling better. Most people that don't have the problem cannot understand the seriousness of such a condition.

We all feel depressed sometimes, maybe because of the weather or something nasty that was said, a horrible neighbour, or because of the fighting and cruelty going on in some other country or cruelty to animals, witnessed or read about. Or grieving the loss of a loved one. But all those emotions, which on the whole don't last, cannot be compared with the absolute despair a severe depressive suffers.

Factors that worsen the conditions

If we come across someone in this condition, we should try to be as helpful and understanding as possible. The problem of their depression can be made much worse by:

- stress;
- setback;
- death or loss of loved one;
- agitation;
- feeling of memory impairment (often a side effect of the medicine);
- feelings of anger;
- feelings of hopelessness;
- lack of self-confidence;
- exhaustion due to sleep difficulties;
- relationship problems;
- financial worries;
- feels unable to cope with minor responsibilities;
- sudden loss of job;
- sexual dysfunction (mostly due to drug treatment);

- insomnia (the same);
- feelings of neglect;
- feeling of injustice;
- lack of proper care;
- the wrong medicines.

When they speak of suicide, take it seriously! The worst thing that can happen to these people, who are often highly intelligent and gifted, is to put them in a psychiatric ward with severely mentally impaired people. Unfortunately if they suffer from any of the points above and have more than 3 or 4 of these listed, they can end up in such a ward albeit initially for observation. They can easily become suicidal and they will then be given more powerful medicines to curb the suicidal tendency, which can lead to more insomnia and confusion, and after several weeks of this treatment when the sufferer seems to be able to cope they will discharge the person. By that time he/she will be in great need of counselling.

They have a great need to talk, they really need to get things off their chest, and these could be private things that they could not discuss with their best friends or partner. As they seem so perfectly normal, calm and able, often that is overlooked. After a spell on the ward it is imperative to keep a close watch on such a patient once discharged. Even if they seem fine, they are not, and how could they be after having been given so many different mind-altering drugs that also caused constipation, allowing the toxins and chemicals to recycle in the body thrice or more?

Aftercare must be provided and followed up. It is not easily possible to help a person in that condition with nutrition and herbs as the psychiatrist inevitably in charge of such a patient will not allow it, claiming the addition of any supplement will interfere with the drug treatment (and some supplements would).

It would be nice if the two could work together.

Note: some of the most modern drugs for depression appear to be similar to a nutritional approach, helping the body to produce more seratonin (a neurotransmitter) the deficiency of which can increase the tendency to depression. They take about four weeks to work and have quite a high success rate, appearing to have little or no side effects unlike earlier drugs given for depression (other than a constipating effect). In the absence of concerted nutritional/naturopathic approach the drugs should not be selected out of hand.

The patient is usually so insecure and frightened of the condition, once worsened, that s/he will follow doctor's orders. The only way naturopathic help can be resumed or given is when the drug therapy has been sufficiently levelled out and the patient understands that s/he will need something to move his or her bowel and try to eliminate the accumulated toxins so s/he can feel better.

Psychiatrists are generally not well informed about herbal or nutritional therapy. They only know what they have studied and experienced with their patients, but they must look at and acknowledge the nutritional aspect, and refer them, or work with the appropriate practitioner. They are very clever people, but they should also open their mind to how diet etc. and especially excess sugar affects these patients, who always crave sugars and always like to drink beverages containing aspartame, caffeine and other harmful additives and colours which cause hyperactivity in normal people. Very rarely will the doctor ask patients about their sugar intake.

Constipation is a disease of mind and body. I know that the National Health Service is severely overstretched and doctors and nurses are overworked and stressed. And in many cases the doctor has a sugar habit too, for those very reasons.

I get 'depressed' about this sometimes, as I have lost a dear friend to suicide.

Michael was a sufferer of the above disability – manic depression. He had suffered several upsets in his life, including severe abuse as a child. Recently he suffered a sudden unexpected loss of employment and problems with a close relationship in a short period of time. I believe he would still be with us today had he been given the counselling he so desperately needed as well as the nutritional help.

The day he ended his life on Earth, he had spent seven hours of his day in the hospital outpatients' ward, waiting to be seen after having been discharged two weeks earlier from six weeks on a psychiatric ward. While in hospital, after 2–3 weeks of treatment, he had suffered several days of insomnia, for which he was sedated to help him get some sleep, after spending seven days awake. Then when he was sent home, supposedly better, with six different anti-depressants to take daily, he felt confused, frightened and insecure.

After a week at home he found it difficult to sleep again, had constant ringing noises in his ears, was constipated, fearful, tormented and desperate. He told me he really needed to talk and he cried a lot. The day he went to wait in the hospital, he was so exhausted from not sleeping for 10 days that he just wanted to be given an injection to sleep. Unfortunately he was not even seen. And after sitting there waiting all day for just someone to see him …

He went home, more desperate, lonely, lost. He called several friends and not finding anyone in, and seeing no more hope, no light on the horizon, only dark clouds, he took his own life with no-one present but his *loving* dog. He was just 38. He had had his birthday just a few days after coming out of hospital and he was also upset that his mother had not even called to wish him a happy birthday.

He had a lot of living to do. He was gifted, talented, likeable, charismatic and good-looking, enthusiastic, bubbly. He was good, kind and generous with everything: time, material things, stuff he had learned he wanted to pass on and had *big* plans for the future – he had been hoping to recover.

He wanted to drink clay again as it made him feel good (he used yellow clay for a short while, which is good for mood changes, helps transmission of nerve impulses to the brain) and take herbs, zinc and B complex, lecithin, minerals, and seaweeds. Michael's irises revealed an inherent thyroid weakness.

Inherently weak tissues or organs do not have a good reserve of the necessary minerals, we need to supply the chemical element to replenish that weak part. An inherent weakness does not necessarily mean one has a disease, but the possibility of one if the body is sufficiently abused.

He had a lot of plans. He wanted to start yoga and meditate and planned to develop his psychic skills. He was a great cook. He loved people and animals and made them feel good, and they loved him – he probably did not even realise how many friends he had. It is a great loss. Life is so precious. The mind is so delicate. When he asked for counselling he was told that the waiting list was one year.

Depression is a hidden illness with the very severest side effects.

28 rules for the body and soul

1. No one is 100% healthy. Accept yourself as you are. You are what you are and that in itself is beautiful. Learn from your *disease* and work to positively improve your stronger points.
2. Increase your awareness, read more, learn, study, attend workshops, take a course.
3. Involve yourself in environmental issues; but don't take on the world's problems. Everyone has their own evolutionary experience on this planet. Remain aware but detached and focused.
4. Do not overeat; avoid high calories and high protein diets; don't eat late at night.
5. Improve your diet; use some of this book's ideas to improve it or consult a naturopathic practitioner to guide you.
6. Do not follow *any* crash diet. They can do more harm then good.
7. *Detox on a regular basis.* If you do, you will find unwanted weight will drop off. Every day we acquire toxins from food, air, water and people and every day we must take that into account. Do not become obsessed about it. (Remove any metal from your mouth.)
8. Do not expect an overnight miracle – it takes time to build a disease and so it will take time to bring back balance. Allow the change in diet and lifestyle to come in gradually; do it with harmony.
9. Avoid constipation of body and mind.
10. Implement stress reduction techniques through meditations and yoga. Get in touch with your higher self; take in quiet time to reflect on nothingness.

11. Exercise rhythmically daily. Walk, cycle, swim, yoga, tai-chi, chi-kung, or just dance; move your body to your music; make love.
12. If possible try to reduce or eliminate the amount of drugs you take, with supervision if needed.
13. Do not think of your age too much. It is only a number. You can think yourself old (and thereby limit yourself of experiencing much of life's amazing possibilities), which in itself will increase the ageing process. Always keep vital in body and mind.
14. Do not give too much energy to your dis-ease – you can think yourself ill. Use a portion of your mind's 50,000 daily thoughts to bring positive change in your life.
15. Value each and every day of your life.
16. Learn to love yourself before you love another. If you dislike yourself, how can you expect someone else to like you?
17. Avoid complacency at all times. Keep it fresh, particularly in relationships; don't take anything or anyone for granted.
18. Avoid retirement, this can turn into a slow way of dying, be a cause of depression ... and decreasing brain-power. You must use your brain. After all your brain is another muscle, that will go flabby if not exercised regularly. Keep actively involved in life.
19. Be compassionate; do something that benefits a total stranger, often.
20. Help elderly people. They are often lost and need help crossing the road, talking to etc.
21. Have kindness for others; a smile can bring sunshine to a life of misery.
22. Children – set a positive example for them, learn from them and nurture your inner child.
23. Keep a pet and be kind to it; it has been scientifically proven that they can prolong your life and even heal your illness.
24. Avoid anger and overheating; it is never worth it and affects colon, kidney, spleen, liver, gallbladder, heart and brain.
25. Avoid watching too much TV and bad news. You can't change these things physically, remember everyone has their own evolutionary experience on this earth-plane.
26. Do the best you can in each situation in which you find yourself.
27. Give away something you truly value and love.
28. In this life we are driven by two most powerful forces. The primary one is hunger for nourishment the second is sexual desire. In order for the last force to be healthy, be sure to nourish the first with care.

Health tips and general guidelines

Water	Drinking 8 glasses daily as a minimum requirement is a very general statement, not necessarily suited to each individual; 2 or 3 glasses daily as well as suitable herbal infusions are a good idea. Listen to your body. Aim for 1000ml.
Oil	Minimise your intake of oils and fats. If you fry at the moment with olive oil, use less and add water. It will make a difference to your health.
Meats	Avoid red meat, eat lamb, organic or from New Zealand from time to time
Fish	Stick to white deep water fish, minimise or avoid shellfish and smoked salmon.
Eggs	Only eat organic free range eggs, 3–4 per week; egg yolk is a good form of lecithin.
Fruits and vegetables	Depending on your condition, eat plenty, organic and preferably locally grown. If you have liver/gallbladder or pancreatic insufficiency, eat more orange-coloured ones, e.g. carrots, apricots; for heart and circulation, look for the red and green ones, e.g. beets, kale etc.; for the kidneys, seek out plenty of yellow ones.
Protein	Avoid high levels from flesh and dairy foods. We are only able to use and store a minimal amount of protein in our body; any excess we do not need is excreted. The liver and kidneys are having to work overtime to deal with this excess, and can enlarge. The chances of osteoporosis and kidney stones increase, calcium is leached from our bones and tissues, and lost on high protein consumption; it ends up in the kidneys where stones begin to form. The purines found in these high protein foods lead to the production of uric acid, which leads to conditions such as gout. Proteins from vegetables are good; high level from beans, artichokes, celery, tofu; medium level from chestnuts, almonds, oats, potatoes, rice, yams, whole wheat; low level from dates, mangoes and coconuts.
Pulses and grains	Include millet, barley, corn, rice, beans, whole wheat, rye, spelt, lentils.
Nuts and seeds	For brain health, take a couple of walnuts and 3 almonds a day (soak almonds overnight and eat them slowly in the morning); sesame, flax, and pumpkin seeds; take a couple of teaspoons of ground-up seeds daily, a good source of minerals and EFAs.
Cheeses	Eat moderately; can be mucus forming and are rich in animal fat; can be clogging to the vascular system; organic hard cheddar occasionally or goat's cheese.
Milk	Avoid cow's milk. Look for substitutes in your health shop, i.e. Rice Dream, goat's milk.
Bread	Avoid too much wheat bread, if suffering from candida eat yeast free breads, made of spelt or rye flour.
Fruit and vegetable juices	Always dilute 50/50 with pure water and cut down, unless freshly squeezed.

Alcohol	Avoid hard liquor; 1–2 glasses of *red* wine can act as a tonic to the heart.
Salt	Avoid table salt; substitute with Bio-salt, or Herbamere from Dr Vogel; use Miso, Tamari and Gomasio.
Sugar	Sugar is a silent killer – do not take; avoid sugar substitutes; use maple syrup, or honey moderately.
Preserves	Use small amounts of organic only.
Pickles, vinegars and spices	Use the macrobiotic variety as they will aid the digestive system.
Iced drinks, ice cream etc.	These create a lot of work for your organs, particularly the poor, often forgotten spleen; your organs are diverted from doing their normal job by having to warm up the ice-cold substances to maintain homeostasis, and funnily enough they do not cool you down, as is widely believed. In India hot tea is drunk to cool down in the heat.

Note: These are general outlines. Consult a professional for your individual specification according to your constitution.

PART II Clay Therapy

How the dust of the earth can miraculously help us restore our health and equilibrium

11 We are born out of the dust (clay)

Genesis 2.7, 3–19.

Clay as a curative medium

Clay therapy is a mostly forgotten therapy. In some countries in Europe clay has been used for centuries, but here in Britain and the States it has been neglected for many years. Now the green clay is becoming popular again for its natural properties and detoxification ability.

Clay has been used therapeutically for thousands of years and has been used as a medicine dating back to ancient times. The Bible refers several times to clay: 'God gave clay to help the handicapped and to give back sight'. 'And the lord God formed man out of the dust of the earth and breathed into his nostrils the breath of life, and man became a living soul'. (Genesis, 2.7)

In old scriptures we read that man is formed from clay giving the body stability, firmness and resilience. In the writings of Pliny the Elder, AD 23, *The Natural History*, which comprises 37 books recording the state of scientific developments during the first century and which is still recognised today, takes in works of over 400 Roman and other writers. Pliny was forever in awe of the power of nature. In these works it states, 'There is a clay soil which absorbs discharges. It is used in medicine, dries and heals damaged skin tissue, can be applied as an eyewash, and removes scars.' He asks, 'What is there that does not appear marvellous, that comes to our knowledge for the first time?'

The ancient Egyptians used clay not only medicinally, but also to mummify their dead. They knew that it was beneficial for its anti-bacterial and preserving ability, and centuries later we can still learn from them. The Chinese used it for many purposes and so did the Greeks. The Romans used the clay to repair fractures, and for their healing bathing rituals.

Humans first learned of clay's usefulness by observing the behaviour of animals as they lived so closely and in harmony with them. They watched how they would roll in the clay if they had an itch, injury, bite or parasitic infestation or they would eat it when their stomachs were upset or had excessive gas or food poisoning, which was not unusual. The indigenous people saw how quickly the animals recovered, and followed their example.

Animals in the wild have a natural instinct and know what they need when illness or disharmony strikes: they can sniff out the exact herb, flower, plant, or piece of clay, and chew it when dizzy, upset or tired. Through learning from and watching the animals, tribal people started using clay for various curative purposes and they even used it to embalm and preserve the dead.

Father Sebastian Kneipp

The famous German Pastor, Father Sebastian Kneipp, (1821–97), used the clay in various forms with his water therapies. He devoted his time more to the detoxifying aspect of the body then to the purification of the soul. He gained a lot of fame and notoriety with his controversial treatments for which he was paid in gold and soon accumulated riches beyond belief. With this money he opened at least three sanatoria: the Sebastianeum, the Kneippiannum and a children's clinic, which were all run by monks and nuns.

'The more I have to deal with sickness,' he wrote, 'the more I am convinced that God the creator of all things has given us the means of a cure, viz. one half water, one half herbs.'

The Church declared him a 'non-holy' person as he continued to gain fame and money through his work but in his locality he was elevated to the title 'Holy Water' man. The most famous of his clinics was located about 80km from Munich, where he had as many as 7000 beds. He discovered the healing power of water and was often seen walking barefoot through the meadows. His most famous clay treatment was the clay and vinegar mask whereby the ailing body was painted all over with the mixture, often giving miraculous recoveries. The 'Kneipcure', as the treatment has become known, is utilised in many spas and clinics in Europe. In Germany alone there are as many as 50 clinics where the cure is practised. There are a few books written about water therapy (see Resources, p. 233 or check out your local bookstore).

During the Asiatic cholera epidemic in 1914, Professor Stumpf, a German, used clay successfully to treat the dysentery associated with the debilitating illness.

Animals, birds … and clay

In modern times we have lost these natural healing instincts, to help ourselves. Our animals are kept inside the house or in zoos and in several countries they are very badly treated and abused. There is less and less natural life, and more and more concrete, urban, artificial and plasticised living. If we gave our animals a chance though we would see that these natural instincts are still alive. They are no longer in a position to find those things they know instinctively will keep them well, but depend on veterinary help and most wild animals are being slowly driven to extinction, as more and more of our natural forests disappear.

Even though zoo animals are fed a diet as closely resembling what they are used to in the wild, it is sadly lacking in what they really need, and therefore they are now suffering from our Western maladies, which even includes cancer. Animals such as bears and monkeys never get cancer in the wild, because they always eat many seeds and obtain the important enzymes and vitamin B17 that way.

It is now quite commonplace to find zoo animals dying of illnesses caused by bad nutrition. If these animals had been allowed to remain in their natural environment, our veterinary surgeons would not be inundated with so many sick, acidified animals, who for years have been fed on coloured meat derivatives which may have contributed to their illnesses, e.g. heart conditions, stiffness, sclerotic processes and cancers.

On a recent trip to Peru, my attention was drawn to a delightful looking bird, the macaw, with beautifully coloured green, blue, golden, turquoise and red feathers (Figure 11.1). Macaws apparently gorge themselves on irresistible sweet berries from the jungle. These berries attract a wide variety of jungle creatures such as monkeys, rodents and birds, who love the sweetness of the fruits and after eating the whole berries, through digestion and elimination of the pulp including the seeds, they are then ready for re-germination and so the jungle cycle goes on. The seeds inside the berries are surrounded by a bitter chemical substance which

11.1 A group of macaws eating clay on the biggest clay formation in Peru in the remote parts of the jungle and almost impossible to reach. *Photograph courtesy of Prom Peru, Lima.*

11.2 A macaw.
Photograph courtesy of Prom Peru, Lima.

is a poison. This substance is put there by nature to prevent the birds cracking open the seeds before they are ripe. The only creatures in the jungle that do eat them are parrots and the macaw. The way they counteract and neutralise the poisonous effect is to eat red clay from a red clay rock-formation. These formations are called 'clay-licks', of which there are many in those regions. It is as if they were put in that place especially for that purpose

The variety of birds that visit the clay licks is immense but the macaw prefers the early morning. They are endowed with a beak so powerful it is said to be the strongest in the entire animal kingdom. So when they arrive all the smaller birds make way for them. Some of these magnificent birds measure 1 metre in length. The clay lines the birds' stomachs, acts as an antidote and protects them from the poisons. The clay is rich in minerals and salts which they need as their diet consists of only vegetables and fruits.

Regular use of clay is of course not something solely reserved for the birds in this area: it has been a habit for the indigenous Andeans for centuries. There is a wide variety of wild potatoes there, some of which are also poisonous. A lot of tribes there still include clay as part of their daily diet. There are at least 25 clay licks in Peru mostly found alongside rivers leading into the jungle. They are mostly in difficult-to-reach locations, which benefits this wildlife and protects the animals from extinction given by nature to protect them. They generally do not like the presence of humans and there is unfortunately an illegal trade going on to capture small chicks sold on the black market against high prices for export.

There are also some clay licks in the heart of the jungle and they are frequently visited by a large number of furry friends, including bears and boars, who all have their unofficial timetable. The jaguars and pumas also benefit by lying in wait for easy prey. These jungle licks are usually found under the shade of large trees, recognised by the foot imprints of the different animal species in the mud-pits that have visited the sites.

Luckily there are many areas left where the animals are quite safe. In the early morning the clay-cliffs are covered with colourful birds as they are all eating the clay at once. It is an amazing, awe-inspiring beautiful sight. This again is a wonderful example of the animal's instinct to survive. Our animals are our greatest teachers when left to their own devices.

11.3 Pictures of my dog, who became 16 in the year 2001.

Teela

It is very easy to change the way our animals are fed at present. Dogs love vegetables and could easily be vegetarian, My dog goes wild at the sight of brown rice and carrots, she is 16 and looks like a two year old (see Figure 11.3). She does occasionally have meat though – and she also drinks clay regularly.

There is little doubt that the cure for disease is still found in nature as it always has been; of course it is to our advantage to combine these things with modern technology. However Man and Nature must learn to respect each other. Think of how many famous naturopathic doctors were ridiculed when centuries ago they discovered things like the pain-killing properties of salicin found in the white willow bark, which has since 1852 been utilised to make the now best-selling drug aspirin. And this prejudice against natural treatment is still strong even now, even though awareness about natural healthcare and demand for organic foods is growing.

There is a tendency to brand harmless natural remedies as dangerous because of one or two cases in which someone may have taken too much of a certain vitamin and has become ill. Then as a result all of these vitamins are banned or are only available on prescription. This happened with Vitamin B6 in 1998. In America it is much worse, as the FDA is at constant war with such natural remedies.

Tremendous advances have been made in modern medicine, open-heart surgery, organ transplants, laser therapy etc. Many lives have been saved. However there is an awful lot of money spent on unnecessary X rays, investigations and drug treatments that in the end can weaken the body or shorten the patient's life. The problem is that only the damage is assessed and not the cause. For example, a swollen knee does not necessarily indicate a problem with the knee or the bone; a malfunctioning kidney could cause it. Meanwhile, painkillers are prescribed and X rays are given. And the problem persists due to failure to get to the root cause.

A couple of weeks ago my cat Lucy, (see figure 11.4) a Devon Rex, 10 years old, started showing symptoms of stress and extreme lethargy, She appeared to be on her litter tray every 5 minutes. I then began to notice some blood stains on white paper sheets, where she had urinated to make me take notice. I realised that she could be suffering from a stone in the bladder, which would cause a frequent need to pass droplets. As an iridologist I had already noticed brown psora/markings appearing in her beautiful green eyes, a sign of underactive or reduced function in a particular area.

This sign appeared exactly on the region of the kidney and the bladder. It must have got gradually worse and was so bad now that I knew that she might need surgery. It is not unusual for cats to get this problem, particularly as they get old, due to their diet, which has a high sodium level. (She has now fortunately taken a liking to the clay water my dogs drink whereas before she had a tendency to drink bath water!)

11.4 My cat Lucy. See the mark in her left iris. In iridology terms, in this particular area, this is an indication of under-activity and congestion in the bladder.

I talked to a friend, who said that the stones could be pulverised by laser now, so she would not need a major operation and it would be a simple procedure. However this procedure is not available for animals. Only humans can have this treatment whereby the stones are quickly pulverised. An X ray revealed a very large stone and she was duly operated upon.

When I told my vet about the mark in her eyes he became very excited and interested in my work. He asked if I would be interested in spending some time in his cat clinic, where he plans to offer alternatives. I thought that was very nice, I love animals and was eager to help.

In an ideal world convention and alternative medicine would combine efforts and advanced technology would work alongside herbal medicine, tonics and good organically grown foods. And only as a last resort would we turn to antibiotics, intravenous drug treatment, steroids and surgery. The devitalised and demineralised foods offered up to patients in hospitals contribute to the repression and depletion of the immune system. In order to recover quickly, they need to be given real food. Food that is alive, with enzymes and vitamins, not the depleted, dead and genetically engineered material, which goes by the name of *food*.

People would recover much faster, on wholesome, natural foods, reducing the need for hospitalisation. Hospital beds would become vacant more quickly, creating a more harmonious atmosphere on the wards (for exhausted doctors and nurses). Many people in hospitals are very constipated, mostly from the medicines they take as well as the diet. Then they are given more drugs to deal with this problem, which weakens them further. There is such a simple herbal treatment for this condition, to tone and restore natural bowel function.

12 Back to nature

Luckily, as we reach the millennium, many of us are turning back to nature. We are fed up with the forced addition of chemical additives, preservatives and hormones in our foods, not to mention the genetically modified ingredients, which are added to almost any bread, tinned food, sausages, or breaded fish, and certainly to any pre-cooked dishes and food substance you care to mention.

Just think of the new breed of insects that could grow from this technology. We could soon be inundated with mutated insects that we do not know how to control. Recent research by Friends of the Earth shows that a bee is able to take pollen from GM plants for up to 20 miles, thereby passing the genetically altered material to neighbouring organic farms, and ruining their crop. This is a scary scenario and there is not enough information or research on long-term effects. It seems like a science fiction horror story.

Fortunately, more health food shops are opening up, with strict rules on GM and pesticides. The giant supermarkets are quick to add organic produce to their range. So maybe this genetic stage may be phased out soon so that we will see a brighter future for our children. I hope so as wild life is already fundamentally changed.

We are now bombarded daily by articles claiming miraculous healing from ancient remedies. Recently an article appeared by a journalist who had just discovered the wonderful healing properties of the herb Kava Kava. A whole page was devoted to this in the London *Evening Standard*. Kava Kava is a wonderful nervine and sedative herb, but here it was being promoted as an aphrodisiac. (It does have very mellow compounds to aid that effect.)

> **Note**
> At the time of writing the movement against GM foods is increasing in Britain, but we also learned that in several Third World countries the farmers are being forced to grow genetically altered foods or lose their plot of land and thus their income. These grains and beans are then exported all over the world and we are not able to tell if they are genetically engineered or not!

Needless to say, the next day when I checked in my new health superstore in Camden I found that the entire stock had been raided, all of the dried herb was gone at £33.00 per kg. And only one bottle was left of the tincture at £15.00 for 50ml. That was not bad for business! Most people believe what they read in newspapers, and even though this particular herb is very good for anxiety, and also helps to get a good night's sleep, it may not necessarily be good for everyone

Almost everyone now knows about the herbs, echinacea and Ginkgo Biloba due to the enormous amount of advertising they have been given. The same happened a few weeks ago when an article appeared about a new treatment from Australia for cellulite, which is a condition that gives an 'orange peel' appearance to the thighs. Cellulite is basically caused by:

- poor diet;
- lack of a vital chemical mineral element (sodium/potassium imbalance) through intake of fast foods;
- wrong fats;
- hormonal imbalance;
- weak connective tissues.

The tablets sold out as soon as they hit the shelves in the UK at £33.00 for a month's supply. Most of us are very gullible. The pill may have an effect for a few days or weeks, but unless we look at our lifestyle, which caused the imbalance in the first place, and adjust our stress threshold, alcohol consumption and other bad habits that triggered the condition, the improvement won't last.

It is a bit like these yoyo diets – you lose it and then you put it back on just as fast. *Now coming back to clay we have a different story!*

Twelve things you should know about clay

1. Clay receives its energy from the sun, water and air.
2. Clay can play a large part in the re-energising, balancing, health restoring and healing processes.
3. Clay is reliable; it stands solid as a rock.
4. Clay is easy to take.
5. Clay is tasteless.
6. Clay is inexpensive.
7. Clay is low profile – neither fancy nor glamorous.
8. Clay is sympathetic.
9. Drugs that were needed can be reduced or phased out over a period of time.
10. Clay is pure: it has no gimmicks or additives.
11. Clay is fantastic – it needs to be tried to be believed.
12. Not many people know this.

It is of course important that you adjust your diet. Don't rely solely on clay to do the job for you. If you continue to eat junk food, consume too much alcohol, smoke like a chimney or use too many recreational or other drugs, don't expect a miracle. Clay is not going to turn around a downward spiral without your help. You need to work with it. Take responsibility for your health, your life, and your body.

Don't expect the doctor to fix every little pain, cough or tickle you have. Doctors can save lives but they are also spending too much of their valuable time giving medicines for coughs and minor tummy upsets which the pharmacist could easily deal with. The surgeries are filled up with cases like that.

When I returned from South America a couple of months after Christmas 1998, I heard that the hospitals were working overtime and completely overloaded with people who had coughs and 'flus. (What a coincidence all this happened just after most of us indulged in the excessive eating and drinking associated with the festive season.) I was horrified. I agree 'flu is very dangerous for the elderly, particularly if they have a lung condition, but there were mostly young people lying there on trolleys in the corridors of the hospitals. Nurses and doctors were desperate and overworked as usual.

Aspirins and antibiotics are not what is called for, they weaken and acidify your system even more while killing off your beneficial bacteria and digestive enzymes, and driving the illness more inward and deeper. These are 'cold medicine', and you need warming up, for example try ginger and honey. (from Chinese medicine we understand allopathic drugs are cold medicine – which repress a condition – and acidify the body.

It is all about balancing your;

- equilibrium,
- pH,
- juices.

Acidity

Most people are too acidic. Acidity signifies: ageing, disease, mucus, catarrh, strange aches, stiffness and sclerosis. We should aim for a better balance; our saliva pH should ideally be 6.8. Clay helps to achieve this balance, together with the right proportion of alkaline producing foods which are found mostly in vegetables and fruits.

When clay is used internally

- An acid condition becomes more alkaline.
- The pH is balanced.

- Detoxifies, absorbs, neutralises germs, bacteria, microbes, parasitic infections and other pathogens.
- Normalising and preventing germs to proliferate.
- Unhealthy cells are eliminated and destroyed.
- Activates the rebuilding of healthy cells.
- Cleanses noxious substances.
- Sedates (nervous system).
- Relaxes (irritable bowel syndrome).
- Absorbs (amoebas).
- Heals (dysentery).
- It has a direct action on the gastro-intestinal channel.
- Not only aids the cure of minor problems such as diarrhoea or constipation but acts on the entire organism.

When clay is used externally

- It is able to absorb pain, swelling, lumps, sprains.
- Aids in the healing of fractures.
- Helps earaches.
- Sore throats (start at the onset).

Scientists are still baffled by the clay's miraculous phenomenon. The clay is not materially absorbed into the blood or cells. It does, however, have an energetic or bio-electric effect on the body.

Clay is composed of ultra tiny colloidal particles. When liquid and in suspension, the clay exhibits a negative charge. Also, other beneficial electrical effects are induced by the various microscopic crystalline structures of which clay is largely composed.

Every element and mineral that is present in the earth's crust is present in the clay. Each of these elements has their own frequency that is registered through resonance by every cell. Bioelectric research has established that in the body toxic material is associated with a positive charge, while negative charges are a major source of healing, regeneration and purification.

Clay's purification aspect is thought to work by delivering its negative charge over an exceptionally large surface area (due to its microscopic particle size), e.g. when consumed in a glass of water. (Always take clay in water; never attempt to take a teaspoon of the powder as it is.) This charge is conducted from the *gut*, throughout the body to neutralise the positive charges attached to the toxic material. When this happens the body is then able to eliminate these toxins. It is then propelled to the channels of elimination taking with it all the noxious material, while continuing to purify, cleanse and enrich the blood.

12.1 Close-up of Macaws eating red clay.

To date, we still cannot fully explain just what it is that makes clay such a miraculous healer. It is a phenomenon that no scientist can yet explain. All they know is that it is a substance that has worked for thousands of years. And we know and see results in a relatively short period of time. Even when analysed and evaluated it is not clear how after a month of use it has managed to increase one's red blood cell count.

13 The therapeutic actions of healing clay

Clay stimulates deficient organs, restoring their failing functions. It really works as a catalyst and is a life substance when immersed in water. Electrolytes are the salts, which become apparent when the clay is in solution, dissolved in stomach acid, and then are able to give a spark to all our cells (Figure 13.1).

The list below is indicative of the beneficial actions that clay possesses, these have been enjoyed and experienced by 1000's of users for as many years

Internal	*External*	*Internal*
1. absorbent	1. absorbent	20. anthelmintic
2. analgesic	2. alterative	21. catalyst
3. adsorbent	3. analgesic	22. cicatrising
4. alterative	4. anti-infection	23. corrective
5. anodyne	5. anti-inflammatory	24. decongestant
6. ant-acid	6. anti-septic	25. deodorising
7. anti-anaemia	7. cicatrising	26. detoxifying
8. anti-bacterial	8. detergent	27. disinfectant
9. anti-bilious	9. detoxifying	28. haemostatic
10. anti-biotic	10. decongestant	29. healing
11. anti-diarrhoea	11. healing	30. hydrating
12. anti-emetic	12. neutralising	31. intestinal regulator
13. anti-infectious	13. prevents seepage	32. ion-exchange
14. anti-inflammatory	14. purifying	33. neutralising
15. anti-oxidant	15. revitalising	34. pest destroying
16. anti-mycosis	16. stimulating	35. purifying
17. antiseptic		36. revitalising
18. anti-toxic		37. stimulating
19. anti-parasitic		

The more exposure clay has to the sun the more its power is increased. This is why sun-dried clay is best. It attracts the sun's magnetism, when exposed to its rays. Then when we apply it to ourselves we receive this energy. Looking at the four elements from which man is made, we see that these elements are dependent on each other. Earth needs water, air and fire, which are all found within our body. Taking one teaspoon of clay in a glass of water returns this balance within.

Clay can destroy bacteria. Contaminated water can be purified by the addition of clay. It deodorises, and absorbs noxious smells. It acts in this way along our digestive tract, absorbing gas and flatulence.

14 Practicalities and chemical structure

Storing
The best way to store clay is in a dry cupboard in the packet in which it comes or transfer it into a pottery, wood or glass container. Never store it in plastic or metal.

When to avoid using it
Internally:
- When receiving orthodox hospital treatment, i.e. chemotherapy or other intensive drug therapy.
- When severely constipated, bowel obstruction (use herbs first), i.e. cascara sagrada.
- With markedly high blood pressure.

Externally:
Avoid using the broken clay poultice near a pacemaker.

What should this clay look like?
It should be finely powdered and the colours can be pale green, red, yellow or white. Broken clay for external use should be in lumps of uneven sizes and light green, red or yellow. Here we mostly use *green* broken clay pieces and green powder, fine or superfine, as green is the most powerful and versatile.

Green and white clays are products of the silico-aluminous sedimentary rocks. They are composed of crystallised elements arranged in a layered structure, ('phyllitous') or in a fibrous structure ('fibrous'), in conjunction with minerals such as iron or aluminium hydroxide.

The green clay belongs to the smectite series (montmorillonites). The green and white clays are phyllitic clays. White clay has less absorption than green as it has a less 'layered' structure. Green clay is made up of one layer of potassium, in a complex form, which becomes 4–5 layers of the other elements. White clay is weaker/milder due to the less layered structure. The absorption of clay depends on these 'layers'.

Chemical structure

Oxygen is a dominant element – the breath of life. It is the chemical action of oxygen that helps to make clay so beneficial and curative. Oxygen relates to the basic element of life (carbon) by combining with all the other elements except fluorine, iodine and chlorine. It comprises a quarter of our body and enters the life process of every cell, allowing for:

1. discharge of electrons (enriching power);
2. transformation of ferrous iron Fe_2+ into ferric iron Fe_3+.

In this case the electrical neutral atom of iron (Fe) comprises 26 protons (positively charged particles) (e+) in the nucleus of the atom and 26 electrons (carriers of negative electrical charges on the outer shell of the atom) (e-). When a positive/negative atom loses or gains an electron, it is transformed into a radical.

An ion is an electrically charged radical, having a positive or negative charge consisting of one or more atoms carrying a unit charge or multiple of that unit. Ions of hydrogen and metals are positively charged; ions of acids and hydroxyl (OH) are negatively charged; these are called anions. As most molecules are divisible into two ions, negatively charged ions travel to a positive electrode and vice versa. They are carriers of electricity, life force.

Clay is not ionised as such, as it is in suspension not in solution. Electric currents carried through water are conducted by the ions in solution. Ions carry electricity, *life*. Life is only possible through ionisation, because all chemical exchange is brought about through this, only ions enter the anabolic and catabolic processes of the metabolism, which alone makes up for lost energy and substance to cell life.

Radioactivity

Clay is made up of very small particles, i.e. colloids, which are small particles made of two or more molecules (usually many) which on the surface exhibit a charge.

Some books state that the clay is radioactive. This is a very complex issue. Radioactivity is represented by several heavy elements such as thorium, radium, actinium etc. These elements are very rare. There is no chance that clay could be radioactive: clay is not active because of radioactivity, but though its possibilities for electron exchange. This electron exchange radioactivity is present in all animals, plants and humans; this is not detrimental but regenerative to all cells and tissues.

The radioactivity found in nuclear power stations is destructive to cells and life in general. Clay can absorb the radioactivity in a body that has been subject to radiation, after first enhancing it due to the negative charge clay emits, like the ionisers we put in our bedrooms or offices. Toxins are positively charged and are drawn towards the negative charge as in clay. Radiation creates free radicals (excess + charges). Clay can remove these charges.

Grey clay

The clay to be avoided for healing is *grey* clay. This is clay of fibrous texture called sepiolite. It belongs to the palygorskytes family. The grey colour of this clay is due to the organic carbon that has not been oxidized. The colour comes from a mixture of eruptive rocks and basaltic ashes. It is often associated with the 'lagoon sediment'.

The mineral salts in the grey clay, Al, Si, Fe, Mg, have the ability to exchange ions rather like the green clay, but it has a structure rather similar to asbestos. We tend to dismiss this clay for therapeutic use. It can contain particles of quartz, from 25% to 75%, and is very cytotoxic due to the formation of hydrogen bonds with chrysotile, which makes it capable of altering cells by releasing enzymes.

The fibrous clays are dangerous for our health as they can develop harmful physiological conditions if taken internally, such as haemolysis, increasing the action of toxins on the organism. Those toxins are poisons, which can provoke the destruction of red blood corpuscles, shortening their life span, pulmonary fibrosis and increases general sclerotic processes.

In the grey clay there is a lot of quartz. This is a very hard mineral that has the property of letting through ultra-violet rays. It is the general shape that silicon dioxide takes. Several varieties exist, which all differ from each other, by the colouring of their crystalline structures caused by impurities. Quarz is a transparent mineral that can scratch glass and steel. It has a conchoidal break and is very resistant to chemical or physical agents.

Avoid ingesting clay that is specially used to make pottery and ceramics. It is of a very different quality even if it may look similar.

Note
In certain impure clays following extraction, we can find quartz, easily visible as small sparkling plates or stones, which do not dissolve in water. Be sure to be aware of this when purchasing clay for therapeutic use, as you must be sure of its purity. This is why it is best obtained from a good source, such as the special green and other coloured clays originating in clean and unspoilt regions of France and Spain, obtainable in Britain and abroad in selected health shops, pharmacies and clinics (see Resources, pp. 218, 227, 230,231).

15 Trace minerals and their function

The composition of fine green clay powder

Magnesium (MgO)	2.25 %	Iron (Fe_2O_3)	4.8%
Calcium (CaO)	9.2 %	Titanium (TiO)	0.71%
Potassium (K_2O)	4.02%	Aluminium (Al_2O_3)	13.45%
Phosporus (P_2O_5)	0.12%	Silicon dioxide (SiO_2)	50–60%

Trace elements mg/kg

Copper (Cu)	28	Cobalt (Co)	20
Zinc (Zn)	99	Manganese (Mn)	0.448
Selenium (Se)	0.160	Molybdenum (Mo)	1.31

As different clays vary slightly due to where they are obtained the above percentages are a rough guidance and do not necessarily add up.

In the presence of green clay regarding the elements Al, Fe and Mg, the element Al replaces Fe and Mg which substitutes iron. The biological activity is due to the freeing of electrons, causing the transformation of iron Fe_2 into Fe_3.

Minerals in the human body

The minerals present in a human body make up between 5 and 7 pounds of the person's weight. Six macro-minerals – sodium, potassium, calcium, magnesium, chlorine and phosphorus – are the main components of this weight. The micro-minerals – iron, zinc, fluorine, iodine, copper, selenium and others – are essential for maintaining good health. Minerals help to compose our bodily fluids properly and aid the formation of blood and bones. They serve as intermediaries in chemical reactions, maintaining bone structure and teeth, and help with muscle contraction. They help to create beneficial physical and mental conditions for our cells. Like protein, fat and carbohydrates they are considerably involved in the process of life.

We can get some of the essentials we need on a daily basis from our diet. However we nearly always need to take a little extra, particularly if the diet is far from ideal. *It is important to have the correct balance in order for the biochemical reactions inside each cell to operate efficiently.* The balance is controlled by *enzymes* on the surface of the cells.

The ions of metals are pumped in and out of the cells by the cell pumps and transported into the body via the intestines and absorbed or secreted by the renal tubules inside the nephron of the kidneys. (The 'sodium pump', for example, in the kidneys is the mechanism which evolved to transport sodium ions out of the cells; this pump action is found in every cell of the body in order to maintain the potassium ions inside the cell; we find 'calcium pumps' in the muscle cells and so on.)

The urinary system when functioning well maintains the balance of water, salts and acids in the bodily fluids. High sodium in the cells inhibits oxidation, slows down the detoxification process and can lead to water retention, accumulations of toxins and acidity. High sodium levels are often found in serious chronic ailments and conditions.

Ions are continually exchanged and lost. We must endeavour to receive them regularly. Deficiencies over a period of time can give rise to all sorts of ailments, including arthritis, diabetes, heart disease and kidney problems. A sodium/potassium imbalance should be corrected when treating chronic disease.

The incorrect dietary intake of minerals is greatly responsible for the modern diseases of the Western world. Minerals occur naturally in the earth and rocks; through them they are passed to the plants and into the ocean. They are eaten by our animals and absorbed by the plants and fish. We get them from our vegetables and meats such as fish and lamb. We used to get them from our waters, but not any more.

We need our macros in larger quantities then we need our micros but they are all necessary in the proper proportion to be able to function at our optimum best.

CHONPS

CHONPS is the acronym for the dry matter which makes up our body and also what makes up proteins, which according to their source are broken down into simple soluble substances called amino acids. CHONPS stands for the elements Carbon, Hydrogen, Oxygen (they make up carbohydrates, fat and protein) where Nitrogen, Phosphorus and Sulphur are contributing elements.

The elements found in CHONPS are not regarded as important as they are organic and do not appear in the ash or left-over residue when the human body is burned. What are left in the ash are seven important micro-minerals, metals and non-metals, balanced by four positive and three negatively charged ions. Deficiencies in these delicately balanced minerals results in tooth decay and degeneration and malfunctioning of organs will occur.

In some parts of the world these mineral intakes vary greatly. We find that in countries where the soil is highly deficient in the micro-mineral boron, there are more cases of arthritis, for example. A lack of chromium can contribute to atherosclerosis (a type of arteriosclerosis). A lack of iodine can result in goitre, which in populations far from the ocean used to be quite common; now, due to the use of iodised salt, it is less common. However, we know it is not so good to add this type of table salt to our diet as this can result in other problems.

Micro-minerals found in the ash of man only amount to about 14 grams. This is only 0.02% of the body. In this tiny little fraction we find 15 of the most important elements as well as six others of which the importance is yet to be established. Some of the micro-minerals are toxic, but when used at proper dose levels they are beneficial and essential. Our present diet is grossly lacking in essential nutrients, consisting of approximately 70% wrong fats and sugars. When we add to these chemicals and preservatives we get ill health.

The general supermarket foods merely provide the CHONPS elements. These provide the bulk base element of our essential nutrients but without a balanced mineral intake the energy gained from CHONPS will be short-lived. The proteins derived from this type of food are deficient in certain essential amino acids. CHONPS without iron, calcium and phosphorus cannot form new blood cells. Without potassium, iron, sodium and calcium we cannot rebuild our nerve cells. A deficiency in these elements will cause a deficiency in the relative cells. If the body is given the right elements, it will regenerate.

When sugar and white flour are refined, all the minerals are removed. The wheat germ removed in the refining process for making bread is high in phosphorus. It is removed to increase the shelf life of the bread. The molasses removed from sugar beets is high in potassium. Minerals and vitamins are generously found in potato peelings, the potassium content of which is at least 60%. Why do we throw them away? A delicious soup can be made from potato peelings; this will help to alkalise the body and gets rid of uric acid, which causes gout.

Scientific research has highlighted that all but eight of the essential amino acids can be synthesised by our own organism, from other sources (clay is a catalyst). The other eight amino acids needed must come from our nutrition. These are leucine, methione, phenylalanine, valine, lysine, isoleucine, threonine, and tryptophan, while arginine is an essential amino acid for the growing child. As all these aminos depend on each other to make our body tissue, if there is an absence of one or two, the others won't work. By using a variety of all the plants, vegetables and fruits, we can ensure that we have a sufficient allowance of high-grade biologically complete protein, to build a healthy body and mind, increase resistance to diseases and create healthy children.

Some health-invoking protein combinations are:

- sprouted grains and seeds mixed with salad leaves and carrots;
- salad with beetroots and organic short grain brown rice;
- green drink (spirulina, barley or wheat grass, with ground up nuts and seeds); add a banana if desired;
- green salad leaves with whole puy lentils and avocados;

See 'How To's (p. 212) for growing your own wheat grass.

More proteins are found in cheese and eggs, which can be eaten in moderation; 'Miso' a fermented soya paste, is rich in amino acids, as are nuts.

Remember that a lot of illness comes about from excess protein from meat stuffs that are not metabolised due to inability to digest and therefore putrefy in the bowel. They are the cause of uric acid. Uric acid leads to gout, stones and other sclerotic processes. Excess protein will make the body lack in physical vitality, lose elasticity of our skin and ligaments, and degenerate the mental and spiritual aspect of our being.

Milk was always thought to be a source of protein and minerals. Now this is no longer thought to be a health-giving food by some nutritional experts (see Part I, esp. Chapter 1, pp. 10–12).

Too little protein is also a cause for ill health. It is therefore advisable to obtain proteins from a good source. When we look at nature she is very good at providing the protein we need and she gives it to us via the interaction of four elements: (1) carbon, (2) oxygen, (3) hydrogen and (4) nitrogen. (Just keep in mind what has been written about CHONPS above.)

Trace minerals are essential and necessary to burn excess calories. They help to strengthen our immune system and balance body and mind. The mind's problems stem from a diet devoid of essential minerals. Nowadays we experience many problems with the mind, causing untold misery and unhappiness. If the brain does not receive the essential chemical elements needed, how can you deal with the stresses and upsets of daily life? If this area is not considered those affected are no use to themselves or anybody else. They are constantly at odds with society or become aggressive and angry, leading to loneliness and isolation.

The problem increases with time, unless the elements are obtained through a simple diet of natural foods and herbs. Harmony can be restored. Consumption of mineral-deficient foods increases the desire for sugar, which will cause more imbalances and affects the concentration as well as increases blood sugar problems, creating mood-swings.

An excess intake of wheat is known to increase a tendency to schizophrenia. A reduction of wheat consumption appears to cause an improvement in those conditions.

Replenishing our Earth

As time goes on we are realising that we must replenish our Earth. Our organic farmers are putting energy and life (humic acid) back into the earth to try and restore the soil depletion. If we can't get more farmers to follow natural farming methods, we will not be able to have natural nutrients in the not so distant future.

It has been found that diets high in refined carbohydrates and lacking in fibre are a contributing factor in colon cancer in the US. The colon becomes clogged and nutrients are unable to pass through the bowel wall. Other problems associated with this diet are:

- the bowel wall narrows and bowel pockets (diverticulae) start to form, which allows food matter to putrefy and lodge in these pockets causing the bloodstream to get increasingly toxic, prematurely ageing us and causing lethargy and depression; you may not appear to be constipated but you are;
- varicose veins, haemorrhoids, obesity, appendicitis, dental problems, cystitis and kidney or bladder stones.

The need to have important minerals in the body which, when combined, act to create a proper ionic environment is becoming very clear. When you take two components and mix them together nothing happens; then add a minute substance and the two main substances start to alter and become something else. The minute substance remains unaltered. At first the minute substance may have altered to activate the two main substances. As soon as that has been achieved the minute substance returns to its original state. This is known as a catalytic reaction.

On another note, we have spoken about the depletion of the minerals in our earth through excessive farming practices, taking the goodness out and not returning any, failing to give the earth a rest from time to time, feeding the earth with fertilisers, chemicals and adding pesticides, all to increase volume and profits rather than quality.

Don't you think that through these processes we have started to get a change in the way people behave toward each other, having lost something so fundamental and basic? We know that the love between a man and a woman is sacred. Opposite charges culminate in the union of body, mind and spirit, a fusion of Yin and Yang, this way fulfilling the higher spiritual evolution of our planet. Why is it that this no longer has any meaning – is it because our earth has become too yang?

Why is there such a lack of depth, is it because there is none left? Is it because the earth has no depth any more and the food and nutrients most people consume and live on are grown on dead earth? The nutrients are growing only on the top level of the soil, and the earth is never allowed to have a rest, to get back to itself. I do think that if we look around and see the destruction of the family unit, so easily discarded nowadays, that this point is a valid one.

Children are maturing at an alarmingly early rate. Doctors and scientists are baffled. Recent newspaper articles are telling us that girls and boys as young as 8 or 9 are reaching puberty. They are clearly too young and immature to cope with this influx of hormones – it is hard enough at 13–14. This will increase the rise of the unwanted pregnancies of young children who are not able to look after their offspring. It will create a whole new type of society. These children are unable to take care of the babies, set the right example or give them the time and love they need.

Is it not possible to see and acknowledge that this unhealthy phenomenon is caused by the hormones in the meats and the pesticides in the fruits and vegetables? Could it be due to the hormones circulating in our water supplies during the last 30–40 years in which birth control medication ('The Pill') has been available? Or could it be the excessive intake of sugar and sugary drinks etc. which have caused a lack of essential chemical elements in our tissues? Or are we just going to say that it is due to the advances in our nutrition and the affluence of our society?

We must take great care that the children we bring into this world are wanted. Children need mature and loving parents who are able to set good examples to them and give them the love, quality time and guidance they need. Parents who will stand by them no matter what. This takes time patience and selflessness. They will be here on Earth long after we are gone, it is up to us to help them become responsible adults, that appreciate being here on Earth and learn to live in harmony with nature and the environment, to keep the Earth a healthy and safe place in which to be while we are dwelling here in the physical form.

Without the above there will be health problems, in particular concerning the depletion of the central nervous system, affecting learning ability, concentration, sleeping patterns etc. We need to guide our children without expecting anything in return and for this we need to be mature. Because we are eating from dead earth, people are becoming shallower; there is no depth, no compassion, no patience and no value, On to the next thrill! – more sugar please. Is it too late or can we turn it around? You tell me.

The action of mineral elements found in the earth

Magnesium

Together with calcium, magnesium is an important aspect in the components of our enzymes.

Functions, benefits and tips
- Activates a large number of enzymes.
- Aids nerve and muscle activity and helps the action of phosphorus.
- Increases the action of our immune system.
- May prevent heart disease, particularly arrhythmias and congestive heart failure.
- Improves the heart muscle after a heart attack.
- Prevents free radical damage to cells.
- Prevents the pituitary (the regulator of all our glands) from hyperactivity.
- Deficiency can cause calcium deposits in the muscles, heart and kidney (stones).
- Helps operate the sodium pump, which helps to regulate the potassium levels and fluids in the body.
- Necessary for proper adrenal function.
- Helps keep potassium in the cells.
- A natural tranquilliser.
- Deficiency leads to depression, irritability, cramps, insomnia and restless leg syndrome, high blood pressure, hyperactivity, teeth grinding, memory loss, anxiety and fear.
- 75% of magnesium is found in bones and teeth; regular intake is important.

Calcium

Calcium constitutes the largest part of the mineral elements contained in the body, in the form of calcium carbonate. It has an osseous formation, and is present in all cells, their activity regulates the intestines and helps coagulate the blood.

Functions, benefits and tips
- Helps to re-mineralise the bones with the help of phosphorus; also needed by the arterial walls and the veins, the heart, the teeth, the epithelial and connective tissues.
- A necessary element for blood and lymph.
- Take with vitamin C; wards off the troubles associated with ageing.
- Postmenopausal women should ensure that they have at least 1.500mg daily with a ratio of 2:1 magnesium.
- In old age the amount needed can be reduced by half.
- Calcium supplement for young girls are just as important; they may protect against disintegration of bone in old age; in fact it is important at any age to ensure 'sufficient' intake.

- Deficiency will give rise to insomnia, muscle spasms, susceptibility to fractures, rheumatism, and hypertension;
- *Never take calcium supplements as a single element. This could lead to calcification*; it should always be taken as part of a multi-mineral complex or use natural nutrition, e.g. a teaspoon of clay in water, inland seawater, algae or chlorella.
- An excess of calcium can lead to arteriosclerosis, sclerosis of tissues and organs such as the liver.
- The element sodium (not table salt) keeps calcium in solution and stops it from becoming hard calcium deposits in the tissues and arteries.
- In an imbalance, sodium is leached from the stomach wall, where the sodium reserves are to help neutralise stomach acids; this causes an acidic condition with problems related to digestive disturbances.
- Goat's milk is a rich source of natural sodium.

Potassium

Potassium is found mainly in the intracellular fluids with small amounts present in the extra-cellular fluid. It is involved with the equilibrium of water in the epidermic tissue and together with sodium distributes fluids on either side of the cell wall.

Functions, benefits and tips
- Regulates the heartbeat. Helps keep the blood pressure in check.
- It is a tonic to the muscles and nerves, essential for life.
- Works well with phosphorus, when it becomes potassium phosphate.
- It is an important mineral salt for the brain and nerves.
- A lack of the element can cause the tissues to retain too much fluid, sodium and fatty deposits.
- A lack also gives rise to excess mucous and phlegm.
- When potassium levels are low the sodium will start to enter the cells, changing the pH balance, which will then be the start of toxic states, which will begin to form dead tissue; this tissue can block the arteries and cause a variety of problems including heart attack.
- Deficiencies can be spotted by the appearance of the following:
  - nails are brittle; teeth are broken and rotten;
  - hair is falling and dry;
  - dry skin;
  - swollen ankles and feet; water retention and oedema;
  - tumours.
  - prolapses;
  - muscular pains, cramps and spasms.
- Inside the corpuscles there should be more potassium then sodium.
- Many of our vegetables and fruits contain potassium; it enters 80% of all our cells and organs.

- The element has a powerful and electrically vitalising energy.
- An excess of potassium build-up can be caused by an inefficient kidney, or by a restricted intake of fluids.
- Potassium is excreted through urination and perspiration.
- Potassium is also lost through diarrhoea, excess in perspiration, and vomiting.
- Using diuretic medication also reduces the levels.
- Alcohol and coffee, table salt, carbonated drinks and sugar also deplete.
- Lack of potassium causes the sodium content of the heart to increase. In such cases it is necessary to supplement the element.

Manganese

Manganese regulates the glands. In our metabolism it helps the fixation of minerals, iron and vitamins. It is a biocatalyst in the formation of enzymes, hormones, and fatty acids, proteins and cholesterol.

Functions, benefits and tips
- Helps the action of the pituitary gland.
- Powerful anti-oxidant, helps to reduce excess steroids in the system.
- Needed for normal development, connective tissues, reproduction, and formation of thyroxin.
- Helpful for asthma, arthero-sclerosis, rheumatoid arthritis and diabetes.
- Helps inner ears imbalance, reduces ringing in the ears, memory loss, dizziness
- Helps the normal functioning of the central nervous system.

Phosphorus

Together with calcium and magnesium, phosphorus constitutes the largest part of the mineral elements in the body; 90% is found in the bones and the element is inside all our cells. Alchemists called it the carrier of light. It occurs in the form of tri-calcic phosphate necessary to maintain the normal concentration of calcium. Calcium and phosphorus in a 2:1 ratio achieves the best results. Vitamin D is also necessary. It plays an important part in the components of co-enzymes, helps in our protein digestion, and regulates the pH balance together with calcium. The light-giving energy is released when proteins are digested through the influence of certain enzymes that become available through the mineral's presence helping to maintain our life force.

Functions, benefits and tips
- Helps protect the heart and keeps the beat regular.
- Helps the nervous system.
- Increases energy levels by helping to metabolising fats and starches.
- Beneficial for the foetus.
- Calcium/phosphorus balance can be disturbed through excessive use of sugar, soft carbonated drinks, and all processed foods.
- Essential for problems related to teeth and gums.

Iron

Iron is vitally important for utilising oxygen and metabolising nutritive elements to the interior of our cells and tissues. It is a component of haemoglobin and enzymes, and a basic element in the blood of all red-blooded creatures; it is stored in the liver, spleen, and bone marrow. It has a powerful attraction with all the other elements, due to its magnetic principal manifested in electric phenomena. This is what makes it the most important mineral in nature.

Functions, benefits and tips
- Vitamin C helps the absorption of iron.
- Excessive use of tannin, as in tea, can lead to low iron absorption.
- Smoking reduces the iron level in the blood.
- Deficiencies can give rise to headaches, anaemia, dizziness, reduced white blood cell count, paleness, tiredness, heart palpitations during exercise.
- More iron is needed during pregnancy
- Some iron supplementation may make you constipated; take folic acid, 200–400mcg, daily, half this dose if not pregnant.
- Will improve lactation.
- High levels of iron are found in molasses, oatmeal, egg yolk and asparagus.

Zinc

Zinc is an essential trace element. It is found in the tissues and places of reserve, the liver and the pancreas. In diabetic conditions the pancreas contains only half the level of zinc as one would find in a healthy one. The enzymes and protein absorption rate in the digestive tract is influenced by the content of the nutrients. It acts on certain enzymes.

Functions, benefits and tips
- Involved with the senses of taste and smell.
- Important for the prostate gland, which contains more zinc then any other organ in the body.
- A deficiency can lead to unhealthy changes in size as well as structure of this organ.
- Helpful for fertility problems, thyroid problems, psoriasis and acne.
- Increases sperm motility.
- Helpful for reducing schizophrenia.
- Helps wound healing.
- Lowers cholesterol levels.
- Helps the immune system.
- Helpful in Crohn's disease.
- Reduces pains in the joints, hips, knees.
- Reduces hyperactivity together with B6 (combined with B complex); this combination is also beneficial when treating infections.

- Deficiency leads to hair loss as well as loss of colour and brittle hair.
- Helps reduce white spots on the nails.
- Helps with impotence.
- Helps with stretch-marks.
- Helps with night-time vision problems.
- Helps with PMT.
- A lack of the element can also be a factor in stress, fatigue and frequent infections.
- Generally recommended intake is 15mg daily.
- An excess amount can lead to depletion of iron and copper from the liver.
- More can be taken during times when suffering from colds and 'flu.
- Depletion occurs through alcohol abuse.
- Pumpkin seeds are high in zinc. Oysters are very high in zinc and are also an aphrodisiac. (Check your source as heavy metals and pesticides etc. can contaminate them.)
- Colostrum is high in zinc; colostrum from the lactating cow is available in capsule form in many health shops, it has received a lot of press lately as an immune-stimulant; there are several books written on this subject.

Aluminium

Aluminium is the third most abundant element in our earth (about 8.13%) after oxygen and silicon. In the form in which it is present in clay it is insoluble and there is no need to be alarmed. It is electro-positive, contains reducing properties and provides salts, which are easily hydrolysible. In the water supply the soluble salts of aluminium sulphate could be harmful.

Functions, benefits and tips
- Calms the nerves, tranquillises and facilitates sleep.
- It is a very good healing agent.
- It is very commonly found in many plants and the foods we eat.
- Due to the many studies conducted, which connect certain diseases with aluminium, particularly Alzheimer's disease, many people are worried when they read that aluminium is found in clay and even discard it; it is wise to avoid aluminium cookware and products with metallic aluminium; when these utensils are heated they release harmful vapours which enter the foods.
- You will see that most of us happily eat foods with colloidal aluminium daily such as lettuce, tomatoes, potatoes, wheat etc.
- Remember each potato that you eat contains at least 50mg of aluminium. This is harmless plant-derived aluminium, e.g. bananas have 97ppm; tomatoes 90ppm; wheat 140ppm.
- It is very commonly found in most basic foods (see Table 15.1).

Table 15.1 Aluminium: plant food

Asparagus	90ppm	Palm oil	90ppm	Bananas	97ppm
Peas	45ppm	Beans	165ppm	Peanuts	75ppm
Brussels	65ppm	Peppers	75ppm	Celery	190ppm
Pineapple	100ppm	Coffee	97ppm	Potatoes	100ppm
Corn	140ppm	Root crops	140ppm	Cucumbers	90ppm
Small grains	135ppm	Soybeans	75ppm	Leafcrops	50ppm
Tomatoes	90ppm	Melons	65ppm	Wheat	140ppm

Source: ATL Agronomy Handbook under Plant Analysis:

It is not surprising that we are a bit confused, about products with plant-derived aluminium! Leading doctors and nutritionists, in Finland did not know the difference either. They made a law that it was unlawful to consume more then 2mg aluminium daily. They did not differentiate between the metallic aluminium and the plant-derived colloidal aluminium. However, when they became aware that the plant-derived colloidal form was not harmful and they realised that it would be unlawful to eat a slice of banana, which would go over their legal daily limit, they quickly changed their law.

A paper published by the Harvard Medical School in 1990 states that scientific studies, which wrongly attacked aluminium as the cause for Alzheimer's, have been reviewed: the symptoms of Alzheimer's in question are now put down to a plaque forming diet and they have now ceased to blame aluminium. This is not really very well known by the general public.

Silica

Silica is the most abundant element in nature. Found in most of our vegetables and grains, it helps the fixation of calcium to help the bones. It is a youth element like sodium.

Functions, benefits and tips
- Encourages elasticity of the arteries and is needed by the connective tissues and cells.
- Affects the lymphocytes, helps repair and strengthen fractures.
- Important for the brain, the nervous system and the sexual system.
- Hardens bones, teeth and nails, makes hair strong. Good for eye health, failing eyesight, cataracts.
- Anti-arthritic, anti ageing; helps dry cracked lips, boils, improves scanty menstruation.
- Helps to remove uric acid and moves calcium deposits. Slows down wrinkling skin, helps tissue integrity, eliminates toxins, works on abscesses.
- Deficiencies show as: varicose veins, arteriosclerosis, brittle, weak nails, epilepsy, tumours, obesity; depression and slack muscles. Herbs rich in silica are horsetail and borage, lungwort and nettles.

The elements below are only essential in tiny trace amounts.

Copper

A deficiency is rare, as it is found in a variety of foods. Copper inhibits the development of a virus. The element is mostly concentrated in the liver and pancreas; an adult body contains approx. 125 mg. As present in clay there is no fear of accumulation due to the presence of all the other elements.

Functions, benefits and tips
- Small amounts help to form haemoglobin.
- Like iron it has magnetism; it has shown to be able to help various skin conditions such as psoriasis as well as rheumatism.
- Excess can cause mental and physical problems and are associated with low levels of zinc.
- Zinc and manganese will help excretion of excess copper.

Cobalt

Very little is needed of this trace element. It is present in Vitamin B12, which is found in animal products. Vegetarians and the elderly often need to supplement Vitamin B 12.

Functions, benefits and tips
- Prevents the formation of acids, which lead to rheumatism.

Molybdenum

Molybdenum is found in all the tissues and is part of the enzymes that help to utilise iron, helpful in cases of anaemia.

Functions, benefits and tips
- Prevents dental carries.
- A lack can cause sexual impotence in the older male.
- Excess can lead to copper deficiency.
- If your nutrients are coming from rich soil there is no need to supplement.

Selenium

Selenium is an anti-oxidant trace element and slows down the ageing process, preserving the elasticity of the tissues and preventing hardening (sclerotic processes).

Functions, benefits and tips
- Helpful in alleviating menopausal symptoms; men hold most of their reserves in the testicles; the element is lost in semen.

- Protects against an excess of cadmium, mercury and copper; 10–100ppb increases the normal growth rate of human cells; appears to reduce the rate of certain cancers.
- Found in brewers yeast, liver, seafoods, broccoli, and eggs.
- Following a natural wholefood diet reduces the need to supplement.

All the above-described elements have an interesting and therapeutic action when taken daily in the appropriate amounts. Remember, our bodies are chemical structures, which need to be rebuilt daily by what we take in.

Problems with our ability to metabolise minerals

These problems can come from the consumption of foods grown with chemical pesticides, which remove all surface minerals and give an unnatural colour to fruits and vegetables. Other causes are as follows:

- Acid rain makes the soil acidic, leaving only a limited amount of minerals available.
- Toxic metals are in the air, food and water. In the workplace, printers and paint manufactures and users expose themselves to a great deal of toxic metals.
- Using table salt in cooking and food preparation increases the chances of arterial hardening.
- Drinking cow's milk gives the wrong calcium, which can cause a build-up of this element. Milk coagulates in the stomach, thereby inhibiting the digestion of other foods such as grains and starches. If the milk drunk was curdled beforehand the effect would enhance digestion. This is the way the Hunza drink their goat's milk.
- A diet which lacks unsaturated fatty acids will create an imbalance in our mineral metabolism.
- Using aluminium cookware causes the metal to be present in the foods cooked in them, creating an excess of harmful aluminium.
- Over the counter remedies for hyperacid stomachs, containing aluminium hydroxide, give temporary relief and affect the phosphate levels.
- High intake of animal foods, wheat and fats and sugar.
- Laxatives deplete minerals in the body.
- Vomiting.
- Constitutional deficiency, a 'miasm' or weakness of organs, can affect the absorption ability or increase the need of a certain element at a higher dosage.
- Excessive and continual stress.

As our earth is so mineral depleted we need to ensure our daily need by eating right and sometimes supplementing with additional minerals, herbs and digestive enzymes.

16 Clay: quality and colours

The importance of quality

Never use clay which has been gathered up from the garden or roadside, and never use clay from a pottery for therapeutic use, or you risk bringing about serious problems. The quality and purity of the clays we use is most important.

The only clays that comply with the proper standards are from France and Spain and available at selected clinics and health shops (see Resources, p. 218). The clay is collected from several protected quarries and reserves, surrounded by luscious pine trees and woods in clean and unpolluted areas. Constant care is employed to ensure the clay's purity.

After a natural process of drying in the sun and wind), a process of careful microbiological and mineralogical control follows. At each extraction the clay undergoes strict analysis. The tests are carried out at external and independent laboratories such as the BRGM, the CNRS (the National Centre for Scientific Research) and the microbiological laboratory IRM 77 in France.

Specimens are examined by X-ray diffraction; the argileceous materials observed are two minerals in similar quantities, Kaolinite and Illite. Examination by electro-micro-diffraction reveals the presence of a third argillaceous zone, Metahalloysite. The clay is composed of crystallised elements arranged in a layered structure. No preservatives are added and no ionisation takes place. It is produced under the strictest quality control.

There are several universities in France where research is carried out to find just what it is that brings about the healing power in the clay. A French Clay Study Group, established in 1979, by a Professor Pezerat, continues to research the physico-chemical structures of clay.

In the winter clay is stored in dry depots and hangars and packaged in various forms, crushed, granulated powdered, superfine, very fine etc.

It is available in clinics and health stores that seek to provide their clients with the best the earth has to offer.

16.1 Sacred stone in Machu Picchu, Peru.

The colours of clay

The different colours of clay have different mineral compositions; therefore they have different effects and are used for different conditions. We know that the green clay is the strongest for detoxification, strengthening the system and toning. We use very fine green and superfine green. The last one is easier to take, as the particles are even finer than fine. The most popular is the very fine green clay.

Green clay, very fine and superfine

The most popular, used for general detoxification and strengthening the entire organism.

Composition of green clay

Silica (SiO_2)	47.0	52.0 %	Magnesium (MgO)	2.0	3.0 %
Aluminium (Al_2O_3)	13.0	15.0 %	Sodium (Na_2O)	0.1	0.3 %
Calcium (CaO)	7.0	9.0 %	Manganese (MnO)	0.1	0.3 %
Iron (Fe_2O_3)	4.0	6.0 %	Phosphorus (P_2O_5)	0.1	0.2 %
Potassium (K_2O)	3.0	5.0 %			

Trace elements

Copper (Cu)	20 ± 10 ppm	Molybdenum (Mo)	< 1 ppm
Cobalt (Co)	15 ± 10 ppm	Selenium (Se)	0,116
Lithium (Li)	3 ± 1 ppm		

ppm = part per million (milligrams per kilo) (that is when the powder is undiluted in water). Green clay is the Illite type of a Phyllitic structure.

Clay parts	60–80%
Illite	65–75%
Kaoline	5–15%
mass volume	0.94g/cm

The tiny trace amounts of these micro-elements are harmless as found in the clay's composition. Copper in clay acts as an anti-infectious agent, selenium is important for hepatic drainage, cobalt is mineralising and known for its anti-anaemic properties. Molybdenum balances the metabolism and lithium is an important element for the brain.

Red clay, superfine

The colour is due to the iron oxide, and results from erosion of volcanic material. After leaching, red clay has lost almost all its silicon dioxide; it contains oxides and hydroxides of iron. This clay has a revitalising and cleansing effect. It is a good tonic and those who will benefit from this clay particularly are those who are anaemic. They can be checked at three-weekly intervals for the rate of improvement (regular blood test).

Red clay is also good for alleviating headaches, especially when caused by stress and which come on suddenly. Take 1 teaspoon in a glass of water. Repeat 30 minutes later.

There is a 'red clay spa' in California where the lucky visitor can spend the whole day running from mineral bath to plunge pool, then to specially designated areas where a mountain of ready prepared clay waits to be applied to any part of the body, after which there are special sun-drenched beds upon which you can lay down and let the clay set.

Afterwards the clay is washed off in the specially made outdoor showers, where clay gel and shampoos help to get it all off the body. Those with blond or greying hair will find their hair will go a beautiful shade of red, which apart from looking like a million dollars at the end of the day, is an added bonus as it is rather a nice red. (Lasts about three shampoos).

Contact Sunny Seminars for details on clay

16.2 Person covered in red clay in the red clay spa.

trips out there and other locations (see Resources, p. 218). This clay has a higher iron content.

Yellow clay, very fine

Very fine yellow clay is very good when recovering from a debilitating illness such as glandular fever, or from the effects of exhaustion and it is remarkably effective for jetlag.

Other benefits
- Stabilises and balances the metabolism.
- Balances blood sugar levels.
- Improves the appetite in anorexia.
- Helps skin problems, itching, psoriasis, acne, and eczema.
- Cleanses toxins from kidneys and bladder.
- High level of iron in yellow clay helps to utilise enzymes, helps anaemia and haemorrhage.
- Relieves rheumatism.

White clay, superfine

Superfine white clay is a kaolinite clay of two layers with a phyllitic structure. It originates from weathered crystalline rocks. The action is milder and gentler for detoxification and healing than the other colours and is suitable for the elderly with sensitive digestion and the young.

Some dentists are recommending this clay after the removal of amalgam fillings, to detoxify this heavy metal from the body. Tests have proven it to be effective in the treatment of salmonella and staphylococcus. Can also be used as a natural talcum powder. It is a good alternative for the reflexologist who normally uses baby powder during their treatment, which is harmful when inhaled by them and their client.

For a sudden onset of diarrhoea, drink a glass of white clay every 30 minutes until better; alternate this with strong peppermint tea.

17 As above, so below

Solar and lunar energy

The spring is full of the sun's energy. The colour green becomes abundant, and brings joy to the heart. The rays of the sun penetrate the sleeping mineral elements on earth, waking them up from their hibernation, stimulating their beneficial action. Without the sun there is no life on our earth. Life starts from the sun, everyone is a ray of the sun, we are the children of the sun, and we are light beings. Without oxygen, light and water, nothing will grow. We are made up of the same elements as the sun and the moon. The sun and the moon help us to attain a perfect pH, which aids the immune system.

The moon helps us to become more alkaline. (Do your planting when the moon is waxing for better results.) The waning and waxing moon creates the tides and the rhythms here on earth. The waning and waxing moon influences the mind and the psyche, like the rhythm of the breath influences the heartbeat which affects the blood flow, governed by the conscious and subconscious psychic power coming through our vital forces. It helps if we can sleep under the light of the moon sometimes. If you can get a chance to do this, it benefits the thyroid and pituitary gland; women benefit by improving their own lunar cycles, particularly if there are problems with the ovaries and uterus.

Every sunrise is a new day to inspire us with fresh ideas and hopes that we are able to manifest on earth. We came to earth so she could reward us with her beauty and riches. A healthy human is aware that he is born from the same source as the fire, earth, water and air, and fully respects this heritage. The person able to feel this cosmic arrangement within himself is a healthy, connected, aware light being. The pulse beating through life is generated by the universe; planets are whirling and pulsating like the plants that grow here on earth, affecting all the living and breathing things.

The earth is female and the sun is male; the moon is female. The earth wants us to be more alkaline. Some people need and are drawn to the sun more then others, some people light up a room like the sun when they enter. We are very closely connected to the sun. When people do not like the sun, or feel unwell in the sun, it is usually due to an imbalance with the four humours in the body, and the heart or kidneys. (Don't avoid the sun completely like so many do nowadays, just avoid getting burned, by using the appropriate sun factor preparation and wear a hat. Avoid the midday sun, when the effect can be too acid. Sun sensitivity increases with the use of certain drugs.)

Purifying the emotions

The kidneys are closely connected with the eyes; by balancing these areas and looking at the emotional/spiritual aspect, we find that unresolved emotions, inability to express oneself, disappointment in love, sorrow, wrong choice of partner etc. has a lot to do with it. We can take herbs to deal with the oedemous swelling associated with the physical side of the above imbalance.

The kidneys are closely involved with our emotional life and relationships. Unexpressed tears and sadness will eventually manifest in a protest from these important organs; toxins are not being filtered sufficiently, water starts to collect in the hands, feet and other parts of the body; the kidneys are having to work harder.

We need to free ourselves from these sorrows. Disharmony will always settle in the heart and kidneys. Bottling up feelings makes the kidneys suffer; it also affects the skin, impurities settle on the skin, rashes, eczema, from the stress of unresolved and disturbed relationships.

If we can bring purity into our emotional side of life, the blood will be purer. The herbs, nutrients, clays and minerals we take will work better and faster. The kidneys will be allowed to fulfil their task, which is to filter toxins. Bottled up feelings not released through tears will seek another outlet, through skin or kidneys. It's OK to cry when you need to.

Good relationships are only possible when both parties have found love within themselves. We are ever influenced by our heritage and culture. There is a need to let go of the ego. Looking for a soul mate is like looking for your God in a physical form. However your soul mate will always be only human and there are bound to be disappointments. The love from another is *not* something we can possess. Never stay in a relationship out of fear or manipulation. You only deny yourself the possibility of finding your true prince/princess.

Everybody wants to be happy and loved; it just gets harder and harder in our hard world. A world that is losing the ways of simple human warmth (a lack of the sun in life). A herb to heal a wounded soul is *golden rod* (like the golden rays of the sun): take up to 3 cups daily. This helps to purify and strengthen the kidneys, reduces the excess water contained in the body from unexpressed emotions (on its own or combined with chamomile, melissa or nettle).

Try to find a solution for the dysfunctional state; find ways for creative expression and joy. Develop an understanding and compassion for your fellow man. A herb for the pain of a broken heart is hawthorn berry. Lime flowers act as a diaphoretic. An infusion is beneficial for reducing the swelling in the legs and feet.

Medicine and astrology

Culpepper the famous herbalist and astrologer from the seventeenth century had an astrological approach to dispensing herbs: he looked at the stars and the moon and the position of the planets, associating certain herbs with different planets and astrological houses, to find the correct herbal remedy for his many patients and was very successful. He made sure he was able to help the poor by working with locally grown herbs which were cheaper then the expensive medicines from abroad prescribed by some of his contemporaries who would only treat the rich. He was able to perfect his way of treating through many years of research and experience.

Avicenna (980–1037), the famous Arabian physician who worked in Baghdad, left his mark on medicine by writing the million worded *Cannon of Medicine*, an oracle from which it is difficult to dissent. He said, 'Astrological influences are very important as both plant and patient are subject to planetary positions.' He took Hippocrates (468–377 BC), 'the father of medicine' who developed Greek medicine, and Claudius van Galen (AD 131–200), 'the oracle of medicine', as his models, both of whom emphasised the importance of working with the planets, prescribing herbs whose properties would correspond to the four elements, as well as looking at balancing the diet, rest, work, pure air, emotional well-being and cleansing procedures, at all times observing the laws of nature.

Disease was looked at as a disturbance of the elements, ether, fire, earth, air and water and the four humours that correspond to the four main fluids in the body. These are known as: yellow bile (choleric), black bile (melancholic), phlegm (phlegmatic) and blood (sanguine), one of which one usually predominates. When there is an equal balance, health prevails. This type of practice was known as 'humoral'.

18 Points to consider when using clay for the first time

- Be discerning and realise that sometimes the treatment can take some time, particularly if the condition has been there for a while.
- Continue until results are achieved or do not start.
- Clay possesses a universal 'panacea' (remedy); it acts on internal and external problems over a short or long period of time.
- Its action will be different according to the stage of development of the present disorder.
- Clay will reabsorb a furuncle, abscess, or whitlow if used from the beginning.

If the problem is of long standing:

- it will help ease the pain;
- will bring the disorder to a head;
- will heal in record time.

More extensive treatments can be obtained in certain clinics.

To give an example where clay works very fast, a Scottish gentleman whose diet was far from healthy, with too much greasy and starchy food, was suffering from acid stomach and was habitually taking antacids. On recommendation from his wife, who was already drinking the clay, he reluctantly drank one glass. To his great surprise he had no further need for his medication: his heartburn and acidity was gone. Obviously if he started to add vegetables to his starchy diet he would improve even more.

The importance of particle size

There are many clay deposits throughout the world; all are rich in the earth's minerals. As they are of different origins they all have different compositions and properties (see the composition chart for green clay in Chapter 16, which sometimes varies). Coloured clays contain a larger amount of certain elements then the white clays.

The clay we use therapeutically is very fine and pure. The clay is not materially absorbed into the blood or cells, but has an energetic bioelectric effect on every cell in the body. Clay is composed of ultra small colloidal particles that when in liquid suspension displays a negative charge. Other beneficial electrical effects are induced by the various microscopic crystalline structures of which clay is largely composed. Each of the elements in the clay has their own frequency that registers through resonance by every cell in the body.

As already mentioned, bioelectric research has established that in the body toxic material is associated with a positive charge, whereas negative charges are a major source of healing, regeneration, and purification. The purification aspect of clay is thought to work by delivering its negative charge over an exceptionally large surface area due to the microscopic particle size, which is what happens when a teaspoonful is taken in a glass of water. The charge we are discussing is conducted via the bowel, right throughout the body to neutralise the positive charges that are attached to toxic material. When this happens the body is able to eliminate toxins.

The smaller the particle size of the clay, the more effectively it works. The surface area is increased. A superfine colloid's surface area can be the size of a small football pitch, the negative element holds on to that surface. The finer the particle is the more electrons are spread through the water.

Bentonite

Some clay like bentonite will congeal when you add water to it. This congealed mass should not be taken internally. You can drink the water once the clay has settled to the bottom of the glass as there will be finely dissolved particles present in that water. The overall effect will be less beneficial than the clay which dissolves easily in water.

Bentonite is mainly used in industry and several people have reported a constipating effect when taking it. The difference between the therapeutic clay (see Resources, pp. 218, 227, 230, 231) and bentonite clay is the particle size and how and where it is formed. Bentonite has very large particles and is often used in colonic hydrotherapy.

Many people are confused about which type of clay to use. Bentonite is mentioned in several books, which promote certain cleansing and detoxification programmes usually including psyllium husks as well. Bentonite can never be used for long-term cleansing, i.e. for more then 2–3 days, while the healing green clay can be used for weeks and months. You can now see how important the particle size is.

19 The power of clay

The therapeutic use of healing green clay is not very well known, particularly in Britain and North and South America. It is still probably one of Europe's best-kept secrets.

- Clay is a life substance that acts as a catalyst for the vital functioning of the organism (a catalyst is a substance that without directly intervening in a reaction can change, due to its presence, the speed of the reaction).
- It facilitates transformations readily accomplished by the organism, activating the immune process and repairing tissues.
- It is a preventative, acting as a stimulant to the immune system as well as a detoxificant.
- It quickens healing and leaves few or no traces or scars.
- It drains and removes accumulated toxins which our stressed and worn out bodies can no longer successfully eliminate.
- It helps to balance a mineral deficiency and reinforces assimilation.
- It restores the balance of the organism; when applied to a vital organ externally, i.e. the liver, the kidneys, or the lower abdomen, the action will be profound.
- Treatment can be prolonged without any danger.
- Clay treatment can be combined with most other holistic treatments, enhancing their effects.
- It encourages a deficiency to become efficient and absorbs an excess, e.g. will supply iron where needed, or remove mercury or lead.
- It only provides what the body needs.

Absorption occurs when an atom passes from one stationary condition to another. It emits or absorbs an electromagnetic radiation. Hydration occurs by fixation of the HO ion, by water on the element. Acceleration is positive; reduction is negative. They work by chemical action only.

Enzymes in relation to clay

Enzymes work both biologically and chemically in the human body. They help to convert vitamins, minerals and amino acids into vital energy. Without enzymes we would not live. As we grow older enzyme production decreases or get lazy.

Enzyme activation or body catalysts

The proteins in enzymes serve as enzyme carrier factors. They are protein carriers, charged with vital energy factors. Enzymes help to digest the foods we eat; they destroy bacteria, viruses and worms. All our tissues and organs are run from metabolic enzymes. The enzymes take fats, carbohydrates and proteins and structure them into healthy bodies. Food enzymes come from raw whole foods; cooking destroys enzymes.

Enzymes perform thousands of metabolic tasks in our system; they are involved in everything we do. The liver, for example, has numerous different enzymes; good health depends on these enzymes to work efficiently. The pancreas is the hardest working organ devoted to distributing enzymes in the body. The enzymes are received from the body cells and the bloodstream but sometimes the body is not able to produce enough enzymes for different reasons.

When organ function is under-active or impaired, clay can be helpful here as the catalyst to kick-start this function. Taking additional enzymes would help restore and re-educate under-functioning organs. Digestive supplements usually contain protease, amylase, lipase etc. (and sometimes HCL (hydrochloric acid) which should be supplemented for a short while if the stomach is unable to produce sufficient levels). They can be of plant or animal origin. Taken after meals, they are essential in any healing programme and should be taken for two or three months to re-educate your system into producing them again. Use them after that if and when needed.

After the age of 40, or even earlier now, it is common to have an under-production of enzymes, mainly due to a diet lacking in vital chemical elements, stress and general depletion. We use up our enzymes constantly: we know about 2700 of them, but there are probably likely to be in excess of 50,000; we lose them in our urine, faeces and through perspiration. They help to make our lungs, kidneys bladder, stomach, bowel, liver, gallbladder, pancreas, lungs, heart and mind work effectively.

Bacteria

The fixation of bacteria on the green clay, taken internally and externally, depends on the absorption phenomenon, regulated by the Oligocene-elements, which act in conjunction with the synthesis of the metabolites. It is the general effect of the physiochemical transformation phenomenon which occurs in the interior of all cells.

We know that all problems and disease states have an underlying cause. An acid body state will seek out alkaline minerals to react with. These are magnesium, sodium, calcium, zinc, potassium etc., all of which can be found in clay. In the body they are stored in bile salts, muscles, ligaments and bones. They will be leached from those parts if there is not sufficient intake via dietary means.

The body, in order to preserve itself, cannot help but try to neutralise an over-acid or over-alkaline state, even if it is at the expense of our organs and fluids. Mineral loss will lead to defects within the bodily structure.

We are subject to so many acids through our dietary intake; regular intake of soft drinks actually diminishes the mineral content of a person's bones and teeth. Excessive alcohol consumption has the same effect. If fractures occur they will take longer to heal. To test what cola does for you, take the bone of a chicken and dump it in a glass of coke, see what has happened to it the next day (is it soft and spongy?)

Older people are particularly affected as young people still have sufficient bicarbonate buffers in the blood. Years of depleting the alkaline mineral stores, by high protein diets and high stress levels, make the brain start to produce acid by-products, oxidising glucose (lactic acid). All stress is a chemical fact, creating lactic acid. Lactic acid is lactate and H+.

If you suffer from osteoporosis and you go to have a blood test to check the calcium status of your blood, you may find that the reading states that you do not have a deficiency. This is due to the fact that as soon as your body registers deficiency it will simply collect what it needs from your body stores, i.e. your bones and tissues, that way maintaining the correct level in the blood. This test can therefore be a little misleading.

Protein is vulnerable to pH changes. Carbohydrates and fats are completely digested; the problems start when the food is not completely oxidised. Which happens when we eat too fast or if the food is overcooked. This slows or impedes oxidation, only partially breaking down carbohydrates and fats, creating acidity. A continual high protein intake results in uric acid crystals, which collect in various organs and tissues; alkaline reserves are more depleted, nitrogen is eliminated directly in the urine as ammonia salt. Ammonia will irritate the bladder.

Protein will be found in the urine. These symptoms will come on gradually and don't always show, except by urine sample testing or until the first bacterial infection arrives. Then the patient must look at the diet carefully and change, to avoid further damage. The psychological, physical and structural problems must be looked at.

The general rule appears again: keeping to a low protein diet is better for overall health. The ideal is 75–80% alkaline forming foods, from vegetables and fruits; 25–20% acid forming foods. Reading the book *Acid and Alkaline* may be useful to gain more details on these types of foods (see Resources, p. 231).

There is no need for concern if at the beginning of treatment:

- pain is more localised;
- increase in temperature is experienced;
- fatigue is persistent;
- wounds appear deeper or more open.

These are all normal symptoms. Resulting from the activity of the clay and its effectiveness. Clay sometimes takes effect by aggravating a bit in the beginning:

1. activating the disorders by draining them;
2. cicatrising (e.g. forming new tissue over a wound) helping the disorder to regress;
3. healing until the disorder disappears.

Clay treatment, for internal use can be taken as follows:

- 3 weeks on, 1 week off, 3 weeks on;
- 3–4 times per year.

As a guideline, start at the beginning of each season, but you are not restricted to these times: start whenever you want. Each case/person is different. And you can continue for some time, as long as a weekly interval is observed every three weeks. That way you can help prevent toxins and bacteria taking over your life.

I cannot emphasise enough the importance of diet, as we cannot rely on clay to absorb all the toxins we willingly ingest. It would be silly to go on a clay cure and continue to eat steaks and drink alcohol. When we drink clay we must increase our intake of fruits and vegetables and pulses; also drink plenty of water and herbal teas. Please avoid red meat and greasy foods for that period. Benefits will be apparent much faster.

If you are new to the idea of detoxification, I advise that you only drink the clay water for the first three weeks, particularly if the body weight is heavy. Also after bowel surgery when people desire to start drinking clay to prevent further damage, in most cases only clay water should be drunk for up to three months before taking it as above. This way the clay will not constipate, whereas, if measures are not taken, depending on the state of your general health and toxic level, you may experience some constipation in the first few days of normal use, blaming the clay for the problem, which will thus put you off continuing with this marvellous way of restoring the body back to health.

20 How to make and apply a clay poultice

With the clay for external use (broken, pieces) we make poultices. The amount of time the poultice is left in place varies, ranging from ten minutes to three hours or sometimes overnight. To make sure the poultice has time to act leave it in place for at least one hour. This ensures a perfect detoxification of a diseased or under-functioning organ, or relieving the pain of an aching joint (if used as prescribed).

If you can't tolerate the plaster for more then 10–15 minutes initially, you can try again in one hour, until you can gradually tolerate it. The number of applications taken daily varies again; once daily is clearly not sufficient. If you can manage from two to four daily the results will be much faster and more efficient. Most people can manage twice daily.

Any left-over clay from the bowl can be re-used; covered over with a damp cloth, it will remain good for 48 hours; otherwise let it dry and break it up; keep in a paper bag or a bowl, to be used when needed.

Once applied, the cold clay warms up and can feel very pleasant as it helps relieve congestion, spasm and pain. Sometimes the clay does not warm up, in which case the problem is probably deeper-seated or of long standing. In these cases it may well be that the clay will not get warm until several applications have been applied, which is when you will experience the benefit. Only when the clay will begin to absorb the deficiencies of the diseased organ will you feel its heat. On the other hand depending on what area is treated, you may feel the effects of the clay very soon. You may experience:

- the poultice warming immediately;
- a feeling of slight or intense tingling;
- irritation after a short while, in which case the exposure time can be shortened.

You can apply the poultice several times a day. Proceed gradually. This way you have time to adjust. You will learn to apply the right dose according to the circumstances. You can apply the poultice hot if desired. Prepare the poultice and heat 'Au Bain Marie' (boil water in a pot and place a colander over it; ensure the colander does not touch the water level; place the poultice on a cloth inside the colander; leave for a few minutes until warm, and apply). Cover over with a dry teacloth or towel. Make sure not to overheat the clay as then its power devalues. You can also warm up the poultice by placing a hot water bottle over it.

Either apply directly on to the skin or put the paste on a very fine cloth; this leaves the area of the skin easier to clean, especially if the area treated has hairs. Make sure you have achieved the right consistency: it must not be runny. Pour any excess water off into your plants. You'll get the hang of it soon.

Keep the poultice in place by securing it first with a small cloth to cover the entire poultice, and then use a scarf or bandage, you can cut old sheets into long strips, the poultice should be thick and cover a little over the affected part. Either way the procedure is very clean and there should be no great need to mop up excess clay, as it will come off in one lump or piece. Be sure to dispose of the used clay carefully. There is no need to wait until the clay is dry as then most of its drawing power is gone when completely dried. It needs water to be effective.

Utensils needed to prepare the poultice

- A ceramic or glass bowl.
- A wooden spoon/spatula.
- Clean water.
- Do *not* use a metal bowl or a metal spoon.

Preparing the poultice

- Take the bowl, pour in the amount of broken clay pieces you think you will need.
- Cover the clay pieces with water.
- Leave to stand for 40 minutes to 1 hour; cover with a damp cloth.
- If the result is too runny you have used too much water; allow some of the surplus water to run away or collect to give to your plants; if still to runny you can add some powdered clay to achieve the right consistency.
- If it is too thick you must add some more water.
- It is best not to stir the substance now as then you disturb the oxygen within the poultice, which will affect the drawing power of the clay.
- Scoop up the required amount on to your prepared cloth, which is laid out on a table or kitchen counter.
- Keeping the area to be treated in mind, allowing at least 2 cm thickness.
- Then with one swift movement apply the prepared poultice to the affected area; clay to be directly in contact with the skin or with a very thin gauze first if the area is hairy. Leave on for the recommended period.

How to make and apply a clay poultice 141

20.1 Clay pieces are placed in a ceramic bowl. Slowly add sufficient water and leave to stand for 40 minutes.

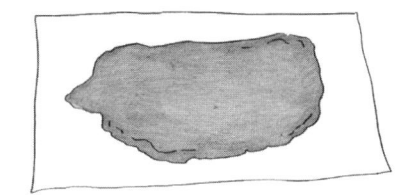

20.2 Prepared clay is placed on a cloth, using a wooden utensil.

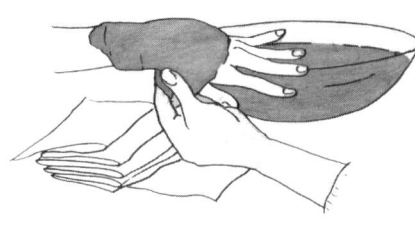

20.3 Poultice applied to a sprained wrist or painful hand

20.4 Enjoying a hand clay bath.

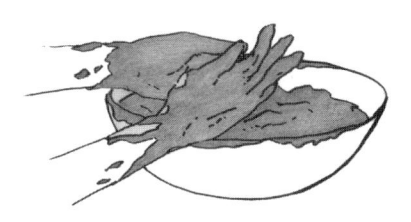

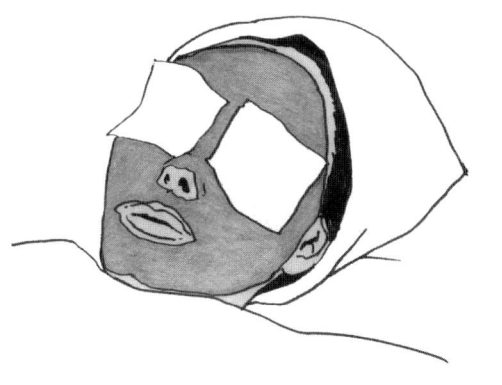

20.5 After application of your chosen facial clay mask relax for 30 minutes.

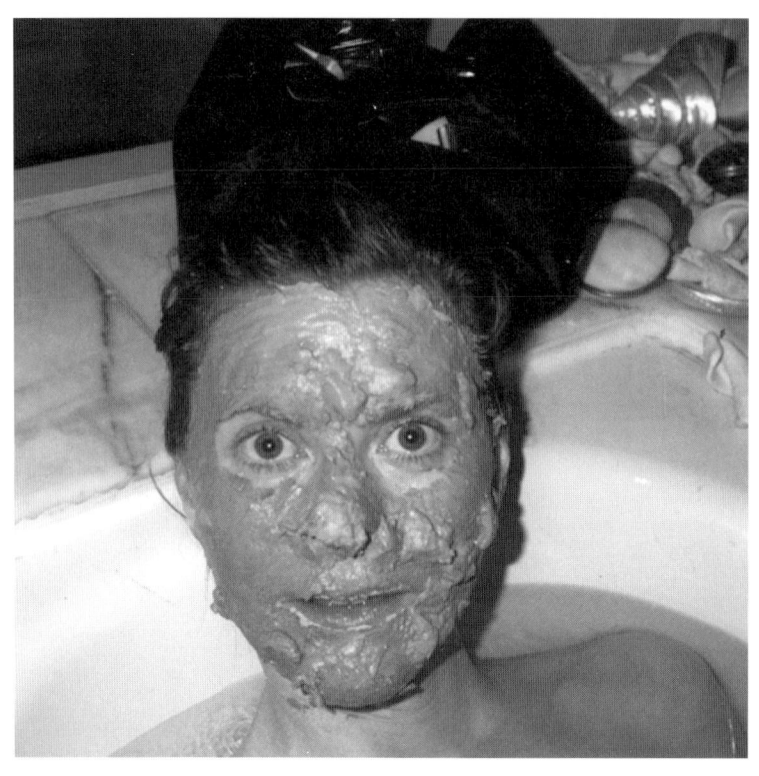

20.6 Relaxing in the bath …

20.7 … Or in the sun.

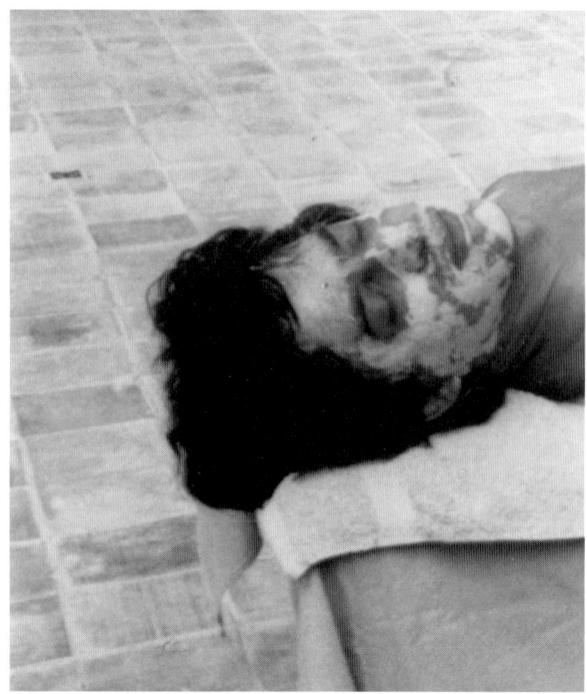

- When finished, and say you are treating swollen glands behind the ears, bend the head towards the floor and the poultice will fall off in one clean drop into your hands; very little or no clay will be left on the skin, which can easily be wiped off. Then drop the used clay in the bin (wrapped in old newspaper) and wash the cloth if you want to re-use it

I have been asked many times if the broken clay can be drunk if ground up, the answer is: *no*, the clay for drinking undergoes a completely different purification process, even though they may have the same elements.

21 How to prepare clay for drinking

Stage I

- Take an ordinary glass,
- Pour in some pure water (use tap water if it is of reasonable quality).
- Add 1 teaspoon of very fine or superfine clay; use a plastic or wooden spoon.
- Prepare this glass in the evening for the morning.
- This way the clay can release its vital elements in the water.
- In the first week only drink the water leaving the clay in the bottom.
- Always take preferably on an empty stomach.

After this first week your organism has had a chance to adapt to the mineral elements contained in the clay.

Stage II

Now you are ready to begin to take the clay and the water together. *Stir the clay water before drinking.* The clay treatments should be taken over a period of about 3 months, twice a year, with 1 week's break after 3 weeks (adapt to your personal need – it can be taken more often as needed). There will always be some clay left over in the bottom of the glass; simply add more water and drink it later, or if you don't want to drink more, do not to waste it: you can pour it over your plants or in your pet's drinking bowl.

Problems

If mild *constipation* occurs, there are several ways to tackle this:

- First only drink the clay water twice daily, prepared as above (Stage I). Once improvement sets in you can then drink the total contents of the glass.
- Clay and water, once per week.
- As it gets better take two complete glasses per week, then three and so on, while on the other days of the week continue only to drink the clay water. (You may wish to look into additional herbal treatment in this case.)

Beneficial for the intestinal flora

The clay will contribute to the maintenance of a complete and well-balanced intestinal flora, dispelling digestive problems. It helps to reduce over acidity in the stomach, relieves headaches caused by poor digestion and improves bowel movement and peristalsis – invaluable for the morning after a party: drink a glass of clay and you can still get to work.

Clay can be successfully combined with all holistic therapies, i.e. homoeopathy, aromatherapy and herbal medicine. There is no point in increasing the dosage of clay: under normal conditions taking it once or twice daily is all that is needed. The clay acts by its presence alone as a catalyst of all organic functions and will help you feel better quickly after 'flu or debility; often dizziness and instability experienced after illness will dissipate. Clay helps to ground you.

Cross-linking

One of the problems that accelerates ageing is blood sugar. Carbohydrates change to glucose after digestion. A high level causes the proteins in our blood cells to stick together. This is known as 'cross-linking'. It does considerable damage to the collagen, elastin and reticulin in the connective tissues. The skin starts to sag and the muscles become flabby, there is an excess of fibrin in the tissues. This sugar creates a diminishing of oxygen in the blood.

We all have a large amount of carbohydrates in our diet. If we had sufficient oxygen around the cells where the glucose is, the glucose would simply be burnt and turned into volatile carbonic acid. No problem of cross-linking. It is not the glucose that should be blamed, it is a build up of acids in the cells that allows this to take place.

Cross-linking and glucose are associated with diabetes, arterial congestion, kidney problems, brain degeneration and lung problems. All are caused by acidic states and oxygen lack. The macrophages (gobblers of bacteria, viruses and poisonous toxins) in our immune system become less hard working as we get older and up to a point they are able to remove those cross-linked proteins, but as time goes on they become quite inactive. Other causes of cross-linking are pollution from water, diet and the atmosphere.

The importance of good water

Clay water can help safely remove the body's accumulation of waste products, which will help the body to maintain youthfulness. Our cells deteriorate due to the accumulation of toxins which are causing acidity and putrefaction. As we age the enzymes that are responsible for breaking down cross-linking decreases: we accumulate more 'cross linkage' as we age and do not have the necessary enzymes left to break them down. Zell-oxygen is very beneficial (resources).

If the accumulated waste products in your system have not yet caused irreversible damage to organs and tissues, then you can expect rejuvenation of these parts. Our body weight is approx. 60% water (male 60%, female 50%); two-thirds of this water is found inside the cells. The rest is found in the plasma, the tissues, the lymph fluid and the cerebo-spinal and synovial fluid. This is why it is important to drink water regularly.

We lose water on a daily basis through urine (approx. 1300ml), sweat (650ml), expiration (450ml) and stools (100ml). Through our diet we take in on average about 1000ml of fluid, in liquids and drinks about another 1000ml and metabolically we produce another 500 ml.

Water helps to sustain as well as protect us.

Ageing is due to wrong pH, and oxygen deficiency. By neutralising the acidity, which can be done through diet and by drinking clay water, damage to the cells is reduced. This is important to consider as we age. Young people are generally more alkaline, produce more necessary enzymes and are able to withstand the onslaught of the various acid-producing states and diets for a while without any visible effects. This does not mean to say they are not damaging themselves. The earlier education about dietary and stress-reducing activities can be given, the easier will it be for them to look forward to a healthier older age. This is usually the last thing young people want to consider. Drinking highly acid forming drinks such as cola are done without any thought of the consequences whatsoever, as is smoking.

A lot of medical conditions and strange viruses are put down to nothing in particular, mostly considered as something that was picked up somewhere. It is really a matter of an acid body state. Increasing hydration is helpful; drinking sufficient pure water is a must. The water for drinking generally recommended in the US is 'reverse osmosis', a system whereby everything is removed. You are left with just pure water.

This way we can add the minerals in which we are deficient, through food-supplementation, diet and to drinking water as tracelytes or clay. Here in the UK we are able to have water purifying systems installed that take out a considerable amount of the chemicals and additives that we should not be forced to swallow (see Resources).

BioCeramica

We have recently been able to obtain the Japanese ceramic disk (written about in the introduction) that can be used to improve water and anything else (even polluted or dead water) when it is placed on top of the disk for 10 seconds. Tests carried out by various institutes and practitioners confirm that the 'BC' (BioCeramica) improves the strength of all kinds of remedies and essential oils, makes foods taste better and last longer, makes a cheap wine taste like a very good wine, reduces the harmful chemicals in toiletries and so on.

The ceramics are made from a clay found in a certain area in Japan. After experimenting for over 20 years with the firing and glazing of the ceramics, they named it 'BioCeramica'. The 'BC' emanates and facilitates living energy within water, influencing a substance without coming in direct contact with it. See Resources (p. 216).

> 'Sometimes illness is Karmic, sometimes it is not'.
>> His Holiness the Dalai Lama.

When we take care of our bodies our bodies will take care of us.

> We must act as if we are completely responsible for our health: whatever we suffer from grew out of something we did or inherited. Self-generated healing comes from diet, exercise and attitude. 'Good health means good memory'; being healthy on this planet is not only for our benefit but has an impact on family, the community, the nation and the planet.
>> (George Ohsawa.1893–1966, founder of macrobiotics).

This is what Ohsawa called *macrobiotics* (big way to be or 'Big Life'). What, in that case, does 'antibiotics' mean?

Anti-life?

PART III — An A–Z Guide to Better Health

Here follows a list of various ailments and conditions as well as ideas to beautify and rejuvenate your body. This self-help listing does not prevent you from seeking proper medical advice or attention. It is purely for educational and experimental purposes but it is hoped that it will help you understand some of the health problems so prevalent today and give an idea of how to work with these in a natural way.

This information is not intended to be a substitute for medical care. Anyone suffering from serious illness is always advised to see his or her doctor. When in doubt always consult a professional.

DISCLAIMER
The writer and her publisher accept no responsibility as far as effectiveness is concerned or indeed any harm that may occur due to the correct or wrongly applied therapies mentioned.

Note on herbs and plant oils
There are certain herbs and plant oils we suggest to combine in the clay poultices, facial masks and clay drinks for internal use; however, the clay can always be used on its own. These are only suggestions to make the treatments in some cases more effective.

Abscesses

Raised toxic areas under the skin, usually filled with pus.

- To the clay poultice, add essential oils, 1–4 drops of lavender, 2 of niaouli, 1 drop of thyme.
- Prepare the clay poultice with water in which 1 tablespoon of elder flowers has been infused.
- Apply warm; try to keep it on for 1 hour.
- Continue with another application after a break of 1–2 hours.
- Do this daily until dissolved.
- Drink yellow clay.
- You will need to assess whether to go on a detoxification programme, as an abscess is toxins wishing to come out through the skin due to congestion in other parts of the body's elimination system.
- Use a hard skin brush daily (see drawings under 'How To's).
- Do not use brush on actual area of the abscess until healed.

Acne

This irritating and embarrassing skin condition usually occurs in adolescence but is not restricted to that period of life; other than having a hormonal cause, it can also be due to constipation, general toxicity, diet, candida and digestive problems.

- Prepare an infusion of elder flowers, with 2 drops of chamomile, lavender or rosemary essential oil (to use as a skin tonic).
- Make infusion of the herb fumitory and drink 2 cups daily; can also be used topically.
- Clean the face with a white clay milk preparation, dissolve 1 teaspoon into $1/2$ a glass of non-fat milk (or water) to which any of the above oils have been added.
- Keeps in the refrigerator for 3 days.
- Followed by an astringent lotion without alcohol (witch hazel, aloe vera lotion).
- Use a green clay mask (tube or prepared from broken clay) 3 x weekly. Add 1 or 2 drops of essential oils. Leave on for 15–20 minutes.
- Eat only natural foods. Avoid sugar and refined flour products, drink 6 glasses of water daily; add dandelion and sage herbs to your diet. Be sure you have regular bowel movements.

- Drink yellow clay.
- Try the clay mask with the addition of 50 drops of 'cloister oil' from a thirteenth-century recipe devised by monks. A mixture of antibiotic and antiseptic essential oils (from Wholistic Research); also available as a balm.

Allergies

An allergy means the body does not want to eat or inhale that which created the allergy. A long-term allergy can result in inflammation of the brain. If you avoid what it is and work to strengthen the general system, the problem will clear between 6 months and 2 years. Allergies can be caused by food, air, drink, drugs, fungus, candida and weak adrenal function.

- Drink green clay while suffering, particularly during the hay-fever season.
- Add local bee-pollen, 1 teaspoon 2 x daily to water or apple juice.
- Check the adrenal glands. Support the glands if weakness is found.
- Take vitamin B5 and B12 with a Multi B complex formula.
- Take 2–3g vitamin C daily. Take digestive enzymes.
- Check your pH balance which should ideally be neutral.
- Many people experiencing allergies are often suffering from alkalosis.
- Add more grains' nuts and seeds, fruits and vegetables to your diet.

Alzheimer's disease

Alzheimer's involves a gradual loss of mental functions, caused by a depletion of neurotransmitters in the central nervous system. A web of entangled nerve fibres starts to surrounds the hippocampus (the centre in the brain that stores memory), making it difficult for nerve impulses to carry messages to and from the brain. The person loses touch with time and space. It is most likely to occur after the age of 50.

- Prevention is the best cure: follow a naturopathic diet and philosophy.
- Avoid food additives, pesticides, processed and artificial foods and drinks, sugar and sugar substitutes, chocolate and animal fats, wheat, 'over the counter medicines' for stomach problems, anti-perspirants and aspirins.
- Cook only with quality stainless steel pots and drink filtered or 'reverse osmosis' water.
- There are always low zinc levels, and a low immune system are factors to be considered.
- A mineral imbalance and low oestrogen levels have been found in female sufferers.
- Thyroid involvement, lack of iodine; seaweeds such as dulse, kelp and spirulina are helpful.
- Vitamin B12 is usually deficient; take individually as well as B complex.
- Take zinc, a good mineral formula, anti-oxidants and borage oil capsules.

- Useful herbs, Ginkgo Biloba (high dose) 1000mg daily, butcher's broom, blessed thistle.
- Lecithin is rich in choline.
- Choline is a lipotropic which helps to sends nerve impulses to the brain; it is also found in egg yolk and is very helpful for the condition.
- Check for allergies and avoid allergens if possible.
- Drink red or green clay.

Anaemia

This is often found in young adolescents or heavily menstruating women, but can occur at any age. It can develop from an unbalanced diet, drugs or parasites. A lack of mineral absorption is indicated and it is closely involved with a low stomach acid (HCL) level.

- Drink green or red clay morning and night for 3 weeks.
- Have yourself tested; you can use applied kineseology or the Vega testing machine or have a blood test; after testing positive or negative, continue clay treatment as needed.
- Apply a poultice to the liver, with herb extracts or essential oils; add 2 drops of basil and 1 drop of thyme; use mint infusion when you prepare the poultice.
- Take lecithin, folic acid and B12.
- Drink Maca: 1 teaspoon in a glass of water or juice.

Angina

Unpleasant and painful condition involving the heart. Worsens under stress or when anxious. There is usually high blood pressure and athero-sclerosis; a feeling of constriction and suffocation lasting about 20 minutes.

- As an adjunct to medical treatment, use orange blossom, hawthorn berry, aniseed, or caraway and Khella infusion; drink 2 cups daily (hawthorn berry tea is extremely helpful for all circulation problems).
- Add lecithin to your diet; lecithin protects the cells from damage and helps to reduce LDL cholesterol (bad cholesterol) and is necessary for proper brain function and helps the memory; it is known to relieve if not eradicate angina.
- Take essential fatty acids; high GLA, i.e. flaxseed oil, 3–4 capsules daily.
- Avoid putting on weight, no fried foods (see under Obesity); reduce sugar, saturated fats, salt and liquor. Avoid or lessen stress.
- Digestive enzymes are helpful; excess gas can cause pressure on the heart.
- Apply clay poultice to back of the neck and the heart.
- Drink green clay (only the water above the clay).
- *Do not* apply a clay poultice near a pacemaker.
- A swollen nose indicates an enlargement of the heart; red vessels on the tip of

the nose indicate high blood pressure. A crease in the earlobe indicates that the heart may be weakened.
- Too much salt is bad for the heart. Excessive joy affects the heart and slows the energy. Find a balance.
- The heart is associated with the element fire:

Colour:	Red	*Taste:*	Bitter
Emotion:	Joy	*Best grains :*	Millet and corn
Sound:	Laughter	*Fruit:*	Blackberries
Adverse climate:	Hot	*Vegetable:*	Garlic
Season:	Summer		

Ankle, broken

- Always check by taking an X-ray to be sure your are dealing with a breakage.
- If applying a clay poultice immediately, as you would do when treating a sprained ankle, you may not realise it is broken; you may have repercussions later on from pelvic misalignment through incorrect treatment of a breakage that should be put in a cast for a short while.
- After removal of the plaster cast you can massage the area with Vita Fons ointment and Lymphdiarral ointment from 'Pasco' (Noma).
- Applying comfrey tincture to any broken bone accelerates the knitting process.
- While recuperating the homoeopathics Calc Phos, Symphytum, and Aesculus are all helpful.

Antiseptic

- Use 2 drops of lavender, 1 of thyme, 2 of niaouli or sassafras essential oils.
- Apply as a clay poultice to which any of the drops are added or prepare as a wash; mix 20g green clay with 50 ml witch-hazel and add the oils.
- Apply with cotton wool or bud.
- Store in refrigerator.

Asthma

Wheezing and breathing problems, including attacks at certain periodic intervals. The causes can be a hereditary miasm, nervous system depletion, changes in the weather, or it can be of emotional origin or due to an allergy. It can also be caused by eating too many carbon foods or because of the environment. Whatever it is, it is a debilitating condition which is on the increase.

- Try these essential oils: 2 drops of thyme, 2 of eucalyptus, 2 of larch pine, and dilute in 30ml sweet almond oil, to massage the chest and the back, or use the oils as an inhalation with a humidifer; here the oil need not be diluted.
- Drink mullein infusion or tincture, coltsfoot tincture, lime-flowers and lemon-balm herb infusions.

A–Z Guide to Better Health

- Lime juice is very beneficial, not sweetened; take 1 teaspoon 2–3 times a day.
- Drink green clay for several months to restore the pH balance which has been upset in this chronic and acid producing condition and helps to clear accumulated mucous; follow the directions under internal use.
- When suffering from a chest infection which usually worsens asthma symptoms, take a mixture of liquorice and golden seal tincture, 20–30 drops 3 x daily (do not take liquorice if overweight or suffering from high blood pressure).
- Poultices can be applied to the pulmonary area when acute with the addition of the suggested essential oils and herbs.
- Drink infusions 3 cups daily; 1 teaspoon per cup of the herb.
- Use digestive enzymes as they too have been depleted as well as taking adrenal support.
- 80% of asthmatics have low levels of hydrochloric acid.
- Vitamin C and silicon are also helpful.
- There is often a lack of manganese; try taking 5 mg 2x daily for a while; this will help to restore the depleted nervous system often found in asthma and will help with the mental side of the problem; some foods rich in manganese are: walnuts, almonds, chestnuts and seafoods; I don't recommend handfuls of nuts which are much too heavy on the digestion; just 2 or 3 daily of each, at the most (pre-soaked).
- It may be best to supplement manganese for a while in combination with other minerals as they are only available in tiny traces in foods.
- Take B Complex to include high levels of B5 and B12.
- Ensure you take your other elements as they all complement each other.
- Add garlic, cayenne and ginger to your diet.
- Avoid saturated fat; too much fat is difficult to metabolise, puts added stress on the liver and can worsen asthma.
- Elimination channels are often weak; the lymphatic system is sluggish, there is often venous congestion, and an overall acid state; check for thyroid health.
- Homoeopathically, the remedy Thuja can be helpful for chronic asthma, particularly when as a child you received a lot of vaccinations.
- The well-known homoeopath, J.T. Kent, states, 'Asthma is a sycotic disease.' Silica is therefore one of the greatest elements for asthma. Silica can be taken homoeopathically as well as in the mineral element form. This is why we have had so many good reports from asthma sufferers who are drinking the clay regularly as it is high in silicon. They have found a reduction in their general symptoms due to the clay's alkalising ability and its relaxing effect on the nervous system.
- The latest help for asthma is the use of a herbal extract from the olive leaf.
- When asthma increases after catching colds or 'flu, symptoms always get worse.
- Zell-Oxygen increases energy and oxygenates the cells. The life-yeast cells in Zell, can destroy any candida that may have developed through the problem. Can be taken in water or juice or combined with a teaspoon of clay.

- Taking 3–8 capsules of 'Eden Extract' (olive leaf) daily for 4-5 days appears to work quite miraculously (see Resources, p. 229).
- Sadness is the emotion associated with the lungs; the sound is weeping and the colour is white. When the grieving or sadness is extreme the lungs can be injured and the condition worsened. Joy counteracts grief. Pungent foods are good for the lungs, but too much will harm. A white complexion often indicates the condition of the lungs. A suitable grain for the lungs is rice. The adverse climate for the lungs is dryness (dry desert, arid atmospheres) and dampness, the season is the Autumn.
- Find ways of relaxation and more time to do things you enjoy.
- See also Chapter 9 on Asthma in Part I.

Atherosclerosis *see also* Angina

The formation of cholesterol, fat and fatty acids deposits along the arterial walls and vessels, particularly those arteries leading to the heart. It is a hardening process causing a reduction in the circulation. Cholesterol is the main cause of AS.

- Cholesterol is produced by the liver, the good cholesterol (HDL) acts to protect; however the intake of too much animal fat, butter, milk, cheese and eggs can produce an excess of cholesterol (LDL, bad fats) and make it harmful; another factor to consider is the unavailability of essential minerals.
- Avoid eating too much saturated fat, found in red meat; this will increase homocystine levels which are a contributing factor.
- Avoid alcohol, caffeine, sugar, salt, and dairy products.
- Take more garlic, green vegetables and fruits such as apples, papayas, red grapes.
- Add generous amounts of cayenne pepper to your cooking.
- Take hawthorn berries infusion or tincture.
- Lime flowers are helpful.
- Drink lemon juice, 4x daily, to thin the blood, 1 lemon in a glass of water.
- Take high GLA in the form of fish oil.
- Drink clay to strengthen the system (avoid if there is extreme hypertension; in which case take another form of mineral supplement, i.e. tracelytes in liquid form).
- Have a low protein diet.
- It has recently been scientifically proven that red wine is beneficial for the heart and arteries.
- A glass or two of good organic wine is thought to be a tonic.
- Benefit from the rays of the sun from time to time, as the sun has the ability to transform cholesterol into vitamin D.
- Take lecithin (a cholesterol emulsifier).

Arthritis

An auto-immune disorder and chronic illness, manifesting as a painful condition of the joints. The condition is worsened by stress and also causes stress. It needs a good naturopathic approach to nutrition which can be of benefit.

When we become too acidic we get sick and can develop all sorts of problems; wherever the acidity is there is inflammation; we call it arthr**is** if it affects our joints, or psychos**is** if it affects the brain; any disease name which ends with '**is**' is an inflammation caused by acidity and also involves mucous.

- Use essential oils of birch tar, chamomile, rosemary, lavender and sage; 2–3 drops of each.
- Prepare a clay poultice, add the drops (choose from 2 or 3 of the oils) to the prepared clay and spread with a wooden spatula. Apply to the affected painful area. Try to maintain the poultice for 2 hours. Continue 2–3 more times daily until improvement. Alternate with a cabbage leaf pack.
- Massage affected parts with peanut oil daily (Edgar Cayce).
- Drink green clay.
- Eat high potassium foods such as dulse, kelp, goat's milk, almonds, mung beans, beet greens, wheatgrass, sunflower and sesame seeds, green olives, parsley and horsetail for short periods, avocados, raisins, and bananas.
- Avoid or minimise animal proteins and fats, sugar, salt, citrus fruits (except lemon), caffeine, tobacco and alcohol.
- Consider curcumin and bromelain combination capsules, which will help reduce swelling and inflammation (Biocare).
- Specially treated seawater is very beneficial.
- Add alfalfa tablets or powder to your daily regime; a rich source of minerals.
- Drink raw fruit and vegetable juices particularly, apples, grapes, celery, beets, carrots, potato, sugarless sour cherry.
- Pineapple juice (always away from all other food and drink).
- Eat garlic.
- Drink goat's milk or Rice-dream.
- Ask your herbalist for celery tablets or tincture.
- Avoid cow's milk and refined flour.
- Multi-vitamin complex.
- Drink clay and psyllium husks regularly.
- There is a general tendency to constipation, causing a toxic overload.
- Eat raw foods, detoxify, go on a 1 or 2 day fast.
- Take Epsom salt baths (not if BP is high).

Baldness

Baldness can be of genetic origin, but it can be the result of the 'family diet', passed down from generation to generation. Continual stress, can make it worse, and some drugs have also an effect on loss of hair. Drinking too much alcohol plays quite a part. It can be caused by an excess production of the male hormone DiHydroTestosterone, DHT, which is not only known as the killer of the hair follicle, it is also involved in prostate enlargement, both of which are not uncommon in men around their 40s or even earlier. The DHT hormone stimulates oil producing glands; these form a coat of sebum on the scalp which helps loosen the hair follicle. It also causes dandruff, which is another form in which toxins find a way out.

- Nutritionally, take a lot of different types of seeds daily such as sesame, flax, pumpkin etc.; grind them in a coffee grinder and add to apple juice, 2–3 teaspoons a day.
- Eat plants that are rich in silica, alfalfa, celery, dandelion, asparagus, strawberries, wheat-grass, cucumber, parsnips; add seaweeds to your diet; make sure your intake of minerals is adequate.
- No table salt or sugar; avoid too much protein and limit your intake of beer; if you must drink, restrict yourself to 1 or 2 pints and drink it slowly.
- Exercises should involve your head to be lower then the rest of the body, i.e. headstands or using a slant board for 20 minutes daily.
- Take a strong vitamin B complex, lecithin, Omega 3 oils; take sea-water, selenium.
- Silica, zinc and iron are the main minerals that are lacking.
- Helpful herbs: horsetail, alfalfa, cayenne, ginkgo-biloba, nettles, saw palmetto.
- Drink yellow or green clay; have a clay pack on your hair/head from time to time with *no more* then 2–3 drops of essential oil of rosemary.
- Eat more alkalising green foods.
- Liver/kidney imbalance; try to improve their function.
- Lower your protein and saturated fat intake; avoid highly acidic foods.

Blood pressure, high

Exercise, excitement and stress could be the cause as well as atherosclerosis. On a high saturated fat diet clumps of cells and platelets start to block small blood-vessels, restricting the normal flow of blood, also raising the BP.

- Reducing the intake of dietary fat is a must.
- Also limit your use of cold-pressed vegetable oils; use only sparingly (even olive oil); never fry your foods in oil.
- Take lecithin capsules 500mg, 2 in the morning.
- Herbs to aid the conditions are: globe artichoke, yarrow, hawthorn-berries, cayenne, garlic.

- The herb ginseng is known to lower high blood pressure as well as increase low blood pressure, due to its adaptogenic effect.
- Reduce your intake of alcohol, salt and sugar; a glass of red wine can be a tonic; make sure it is organic.
- Avoid getting overweight.
- Consult your local herbalist as there is a lot that can be done with herbs.

Blood pressure, low

- A herbal formulae to aid low blood pressure: cayenne, ginger, parsley, goldenseal, garlic and Siberian ginseng.
- Avoid cholesterol producing foods
- Increase exercise, yoga, pilates.
- This condition needs adequate rest.
- Benefits will be obtained from regular use of freshly made celery soup.
- *See also under* Angina.
- Zell-oxygen is beneficial.

Blood purifier

Toxic blood reduces your energy level; you become sluggish in mind and body and your skin loses its colour. This comes mostly from a toxic colon or tired kidneys.

- Herbs: alfalfa – take up to 6–12 tablets daily; crack them between your teeth before swallowing.
- Use tincture of globe artichoke, chaparral or birch, or try 10 ml Safi, an Ayurvedic herbal tincture daily (available from Indian food stores).
- Drink green clay powder in water with 20–30 drops of the tinctures, or Safi.
- Take colon cleansing herbs; *see under* Constipation.

Brain health

Without our brain we are nothing. How can we keep our brain in healthy and optimum condition for as long as possible? One of the most destructive effects on the brain is an excess of wrong fat consumption. Fat plays a great part in the slowing down of the cerebral circulation, as well as being responsible for adding free radicals.

To remain healthy of mind and keep proper brain function, *avoid all saturated and hydrogenated fats and margarine.* These fats accumulate and do not dissolve in your system. They affect all your cells everywhere in the body. It is thought by many people that margarine is less harmful than pure butter. This is a fallacy and an advertising trick. The sales of margarine are huge for that reason. All margarine is made with hydrogenated fats.

- Avoid hydrogenated fats at all times; it is very bad for the cardiovascular system.

- Avoid frying in oil; as soon as the oil is heated it becomes carcinogenic no matter what oil you use.
- Other ways to poison your brain are to take any form of artificial sweetener; see Part I, Chapter 4.
- An excellent food to keep the brain healthy is lecithin. Take this in the morning or at lunchtime for best results.
- Other beneficial brain nutrients are B vitamins, including 100mg niacin (B3).
- Zinc: at least 30 mg daily.
- Take a form of amino acids complex daily; L Carnitine, although considered non-essential, helps to oxygenate the blood; Spirulina has the full spectrum of all the amino acids.
- Coenzyme Q-10, is good but prohibitive due to its expense.
- Zell-oxygen improves brain function and helps digestion.
- Drink superfine green or red clay.
- Herbs: ginkgo biloba, ginseng.
- Take up yoga for stress relief.
- Try sound healing to relieve the pressures we accumulate (see Resources, p. 231 and Part I, p. 81.
- *See also* Udo Erasmus's *Fats that Heal, Fats that Kill* (Further reading, p. 232),

Breasts

- For lack of tone after childbirth or weight loss, use red or green clay: add to 1kg red clay, 4 drops of sage and 3 drops of myrrh.
- Reduce drops of oil accordingly if using less quantity of clay, i.e. 300g, 1–2 drops sage and 1 drop myrrh.
- Prepare the breast-mask, making sure not to make it runny, so add the water slowly, then add the drops of essential oil and apply to breasts with a brush or hand; aim for a 1cm thickness.
- Leave for 20–30 minutes; take most of it off by hand and what remains on the body can be washed off in the shower.
- Repeat daily for 15 days, repeat again 2 months later. (For this application it is most economical to order the 30kg sack available by special order only.) A herbal formulae would further help the problem (see Wholistic Research and the Nutri Centre, pp. 227,230).
- Take Evening Primrose Oil as well as vitamin B6. May increase breast size if taken for long periods; particular essential elements are calcium fluoride and silica.
- Massage the breasts with a mixture of 30 ml sweet almond oil and 10 drops of cypress essential oil. Circular movement up to the neckline.

Breast feeding
- To increase lactation: drink fennel tea infusions, 1–2 teaspoons per cup, 2 cups daily; massage the breasts with almond oil and glycerine with added essential oil of fennel; add 10 drops to 50 ml.
- To suppress lactation you can use essential oil of jasmine diluted as above.
- Use an ointment prepared with calendula and echinacea for sore nipples.
- Jasmine essential oil is helpful during the painful contractions of childbirth, (massage into the lower back). Dilute 15–20 drops in 50 ml base.

Breast lumps
Always examine the state of lymph, intestines and spleen. These meridians run through the breasts. Intake of wrong dietary fat is another consideration which can cause oestrogen levels to increase as is consumption of vegetables and fruits that have been contaminated with pesticides. When one or two of our elimination channels get sluggish or blocked, toxins find other ways of release via blood and lymph and stagnate in various parts of the body.

Imbalances of the large intestine, such as diarrhoea or constipation, cause the tiny lymph vessels (the peyer's patches found in the lower parts of the small intestines) to absorb more toxic waste. These are then driven upwards; towards the neck and shoulder, between the clavicles are the lymph ducts, that excrete lymph fluid in the blood right around the area of the breasts. This can lead to a toxic build-up causing the lymph fluid to stagnate in the breast-tissue. It is vital to improve the flow of blood and lymph.

- Avoid bras which are under-wired and made of synthetic material.
- Also avoid using highly perfumed anti-perspiration products.
- Exercising on a bouncer is helpful.
- Lower alcohol intake.
- Reduce saturated fats.
- Increase dietary fibre.
- Follow the general health principals outlined in this book.
- Learn how to sprout your own seeds and eat them daily.
- Take blood and lymph cleansing herbs: red clover, chaparral, dandelion, blue flag, sea-vegetables, barley and wheat-grass juice. See 'how to' for preparation.

Helpful poultice
- Boil the leaves of a large organic cabbage in 1 litre of water for 30 minutes.
- Pour the strained liquid over your broken clay pieces.
- Add 2 tablespoons of ground up flax/linseeds, and $1/2$ teaspoon of cayenne powder, or a tablespoon of the powdered herb poke root.
- Apply the poultice to both breasts, and leave for at least 2 hours or longer.
- If you like you can wear an oversized old bra over top of the poultice, so you

- can continue to do what you have to do during the day or sleep with it.
- Try this once daily for a while, until improvement sets in.
- Drink superfine green clay and take the herbs and lecithin.
- If in doubt be sure to seek professional guidance and advice.

Bronchitis

Bronchitis involves severe coughing and congestion of the bronchial tubes. The bronchioles become blocked making it difficult to exhale. Stale air actually becomes trapped inside the lungs which, as the problem progresses, cause the bronchial tubes to become flabby and weak. It mostly occurs during the cold and damp seasons. The condition can become chronic, and there can be a constant cough; symptoms are usually worse on rising.

- Use a humidifier with oils of pine and niaouli, 3 drops of each in a small teaspoon of almond oil, anti-catarrhal, to relieve congestion and help the breathing.
- Use 2–3 drops of eucalyptus (not at night), in a warm foot bath for 10–15 minutes.
- Take mullein extract, poppy extract and niaouli oil, 2–4 drops.
- Prepare a clay poultice, with mullein and poppy infusion or diluted extract and apply to the pulmonary area; add the drops of oil, 2–3 x daily when acute.
- Also drink the green clay.
- Helpful herbs: take mullein, Irish moss and balm of Gilead, as tincture or capsules.
- Take anti-oxidants, amino acids such as methione.
- Selenium, vitamin A, lecithin, vitamin C and E.
- Try McTimoney chiropratic treatment to help release the congestion.
- Silica and calc fluor.
- Breathing exercises are helpful; sit comfortably on a chair or upright in bed, inhale to a count of 7 and exhale to a count of 10; lower the number if that is not possible, exhaling always for longer to expel stale air; try for 5 minutes

Burns

- Immediately apply pure lavender, essential oil drops to the burned part if minor.
- It is a good idea to keep a bottle of lavender oil in your kitchen to apply when sudden burns occur; also keep one in your first-aid kit as well as a clay tube.
- Follow with clay poultices and aloe vera gel if the burn is minor.
- Severe burns: call emergency, or go straight to the hospital.

Calcification

Calcification can be caused by a variety of factors. Check your diet, you may be taking in too much protein and lack natural sodium from your food supply. It can also be a cause of impotence.

- Apply poultices of broken clay to the area affected.
- Increase your intake of essential fatty acids, in the form of freshly ground flaxseeds, 3 teaspoons daily, or in supplement form from the health shop: take several capsules daily.
- Take celery seeds. Also in tablets or tincture for a while.
- Homoeopathically try calc carb (*see also* Stones).

Canker sores

When the immune system is low, they will often appear; also from stress and trauma, too much acid forming food and an excess intake of citrus fruits, as well as a deficiency in vitamins and minerals.

- To treat: rinse the mouth with warm water to which has been added 10 drops of tinctures of liquorice, black walnut and goldenseal.
- Prepare: 2 parts liquorice, 1 part black walnut and 1 part goldenseal; take 20 drops of tincture 3 x daily.
- Apply a pinch of powdered goldenseal to the sores in between.
- Drink 2 glasses of clay daily until gone.
- Take acidophilus and vitamin C, 1–2g daily.
- The herb chaparral is very helpful; use as ointment or drops.
- L Lysine tablets (an amino acid) 500 mg; take 1 in the morning.

Catarrhal conditions

- Helpful herbs: slippery elm powder, marshmallow tincture, Irish moss tincture, lavender, powdered herb or essential oil.
- Prepare a gruel of slippery elm and drink quickly while warm.
- Drink 2 glasses of green clay daily.
- Take marshmallow and Irish moss tincture: 20–30 drops 3 x daily.
- Apply poultices to congested areas with addition of the infused herbs and lavender powder or oil.
- Other useful herbs are: balm of gilead and mullein.

Cellulite

A problem suffered by many a woman, mostly visible on thighs and hips, as a pitting of the skin rather like an orange peel. It is caused by a weakening and thinning of the corium. This allows fat cells to accumulate in the layer of skin, around the area of the thighs and buttocks. The connective tissue walls, between the fat cell chambers also become fragile, causing the area to get bigger and spongy. There is an accumulation of toxins, due to problems with the eliminative channels.

- Helpful baths: take baths with the herbs rosemary and sage, 1 tablespoon of each; infuse in a litre of water and add to bath.
- Also take seaweed baths, prepare 2 hands full of bladderwrack to 1 litre, boil for 20 minutes, add to the bath (helps relax and alleviate pain as well).
- You can also alternate by adding a handful of clay to the bath; relax for 20 minutes, 2–3 x weekly.
- Internally take herbs to move the bowel.
- Reduce your intake of refined carbohydrates; eat food in its natural organic state.
- Take essential fatty acids and enzymes.
- Avoid salt, sugar and saturated fat.
- Consider also adding seaweeds to your diet; this will benefit your master-gland, the thyroid.
- Try lymphatic drainage massages using essential oils of rose geranium and rosemary, 5 drops of each to 30ml base oil.
- Useful herbs, gota kola 90mg and horse-chestnut 150mg daily.
- Prepare an ointment with the herb cola vera; your herbalist may be able to prepare this for you.
- Use silica rich herbs for the strength and restoration of the connective tissues.
- Helpful mineral element: calcium fluoride.
- Drink yellow clay and follow on with green clay.
- Take lecithin (emulsifies fats).
- Use the skin brush – see 'How To's for instructions.

Chilblains

The herb cayenne helps the circulation enormously, thereby reducing the side effect of impaired circulation, which can result in chilblains. Use the herb as an infusion:

- Add to $1/2$ teaspoon one small cupful of boiling water and infuse for 5–10 minutes.
- Build up to around 2 teaspoon daily in divided doses; also use in your cooking.
- Rejuvenates your arteries and veins and opens the tiny capillaries leading to your hands and feet.
- Keep yourself warm and wear gloves when needed.

Chin (double or fatty)

- Prepare a base cream with beeswax, almond oil and a little cocoa-butter.
- Melt 1 tablespoon of beeswax and 1 teaspoon of cocoa-butter together, 'Au bain Marie'.
- Take the container off the heat and add 50 ml of almond oil; mix all together and add 5 ml of extract of ivy when the mixture is lukewarm; use nightly.
- Clay masks: take 4 tablespoons of very fine green clay, to which you add infused ivy leaves (2 tablespoon to a cup) and 1 tablespoon of kelp.
- Apply to area above and below the chin-line, and secure with a cloth and safety pins; leave on for 1 hour, 3–4 x weekly.
- Exercise and change your diet.

Cholesterol

Cholesterol is an essential substance naturally produced by the body at 500–1000mg daily. It is utilised by the liver, intestines and various tissues and converted to steroid hormones, bile acids and pro-vitamin D. Through most of our diets another 1000 mg would easily be added. There is only so much excess cholesterol that can actually be processed. The amounts not processed start to irritate tissues and cause inflammations and plaque (*see* Artherosclerosis). The average cholesterol level in the Western world is 210mg %; this is considered normal but at the same time you have a 50% chance of heart disease.

- Avoiding animal fat, rich foods and increasing fibre rich foods could help to lower this level.
- You can measure your serum cholesterol levels at regular intervals by having a test with your doctor.
- After a change in diet you will find the level will reduce.
- The ideal level to maintain heart health is 160mg %.

Coeliac disease

This can be a problem in early childhood or starting in the third decade of life. Avoiding cow's milk from an early age is recommended. The main problem associated with the illness is an intolerance to gluten; there is a malfunction in the lining of the small intestines which manifests in the inability to absorb fats, resulting in fatty stools. This can be corrected when gluten is avoided.

- Never have hot liquids: they worsen the condition; always check with a finger to make sure the temperature of the liquid is mildly warm.
- There is a lack of minerals (particularly zinc) and vitamins through poor absorption ability.
- Take care of the immune system.
- Take superfine green clay.
- Helpful herbs are: dandelion, chamomile, ginger, slippery elm and golden seal.

Congestion, leading to sluggishness

Apart from following some of the suggestions in this book with regard to your diet etc., massage the following points of the body on a daily basis:

- First have a warm sage footbath; relax for 20 minutes, maintaining the temperature by adding more warm water (see Dr Hauschka, Resources, p. 225).
- Starting with the soles of the feet (where you may find some uric acid crystals), rub the roots of your toes with the thumbs; there may be painful areas which will alleviate, use a bit of oil if desired. *Suggestion:* mix 50ml almond oil with 10 drops of rosemary and 10 drops of rose geranium or just almond oil.
- Continue twice daily until there is no more pain, then keep it up twice weekly.
- At the inside of the ankle, above the ankle bone, is another area of congestion; again apply reasonable pressure upwards and downwards; these areas may be painful at the beginning.
- The inside area of the thighs is another area often overlooked; apply pressure here all the way up the thighs 3 or 4 times.
- Until improved do all these twice daily. This will relieve some of the work your heart has to do pumping all the blood around the body; it will also restore your energy and health.
- This is an easy and inexpensive way to help yourself.

Constipation

The state of your stools is an indication of your dietary intake, i.e. if they float, you eat too much greasy food; if they are small and dry you are dehydrated and need to increase your fluid intake. Dr Bernard Jensen stated: 'We should have a bowel movement as many times a day as we eat meals.' That would mean at least 3 movements daily. How many of us can say that is the case? See his book, *Tissue Cleansing through Bowel Management*.

- Useful herbs (there is quite a selection): marshmallow, cascara sagrada, peppermint, dandelion infusion, senna (used alone can cause cramping combine with marshmallow), aloe vera juice and artichoke extract.
- Essential oil: niaouli – massage the abdomen in a clockwise direction with 5 drops of niaouli diluted in 30ml of base-oil, almond, sesame or olive oil.
- Drink the surface particles of the green clay in the morning and evening; after 2 weeks drink it all, but only if the bowels have started to gain regular movement; If not then continue only to drink the particles.
- For 10 days per month you can also take psyllium husks: 1 tablespoon, 2 x daily in a little water or juice; drink quickly as it jellyfies in seconds; this will assist the clay treatment and work in conjunction with it; acting like a broom in the colon it will sweep accumulated hard particles stuck on to the colon-wall down towards the exit.

- Add local pollen to your diet for 6 weeks; start with 1 teaspoon daily and increase to twice daily after 1 week, taken in a little water or juice (some people may have an allergy to pollen, if so discontinue); this helps restore the intestinal balance and assist in the oxygenation of the cells.
- Take a herbal formulae to maintain natural bowel function, ask the advice of a qualified practitioner.
- Consider colonic hydrotherapy or enemas (see 'How To's and Resources, p. 209) to which fine green clay has been added.
- Poultices can be applied to the abdominal area for 1 week at the beginning of the programme; 1 or 2 x daily, leave on for 1–2 hours; prepared with infusions of one or two of the above herbs and adding 2 drops of the oil.
- Exercise: try yoga, aerobic bouncing, swimming, dancing and walking.
- Daily dry skin brushing is recommended.
- Note: constipation is an extremely common world-wide problem caused by wrong dietary habits. It produces a very acid and toxic state in the body.
- The pH of the blood should ideally be 7.4; the saliva's ideal measure is 6.8.

Coughs, accompanied by a cold

Sometimes coughs can occur from inhaling poisonous fumes, cement dust, builders or wood dust; always avoid any space where toxic gloss paints or chemical sprays are employed (even hairspray) and certainly anti-perspirant sprays, fly killer sprays etc. They can all trigger off a cough attack which can be prolonged if the irritant continues to be used, resulting even in bronchial type of conditions. This is apart from the other detrimental effects inhaling these poisons can have on your health.

- Essential oils: juniper berry, drops x 4; thyme, drops x 1; dilute in a teaspoon of almond oil.
- Prepare a clay poultice; add the oils, apply around the throat area, leave the poultice for 20 minutes and repeat 3 times with one hour interval if severe, otherwise if mild once or twice.
- Alternate application between throat, chest and forehead.
- Drink syrup made from thyme and liquorice; at the onset eat a few umeboshi plums (health-shops, macrobiotics section); this sometimes works fast depending on the toxic levels of the person.
- Drink infusions of mullein flowers and thyme, 3 cups daily.
- Drink green clay.
- Chew slippery elm lozenges.
- Take extra vitamin C and garlic capsules.
- Take zinc and propolis lozenges. (Lamberts)

Crohn's disease

Crohn's disease is an inflammatory disorder, mostly affecting the small intestine but it can include the entire GI tract. Diarrhoea will occur, with associated fevers, anorexia, flatulence, abdominal pain. See also (IBS). Apart from dietary considerations, high in acid producing foods and a high protein intake, evidence shows that it is associated with low immune function. Hereditary factors are also involved. In diets followed by indigenous people Crohn's disease was nonexistent, which shows that diets rich in plant foods are definitely very important.

- Avoid wheat for a while; the bowel flora is usually disturbed, there is an increase in prostaglandin levels, causing pain and cramping and there is a lack of mucin (glyco-proteins).
- When suffering from an attack resort to eating organic baby food.
- You can also try 'Whey to Go' a natural amino acids and vitamin powder from 'Solgar' (healthshops), to sustain you.
- Avoid spicy and greasy foods, pepper, tobacco, caffeine, alcohol, carbonated drinks, chocolate and all animal products except for some white fish.
- Eat vegetables such as broccoli, carrots, celery, kale, spinach and turnips.
- Take psyllium husks as that will reduce the diarrhoea and lifts out the mucosal irritation.
- Treatment with demulcent herbs and Omega 3 oils, flaxseed oils.
- Recommended herbs: marshmallow, slippery elm, poke root, peppermint, ginger root, chamomile, golden seal; selecting a mixture of about three of the above would be of help; golden seal should not be used for long periods of time, i.e. 7–8 weeks, change the combination at intervals.
- Acidophilus is very helpful – but avoid the over the counter convenient little drinks such as Yakult, as they contain sugar and their acidophilus content is minute; they will provide very little improvement to your colon health; you need billions of these beneficial bacteria: you can obtain the correct products from reputable health suppliers such as the Nutri Centre in London or other good health stores, where you will find that the powders or capsules are stored in the refrigerator, where they are meant to be kept.
- Go for high complex carbohydrates, low sugar and refined foods.
- Minerals: take the full spectrum, including zinc, B complex. B5, vitamin E, vitamin C, kyolic garlic (a supplement of concentrated garlic is useful).
- Take superfine green clay.

Debility

This usually occurs after illness, or stressful periods, leaving the patient in a state of exhaustion.

- Massages with essential oils, lemon or bergamot, 2–4 drops; sage or basil, 2–4 drops.

- Add to 30ml massage oil, sweet almond or grape-seed.
- Take spirulina powder or capsules.
- Drink yellow or green clay.
- Take care of liver, kidneys, adrenals and the thyroid with herbs.
- Check your digestive enzymes are working efficiently; if not use a supplement.
- A short course of protomorphogens is good for glandular rejuvenation (available through your practitioner).
- Try the olive leaf extract herbal capsules (see Resources, p. 229).
- Take the herb Maca for about 3 months (1–2 teaspoons daily of the powdered herb).
- Take porridge for breakfast.

Diarrhoea

This is generally the result of food poisoning, bacteria, worms or insect bites.

- Prepare a glass of green or white clay and drink 2 hours later, 2–3 x daily.
- Make an infusion of agrimony leaves, drink 3–4 cups daily until improved.
- Peppermint tea can be drunk intermittently.
- Eat grated apple if tolerated, and eat one or two umeboshi plums (Japanese umeboshi plums are available in the macrobiotic section of most health stores; they are salted and aged for 3 years and help the body to become more yang.)
- Eat organic brown rice when improving.
- Take acidophilus and avoid becoming dehydrated; drink plenty of water.
- If diarrhoea continues for more than 2 days, you must consult your physician.

Digestive problems

These include flatulence, lack of enzymes, lack of absorption of nutrients.

- Change your diet: processed foods are hard to digest, as they are dead and lacking in enzymes; instead of nutritional assimilation we get a process of putrefaction and fermentation, mineral disturbance and a lack of vital elements including natural sodium.
- Helpful herbs: caraway, cumin, fennel, chamomile, peppermint infusion.
- Drink very fine green clay for a while; this will help to restore the electrolyte balance and act as a catalyst to encourage our natural digestive process back to action.
- Lack of digestive enzymes is strongly indicated; supplement these for a while.
- Acid/alkaline balance disturbed; take alfalfa, and you may need acidophilus.
- Zell-oxygen.

Diverticulitis, bowel pockets

Irregularity of bowel movement can give rise to cramps and pain similar to IBS. Alternating diarrhoea and constipation can develop stricture in parts of the bowel and can cause inflammation in these pockets. This can sometimes result in perforation. The cause is a diet of mainly meat and high intake of saturated fats, with a low intake of dietary fibre. The bowel pockets fill up with a putrefying mass which hardens.

- The best way to clean up is to go on a supervised fast, taking specific high fibres such as psyllium husks.
- Anti-spasmodic and demulcent herbs can help: slippery elm and marshmallow.
- Take care of spleen and liver.
- Drink adequate water.
- Carrot and beetroot juice; papayas and bananas.
- Drink superfine green clay.
- Have occasional colonics and regular enemas.
- See Figure 22.1.

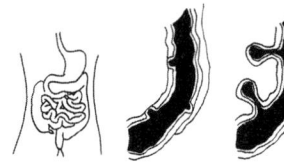

22.1 Large intestine and bowel pockets.

Ear aches

These are very common in young children. Known as otitis media, they are usually of viral or bacterial origin. Otitis externa is caused by water entering the ears while swimming.

- Prepare mullein eardrops, 4–6 drops 4 x daily (see Appendix 2, p. 209).
- Use the special ear candles found in most health shops; they help remove excess wax and are soothing to the pain.
- Apply clay poultices (made with infusions of lavender or chamomile flowers) behind and under the earlobe and cover with a thin cloth.
- Always check kidney and bowel health.
- If the infection has got out of control antibiotic therapy should be sought, always followed by a course of acidophilus.
- Consider the strong indication for dietary involvement.
- Increase intake of carrots due to their anti-inflammatory properties.
- Avoid sugar and fizzy drinks.
- Levisticum eardrops from Wala are excellent for dissolving excessive wax.

Eczema

Eczema can be of fungal, bacterial, parasitic or genetic origin and can be caused by an excess of saturated fats, through allergies and elimination problems. It can be exacerbated by emotional problems and upsets or nerves, i.e. exams.

- There is usually a deficiency of vitamin B complex.
- To treat externally: mix green or yellow clay with equal amounts of spirulina powder.

- Make a mask with warm water, apply to the affected area, cover with thin gauze cloth, leave for 20–30 minutes, once or twice daily; Wash off gently with lukewarm water.
- Add clay powder to the bath, 50–100 g. with added seaweed extract.
- Boil a handful of seaweed in 1 litre water for 15 minutes; leave to stand for 30 minutes; strain and add to the bath.
- Use wheatgerm oil on dry patches.
- Make infusions of burdock root and walnut leaves and drink 2 cups daily,
- Internally take yellow or superfine green clay.
- Liver detoxifying herbs such as milkthistle and burdock root are recommended.
- Add essential fatty acids to your diet such as evening primrose oil.
- Take lecithin capsules or granules; take nervine herbs when needed.
- Find ways of harmonising and balancing your life.
- Bach flower remedies can be helpful.

Eyes

Eye health depends in many ways on the proper functioning of the liver, spleen and kidneys. Our eyes can get very sore or itchy from dust or other allergens. Decline is all due to a sclerotic process as a side effect of ageing; tiny vessels can become blocked with plaque, due to a high fat diet. Leaky gut can be another cause. Bacterial poisons can pass through the bowel wall, creating toxins in the liver and other areas.

Parasites, commonly found around the teeth and gums wherever there are root canals and fillings, can find their way to the eyes through the sinuses. Once in the eye they can create all sorts of irritations to the actual eyes and the surrounding skin causing itchiness, swelling and very dry skin (Dr Schweitzer, HLB test).

- *To treat*: purify the blood; herbs such as sarsaparilla, euphrasia, berberis vulgaris are helpful.
- Improve your diet; eat more vegetables and fruits of yellow and orange colours, e.g. apricots, carrots etc.
- To relieve; make a liquid from an infusion of chamomile flowers, 1 tablespoon to a cup and add 1 1/2 tablespoons of green clay.
- Drench a cotton wool pad in the liquid; squeeze out excess; apply the pads, one to each eye, or treat one eye as appropriate; lie back and relax for 20 minutes.
- You can prepare an eyewash using an ordinary eye bath, from 1 teaspoon of 'Bancha' tea per cup (available from the macrobiotic counter in your health store) or apply with cotton bud to the corners of the eye; store the remaining tea in the refrigerator for later use (keeps 3 days).

- Drink superfine green clay daily, and itchy eyes are a thing of the past.
- Helpful vitamins: vitamins A, B, C, D and E; try to find a good multi-supplement.
- Avoid pre-packed and pre-cooked meals; vinegar, sugar, salt, fried foods, refined foods such as breakfast cereals, soft drinks.
- If suffering from cataracts include extra vitamin B2 tablets with B complex.
- Rinse the mouth with a mixture of black walnut and wormwood tincture, 20 drops to 1/2 glass (parasites).

Eye bags

Sometimes hereditary, indicates kidneys, bladder, spleen or liver congestion, lack of sleep, dehydration, too much worry, excessive stress, drugs, alcohol, smoking, lack of oxygen, frequent transatlantic travelling, sexual excesses, parasites, exhaustion. All or some of these may soon start to show up under the eyes. (Don't worry yourself too much as it can look very attractive sometimes.) It is a sign of general toxicity, congestion and/or exhaustion.

- Externally help by preparing a mask with very fine green clay and olive oil.
- Spread under the eyes with a wooden spatula, and relax for up to 1 hour.
- Due to a lack of circulation, such as is found in low blood pressure, you may find help by taking 1–2 teaspoons of cayenne pepper added to your daily regime; this opens the tiny capillaries allowing fresh oxygenated blood to enter those areas.
- Take time off for yourself; get some pampering.
- Take care of kidneys and liver; purify the blood.
- Herbs, e.g. sarsaparilla, golden rod (you may need to consult a qualified herbalist).
- Drink superfine green clay for a good long while. Detoxify, take a supervised fast.
- Take it easy, don't take on too much alone.

Fever

Fever is the body's way of reducing a toxic overload. After fever the body is usually stronger. It is when the fever is suppressed that the symptoms will last longer, and there is weakness.

- To reduce, use: oils of chamomile, 4 drops; thyme, 2 drops.
- Apply poultice to the head and neck and change frequently, one hour on, one hour off.
- Add one or the other essential oils.
- Sponge the body down with cold clay or clear water, several times daily.
- Apply cold wet towels drenched in clay water and wrung out.
- Stay with the patient if delirious.
- *Always call the doctor if temperature is alarmingly high.*

'Flu

- The virus should be taken care of with fasting and herbs.
- At the first sign of 'flu take echinacea every 15 minutes; if the 'flu is treated immediately, it will go away.
- Once it has taken hold, make an infusion with elderberry and peppermint herbs.
- Drink a cup every half hour, while keeping wrapped up in bed (there will be increased perspiration).
- Repeat in the morning; 'flu won't last long if these measures are applied.
- Have a very light diet with vegetable soups and herbal teas for a couple of days.
- Take superfine green clay, three x daily.
- Inhale clay water if nasal passages are blocked.
- Herb tincture; balm of Gilead very good for the catarrh associated with 'flu.
- Ginger, liquorice, bilberry, golden seal and eucalyptus are also good herbs for 'flu.
- Take lemon and ginger hot drinks, and more vitamin C and garlic.
- See Resources (p. 229) for 'flu formulae from Tigon Ltd.

Foot care

Feet are often neglected, overused and taken for granted.

- To treat: prepare a foot-bath with infusion of peppermint leaves.
- Take 3 handfuls of the herb and infuse in a litre of boiled water for 30 minutes.
- Add to a foot bath with a further 2 litres of warm water.
- Add 2 tablespoons of sea salt, and 2 hands full of broken clay.
- Soak your feet in the foot bath for 20–30 minutes.
- Dry well and massage the feet with a tiny bit of almond oil over the top and sole.
- This is a relaxing refreshing treatment and relieves tired feet.
- Helps take away dryness and cracks in the skin.
- You may re-use the same water up to 3–4 times.
- You can also try the herbs chamomile, melissa, lavender flowers, rosemary in the same amounts as peppermint.
- Dr Hauschka's sage footbath is also recommended – *see* Circulation.

Furuncle

Also known as a boil, it is a sign of toxins in the blood.

- Look at your diet, sugar, salt etc. as described previously under other headings.
- Calendula essential oil, 2–4 drops or extract from the flowers.
- Can be used by itself or with walnut tincture added to a clay poultice.
- Herbs: bilberry, burdock root, blood root or borage extract; apply externally to the affected area.

Glandular fever, mononucleosis

This is a viral infection of a highly acute nature. The throat is sore, the lymph glands swell up and there is fever. The patient is very ill and needs a lot of rest. In severe cases the throat swells up to such an extent that the patient is unable to swallow. In these cases hospitalisation may be necessary for a couple of days. The virus is associated with Herpes and Epstein Bar. It is thought to be transmitted by kissing and is quite common for teenagers.

- Apply 1 drop of eucalyptus, 1 drop thyme, 2 drops of lavender (dilute the drops in a teaspoon of almond oil) 3 x daily, onto a thick green clay poultice, and wrap right around the neck making sure the poultice is covering the swollen glands. Keep the patient warm.
- Repeat until swelling is reduced. 2 or 3 x daily (omit the essential oils after the first session of the day).Reduce the applications as the condition improves, from 1 -3 weeks.
- Drink yellow or superfine green clay 2 x daily.
- Take zinc and Propolis lozenges.
- In most cases antibiotics are necessary. Be sure to repopulate the friendly bowel bacteria afterwards, by taking beneficial bacteria in a course of acidophilus for at least one to three months or longer.
- After this debilitating illness the patient must take excellent care of the liver, for no less then one year. Protomorphogens as well as specific herbs should be given. This aspect is very important.
- It is not uncommon for the after effect to show symptoms such as those of ME, if these measures are not applied. There can be exhaustion, lack of energy and motivation and depression.
- Caring for the liver will help to alleviate these post glandular infection problems.
- Take inland seawater (see Resources, p. 228) and trace minerals.
- In case of the adrenals having become exhausted this should also be addressed.
- A series of acupuncture sessions will be of help to restore the patient. Combined with the above treatment:
- Helpful herbs: milkthistle, berberis vulgaris.

Gum disease

Can be caused by a lack of calcium and other minerals, vitamin C and E and a lack of hydrochloric acid (stomach acid).

- Check around any of your crowns, where the problem often begins (*see also* Eyes, above).
- Gargle with tincture of myrrh, sage, thyme or black walnut, with 1/2 teaspoon of yellow clay powder in some warm water.

- Drink 1 teaspoon of the clay once daily.
- Digestive enzymes are lacking.
- Floss your teeth and have them regularly cleaned and checked.
- Find out how the metal in your teeth affects your health.

Hair care: with clay

Hair health improves with proper dietary intake, digestion and assimilation and a good kidney function. Always take that into account with ongoing problems.

To increase volume and for stronger hair
- Aim to have your hair cut on the day when the moon is waxing.
- Combine clay therapy with the herb sage which is a known strengthener of the hair, tones the scalp and helps prevent hair-loss.
- Add 1 litre of boiling water to 3 tablespoons of organic Sage leaves, infuse for 30 minutes.
- Allow to cool, mix the strained infusion into a smooth paste by adding powdered green or red clay.
- Apply to scalp for 30 min. to 1 hour (you need about 300ml per treatment of the infusion so keep the remainder in the refrigerator).
- Afterwards take off most of the clay paste by hand and follow with shampoo.
- You can rinse your hair with sage infusion alone, no need to add clay every time.
- Remember that red clay may give blond or light hair a slightly red tint which lasts up to 3-4 shampoos. Avoid this if you do not like that. (Does not apply to black or brown hair.)
- Use sage infusion as a hair-rinse; do not wash out; good when scalp feels irritated.
- Use clay pack once per week or when desired or needed.
- Falling and weak hair could be due to a hormonal imbalance, weakness of the kidney function, stress, drugs or a lack of essential chemical elements.
- Drinking Zell-oxygen increases hair growth and improves condition.

For dry brittle hair
- Treat your hair to a white clay mask once per week.
- First apply a wash of almond oil to the hair; saturate a cotton wool bud or use a paintbrush.
- Leave on for 2 hours; wrap in cling-film.
- Then without removing the oil, follow with a clay mask which you can leave on for 1 hour.
- Prepare the mask with 2–3 tablespoons of white powdered clay.
- Mix with chamomile infusion until a thick paste has formed.
- Apply with hands or brush.
- Let it dry naturally; take off most of it with your hands before shampooing.
- Drink golden rod tea.

For greasy hair
- Use a green clay pack once a week with oils of grapefruit and bergamot, 2 drops of each.
- You are lacking in essential fatty acids and chemical elements.

Dandruff: very common and embarrassing
- Apply a mixture of 30ml almond oil with 3 drops of lavender, 3 drops of geranium and 3 drops of rosemary essential oil to the hair.
- Leave on the hair for 1 hour; wash off with a mild shampoo.
- Have a yellow or green clay hair pack once or twice per week or use the newly available black mud hair pack.
- You may need to consider going on a detoxification or a fast, as dandruff flakes are just another way of toxins finding a way out; the diet could be too greasy.
- Undigested protein and a mineral imbalance: take a good digestive enzyme and add essential fatty acids to your daily regime.
- Make sure to rinse your hair well after shampooing: many people are in a hurry and do not rinse well, which can also contribute to dandruff due to the irritant left on the scalp from most ordinary chemically made shampoos.
- Continual dandruff will have an effect on the amount of hair loss one experiences.

For shiny hair
- Mix 3 tablespoons of clay powder with sufficient water to make it into a thick paste.
- Massage into scalp and hair, leave for 5 minutes and rinse well; don't use shampoo; this is a treatment (if hair is treated/coloured you may need some conditioner); do this 2 or 3 times per month instead of your normal regime.

Halitosis

Gastro-intestinal disorder, intestinal sluggishness, constipation, lack of dental care or plaque formation can contribute to the unpleasant odour. *See also under* Digestion. The embarrassing problem can be caused by an inability to digest proteins and due to wrong food combining. It is a sign of gastro-intestinal toxicity.

- Start to drink the green clay as described under constipation.
- Add 6 alfalfa tablets to your daily regime; crack them with your teeth before swallowing.
- Take tincture of Chondrus Crispus (Irish moss).
- Drink peppermint and fennel tea.
- Rinse the mouth, with $1/2$ glass of water to which you have added 20 drops of black walnut tincture.
- Consider adding digestive enzymes to your diet for a while, including beta hydrochloric acid.

- Look into the various books available on food combining; are you eating too much pasta, bread and tomatoes?
- Drink more water (find your optimum level).

Hand care

- To maintain beautiful hands, give your hands a regular hand mask; see Part II.
- You need sweet almond oil, and superfine green clay.
- 1 teaspoon of lemon juice or 5 drops of lemon essential oil.
- To prepare: take 4 tablespoons of clay, 1 tablespoon of almond oil.
- Mix together, add lemon drops; if needed add some mineral water to make a thick paste.
- Apply to top of hands and leave for 20–30 minutes; wash off with warm water.
- Apply lemon hand cream to your hands daily and have the hand mask on a regular basis, particularly if hands are often immersed in water.
- Make your own, by adding lemon essential oil to a natural base cream, 20 drops to 100ml or mix almond oil and vegetable glycerine in equal amounts and add the essential oils.
- Use a natural moisturiser or oil every time after you have washed up or similar.

Hangover

- Drink 2 or 3 glasses of red or green clay the morning after, 2 hourly.
- Take 3–4 slippery elm capsules; also have a couple of glasses of carrot juice (with wheatgrass, optional) in between.
- Or try the Ayurvedic way if you are brave, which is to infuse 1 teaspoon of peppercorns in a cup of boiling water; drink slowly.

Headaches

Headaches can be caused by a variety of factors (see Part I) from allergies, trauma, eyestrain, intoxication, alcohol or drugs, problem teeth, lack of circulation to digestive problems, stress and worry, toxic fumes or long-term use of the computer and mobile phones (if due to the last go and take a walk in the park or on the beach, get some fresh air, leave your phone at home and protect yourself from EMFs with the devices available).

- A chocolate, cheese or wine habit could be involved, or very greasy foods.
- Drink a glass of red clay at the onset, followed by another glass 2 hours later.
- Apply poultices to the head and nape of neck, with 2 drops of lavender or Melissa essential oil.
- Drink peppermint and lemon balm infusions; rest with the eyes closed.
- Take lecithin capsules, 2 or 3 daily.
- Neurapas from 'Noma', 2 tablets 2 or 3 x daily; they are very helpful and contain St John's wort, valerian and passion flowers.

- Take B complex and higher levels of B2 and 3.
- If continual it is necessary to seek appropriate medical advice.
- Investigate the possibility of parasites.
- *See also under* Congestion, leading to sluggishness, for massage treatment to the feet; get a head massage.

Heavy metal poisoning, through amalgam fillings

Have fillings removed and replaced, if you feel or have discovered that they could be affecting your health. If you have had them removed you can follow this regime.

- Drink white clay and mix with apple pectin powder; for 10 days drink the mixture twice daily: 1 teaspoon of clay and 1 tablespoon of pectin in the water.
- Continue drinking the clay by itself for 11 more days; have a break for a week and start again as at first; continue this for several months.
- After 6 months carry on with yellow clay in the usual 3 weeks on, 1 week off mode.
- Check for improvement through Vega or applied kineseology testing, after the fillings have been removed, from 9 months to 1 year later.
- Also take vitamin C, up to 3g daily, multi minerals and selenium 200mcg, Vitamin E 400iu; digestive enzymes and essential fatty acids.
- For extreme fatigue follow the guidelines under ME.

Hypoglycaemia (low blood sugar)

The organism is unable to maintain a constant blood sugar level. The person affected feels faint or dizzy at certain periods throughout the day and rushes for a sugar fix. This will temporary raise the level making him/her feel good for a very short time, after which the level drops again. If this continues it becomes more difficult to balance and the blood sugar level will stay low, robbing the person's vitality and affecting the pancreas, spleen and kidneys.

- To work with this positively, have various small meals throughout the day.
- Eat complex carbohydrates and protein.
- Have a high fibre breakfast: millet, oats, spelt, rye, rice cereal, sprouted barley or a good muesli cereal (pre-soaked).
- Take chromium picolinate 200mcg in the middle of the day.
- Drink diluted, concentrated seawater (see Resources, p. 228) with green or red clay.
- Reduce your intake of concentrated fruit juices (hypoglycaemics are invariably drawn to these) and dilute them at least by half with water.
- Resist the urge to buy sweets, instead eat raisins, certain nuts or an apple.
- Avoid sugar altogether; alcohol, fried foods, all processed foods, very sweet fruits, and all white flour products.
- Eat plenty of avocados, beets, parsley, turnips and carrots.

- Helpful supplements are: spirulina powder (taken between meals will help stabilise blood sugar), 2 teaspoons daily in juice; flaxseeds, 2 ground up teaspoons; kelp tincture or powder and bee-pollen (if not allergic to it) 1–2 teaspoons daily.
- Fruits: apples, grapefruits, kiwis, blueberries and cranberries.
- Take pancreatic enzymes.
- Niacin 500mg daily in the morning, with B complex.
- Adrenal support: protomorphogens or a herbal alternative containing liquorice (do not take liquorice if you have a high BP).
- Take care of liver and pancreas, drink dandelion and Bancha tea (macrobiotics section in your health shop).

Impotence

Impotence is generally thought to occur due to stress and circulatory problems. Other factors to consider are alcohol abuse, drugs, smoking, years of wrong nutrition and surgery. The other side is the psychological aspect and could be caused by nerves, depression or a partner that doesn't turn you on. The facts are that there are problems, as was shown by the huge demand for Viagra, the new potency drug that came out a couple of years ago; however, several elderly men who took the drug died due to strain put on the heart from the excess sexual activity suddenly experienced after periods of abstinence due to their erection problems, because of this it has lost a little popularity.

- To improve naturally, follow the general ideas on diet written about here: plenty of fresh and organic fruits and vegetables.
- It would be helpful to take courses of superfine green or red clay.
- Effective herbs: cardamon and cinnamon, gingko biloba, saw palmetto and damiana.
- Essential oils to chose from: clary sage, sandalwood, sage, coriander, cypress, ylang-ylang, jasmine and vetiver.
- The Peruvian herb Maca grows high up in the Andean mountains under freezing conditions; it is a nutrient root consumed by locals on a daily basis and is gaining increasing popularity as an aphrodisiac by many people; strong alcoholic drinks are frequently consumed, which is why the herb is widely used to counteract the loss of potency caused by drinking; it is also excellent for women; *see* Menopause and ME; it is a general tonic for the whole system; *see also* Calcification; Baldness.
- If suffering from a weak nervous system take the herb only occasionally or take less then the recommended dose as it may be too stimulating.
- There is an aphrodisiac herbal formula which is made with rum, from ancient Inca recipes; it is known as the 7 roots drink and is apparently very powerful; enquire from your herbalist; buy it in Peru.

Infections, viral or bacterial

We are more prone to infections when run down, depressed, after a shock, recuperating or stressed.

- Make sure you have extra zinc at this time, as well as more then your usual intake of vitamin C.
- You can use the herbs elderflower, peppermint and boneset to reduce fever and take away the pains all over the body.
- Take 1 teaspoon of green clay in water twice daily.
- If you feel a cold coming on you will benefit immediately from taking $1/2$ teaspoon of organic echinacea herbal tincture in a little warm water, before it takes hold; take $1/2$ teaspoon again 2 hours later; once the cold has set in echinecea will not be of benefit; then you are better off with golden seal and vitamin C and drink the herbs described under 'Flu.
- If you are working or studying surrounded by a lot of people prone to catching 'flu, you could take echinecea as an immune-system enhancer: 10 drops 2 x daily, (for a short period 3–5 days – don't take the herb continually: it won't be effective when you really need it).
- Liquorice and golden seal tincture are of benefit for respiratory infections.
- Useful essential oils: 4 drops of lavender, rosemary or juniper berry and 1 drop of thyme.
- Add mixture to 1 pint of cabbage juice and mix with the clay to make a poultice, or dissolve the broken clay pieces in the liquid; apply to the affected area.
- *See also under* 'Flu.

Insect bites

Sweet bodies are more prone to being bitten.

- First, always try to protect yourself from being bitten, by using preparations based on citronella, when in infested areas.
- Avoid eating sweets, sweetened foods and drinks.
- Start eating less of anything sweet, 2 weeks before travelling.
- Add more garlic to your diet and take 1 umeboshi plum daily.
- Once bitten, use the clay-tube which you should carry with you at all times when in areas where you can expect to be bitten; pull out the sting if from a wasp or bee, and apply the clay paste immediately.
- Use a thick clay paste, on its own or with 2–3 drops of lavender oil (always make sure you have diluted the oil used on insect bites with a little almond oil, otherwise they could burn the skin which has now become more sensitive, although lavender is quite safe undiluted); cover the clay paste with a plaster.
- Clay tubes are ideal for all types of emergency use including burns; keep one in your backpack, or first-aid kit.

- If bitten by a bee, watch what develops and prepare to seek help if the bite gets really swollen; you may need an anti-histamine.
- If not treated, and there is more than one bite, it can result in anaphylactic shock if the person is sensitive or allergic to the bite; treat as an emergency; seek help immediately; adrenaline is needed.
- For mild situations and instant help, use the clay paste as instructed above.
- When bitten by a mosquito in the tropics, and you have not used any protection; also use clay paste immediately.
- Take wormwood capsules or tincture, daily as a preventative, if not already doing so.
- Drink Cassia herb tea for at least 1 week after being bitten (pack the herb in your travel kit).
- Homoeopathic formulas are available to take beforehand and while in the areas where the possibilities of bites are high (enquire from your homoeopathic pharmacist).
- I always take a high-level B complex as that seems a bit of a deterrent.
- If you develop a high fever after a bite, get yourself checked out at the tropical diseases section of your hospital; the mosquitoes are getting increasingly resistant to anti-malaria drugs, new ones are being developed and several are under research.
- There are a couple of anti-malaria tablets available through your GP which seem fairly effective taken once per week; one is called Larium, which works in parts of Indonesia and SE Asia (to be avoided by people prone to depression; can cause certain neurological disorders; check with your doctor or pharmacist) and there is doxycycline (to be avoided when pregnant); start 2 weeks before travel (they must be given with consideration to the chosen part of the world as different mosquitoes are repelled by different medications); these medications have certain side effects in some cases and can create nausea, headaches, fevers and brain problems; your doctor will advise you; you have a choice: do without and take a risk or put up with the side effects.
- You are advised to take the above herbal precautions as well; see also Part I, Chapter 7, Mosquitoes and malaria.
- Recent research has shown good results with the use of olive leaf extract capsules for the treatment of malaria and dengue fever; take up to 8 capsules daily for a week (see Tigon's Eden extract in Resources, p. 229).
- Take 2 wormwood, artemesiae annuae (Chinese 'Qing Hao', capsules, 2 x daily; the extract kills the malaria parasite), East West Herbs. 1 clove capsule, 30 drops of black walnut tincture and high doses of vitamin B daily when travelling abroad in affected regions.

Insomnia

- Avoid eating late at night, particularly spicy or heavy meals, as problem with digestion could be the cause and keep you awake.
- Anxiety, stress, worry, depression, liver and gallbladder problems are other causes and there are many.
- Exercise will help, preferably in the morning or early evening such as swimming.
- Try the yoga Sun Salutations (see p. 78) in the morning and some gentle stretches in the evening.
- In psychological cases help should be given.
- Helpful herbs: valerian, passionflower, hops, lavender, chamomile and lemon balm; take a mixture of 2 or 3 of these herbs 1 hour before bed (infusion or herbal capsules).
- Hot salt water foot baths with 3 drops of lavender or clary sage essential oil.
- Deep breathing exercises.
- Drink superfine green clay to normalise the equilibrium.
- B complex and spirulina taken in the morning are helpful.
- Check that your mineral intake is sufficient.
- Eat organic as pesticides play with your hormones and are a contributory factor.

Note: as people get older they tend to sleep less and need less sleep; (the pineal gland produces less melatonin in the brains of the elderly) sometimes they doze of in the afternoon; it is not surprising then that they cannot sleep at night. This is not what I would call insomnia, although the sufferer classifies it as such.

Irritable bowel syndrome: IBS

This is also known as spastic colitis and is a problem of the large colon which is quite common. As soon as something is eaten the sufferer experiences abdominal pain and swelling, alternating constipation and diarrhoea with mucous. Some say it is caused by stress, anxiety, allergies; also various psychological and physiological factors contribute to the painful condition.

- There is no doubt that clay is of great help here: 2 teaspoons of superfine green, daily in water, either drank as the clay water by itself or the whole glass (one would have to experiment).
- Take psyllium husks and other dietary fibres, preferably not cereals, but vegetables, fruits, bran, beans etc.
- Useful herbs: slippery elm, peppermint, ginger, chamomile, valerian, lemon balm.
- Cut out wheat and milk for 1 month; if you feel better on this continue for longer.

Jetlag

Air travel is very stressful and toxic, particularly long hauls.

- Avoid drinking alcohol on board, it is very dehydrating and adds to the acidity in the body which is already increased from flying.
- If suffering from nervous tension take some nervine herbs before travel to relax you.
- Take spirulina tablets during the flight and drink plenty of still water.
- Drink a glass of yellow clay before the flight, on arrival and when you wake up; continue for 3–4 days.
- Melatonin tablets always work effectively for jetlag; they are only available in the States and are best for long hauls; to be taken for about 2 nights, at 2, 3mg tablets for transatlantic flights, at your destination's bedtime.
- Before going to bed use 4 drops of lavender and 2 drops of neroli essential oil in your bath, to relax the nervous system and help you adjust.

Kidneys

- If congested; apply warm clay poultices to the kidney area with 2 drops of ginger essential oil, leave for 20–30 minutes; alternate with ginger-water compresses.
- To prepare, grate 2 teaspoons of ginger, put the ginger in little muslin cloths and tie with a string, add to 1 litre of boiling water and leave it there for 20 minutes.
- Squeeze the muslin ginger balls, and also use small towelling cloths, saturated with the ginger water and apply balls and cloths to kidney area, as hot as can be tolerated; repeat as soon as it cools down; immerse the same in the hot ginger water and continue for 5–15 minutes.
- Useful herbs: juniper berry, golden rod, and a short course 3–4 days of uva ursi.
- The kidneys rule the adrenals and sexual organs and are associated with the element water; the desired taste is salty, but too much will harm; the sound is groan, the colour is black to dark brown; the emotion is fear – a little salt on the tongue can help in sudden attacks of fearfulness, strengthening the kidneys, which will reduce the fear emotion; the adverse climate is a cold one.
- Your kidney's health is reflected in your hair.
- Good pulses and grains are buckwheat, rice, adzuki beans and lentils.
- Beneficial fruits are chestnuts, your vegetables of choice are coloured green.
- Why do we get problems with these vital organs, our kidneys? See Part II, Chapter 17.

Liver problems

Liver problems are so common: the liver is always working overtime filtering our dirty blood. We are constantly upsetting this important organ with our wrong eating and drinking habits and our turbulent emotions. The liver has as many as 500 functions, from producing bile to storing nutrients, metabolising fats, synthesising cholesterol and its subsequent breakdown into bile salts; detoxifying and draining the waste of incoming toxins from pollution, drugs, hormones, additives and poisons. We must try to take good care of this vital organ.

- Useful essential oils, 4 drops of peppermint or lavender.
- Drink infusions of milk-thistle and blackcurrant leaves or take the tincture, 3 x daily, 20 drops.
- Apply a clay poultice to the liver area once in the evening for several days, adding the above drops of essential oil.
- Drink green clay but only the surface particles initially, prepared as instructed under Constipation until improved.
- Have a coffee enema from time to time; this will help the liver to produce more bile to help your digestion and absorption, in particular if dealing with fats.
- Useful liver herbs are dandelion and sassafras; globe artichoke can be eaten or is available as juice or in capsules.
- Take lecithin granules or capsules, digestive enzymes and essential fatty acids.
- Ongoing problems should be treated by a qualified naturopathic physician.
- The liver is associated with the element wood, the emotion is anger, the sound is to shout, the counteracting emotion is control, the colour is blue or green, the adverse weather condition is windy, and the season is the spring; the taste is sour.
- A good grain is whole wheat and your fruits are the plum and the papaya; the beneficial vegetables are leeks and beetroots; season your salads with horse-radish, and drink carrot and parsley juice.

Lymphatic congestion

The lymphatic system is very important to us as it helps to keep our immune system in good order; it involves many systems and organs. We have three times more lymph fluid in the body as we have blood, which may give some indication of its importance to our general health. The lymph fluid is a watery substance derived from the blood; it is not moved around the body by a pump, unlike the blood which has the heart to do that job. The fluid flows in the spaces between our tissues and cells, and carries various substances back to the bloodstream. It is composed of water, lymphocytes, digested nutrients, salts, hormones, carbon dioxide and urea.

The largest lymph vessel is the thoracic duct which is where the fluids always end up. Here the fluid is emptied into veins in the upper thoracic area. The lymph fluid needs to circulate in order to work well; one of its functions is to mop up bacteria and viruses which are caught in the lymph nodes. When the nodes swell up as they do, then we have a virus or acute infection; we therefore know that the lymph system is working.

Lymphocytes originate in red bone-marrow; some travel to the thymus where they become T cells and help to eliminate infections, the others become B cells which produce antibodies, and are involved in fighting and destroying invading pathogens, viruses and bacteria. They are found in the main organs involved with the lymph system, which are the spleen, thymus, tonsils, adenoids and appendix. When we have any of these removed our immune system is more compromised.

We can help the fluid flow a bit better – as it is easy to get congestion and stagnation, particularly by those with a sedentary lifestyles – by exercising, walking, and using an aerobic re-bounder, which will create a great improvement. The thymus gland has to function well. This gland is also involved in the support of the immune system. However from puberty onwards, as we grow older and when under stress the thymus tends to shrink. In the small intestines we find specialised lymph vessels which are called lacteals; they assist in the absorption of fats.

- A good healthy adequately nutritious diet is essential, including a multi vitamin and mineral supplement.
- Also take vitamin C and drink clay from time to time.
- Lymphatic drainage massage is sometimes needed; use rose geranium and rosemary essential oils.
- Drink sufficient water.
- Take clay, superfine green.
- Particular herbs are: chaparral, pau d'arco, garlic, turmeric, cumin and blue flag.

ME (myalgic encephalomyelitis)

A fairly newly acknowledged condition that manifests in the sufferer feeling totally exhausted and miserable. It usually occurs after viral illnesses, respiratory viruses or problems involving the GI tract, chronic infections with EBV (member of the herpes group of viruses) or after inoculations. Once brought in contact with EBV the infection lies dormant and when the immune system is weakened the symptoms will reappear and could worsen. It is not psychosomatic as was first thought: people suffering from this debilitating problem are in a lot of cases really unable even to get up in the morning. There is a specific blood test which will confirm PVFS (post viral fatigue syndrome).

- To help the person recover quickly, rest is of course the first priority, but exercise is an absolute must as being sedentary will only make it worse; try to do some even if it is hard at first; help can be given by certain foods, tonics and herbs.

- Proper adrenal and the thyroid function should be considered, as should colon health which often becomes sluggish; check for hypoglycemia.
- Helpful foods are seafoods, and follow the macrobiotic principals, i.e. millet, brown rice, buckwheat, vegetables and fruits; avoid gluten for a while.
- Helpful nutrients: spirulina, zinc, magnesium, acidophilus, evening primrose oil; and a strong combination of essential fatty acids.
- Follow some of the suggestions outlined in Part I, Chapter 2 on Candida.
- Alcohol should be avoided as even one drink can make symptoms worse.
- Also smoking has a detrimental effect.
- Yellow, green or red clay can be taken, twice daily.
- The herb Maca from Peru which grows in the coldest and highest regions of the Peruvian Andes, has been tried out here on the above patients, with wonderful results; the powdered root is best at 1–2 teaspoons daily; it will give an energy boost to anyone who is tired and is very rich in vitamins, minerals and amino acids; AK tests and several people who have tried an initial batch of the herb have shown it to be superior in quality and strength to others tested (Resources, see Nutri Centre or Wholistic Research).
- For those with a weak nervous system the herb could be over-stimulating; try reducing the dose to 1/2 teaspoon daily and alternate with mistletoe leaf extract weekly; mistletoe is calming and toning to the nervous system, anti-spasmodic and helps the endocrine balance.
- When taking any herb always take one day off per week.
- Take a bowl of porridge in the morning 2 or 3 times per week, rejuvenating for the nervous system and helpful for this condition.

Menopause: the cessation of the female cycle

This usually takes place in the late forties to early fifties and sometimes earlier. Some women sail through the menopause with no symptoms whatsoever. Others (at least 70%) suffer terribly, due to the changing hormones, from hot flushes to depression, lack of energy, low libido, heart problems and osteoporosis, often rushing to their doctors for the little helper HRT, which seems to be good for some women. However it is said to give rise to certain types of cancer, i.e. uterine cancer, by some researchers. When given to increase bone strength, the pros do not outweigh the cons.

- In recent years and through the work of Dr John Lee the use of wild yams has been widely researched and found to be effective in treating the menopause naturally.
- When oestrogen levels drop, the following plant foods are recommended: Tofu and other soy based foods, yams, apples and carrots; these have the ability to normalise an oestrogen excess as well as correct a deficiency.
- To increase calcium, eat calcium-rich foods, i.e. 2 teaspoons of ground-up sesame seeds, 3 almonds daily (soaked overnight); lots of leafy green vegetables.

- Through diet and supplements aim to get calcium and magnesium at a ratio of 800–1000mg/400–800mg and vitamin D at 400iu daily.
- Royal jelly is a good tonic. Try Royal Oil (*see* Tigon Ltd, in Resources)
- Taking care of the liver is a must: dandelion tea and milkthistle tincture are of help.
- Check the adrenal function: the glands could be weak; if that is the case symptoms will be worse, they are involved in the hormonal balance; find a way to restore their optimum function; liquorice, the herb, is a good choice.
- Drink red or superfine green clay.
- Externally you can have helpful baths: add 300–500g of green clay to the bath, 2 times per week when suffering from flushes and other associated discomforts; prepare an infusion of the following herbs: 1 tablespoon of chamomile, kelp and witch hazel leaves, added to 1 1/2 litre water; boil the herbs for 15 minutes and add to the bath water; take 2 baths like this per week, alternating these with the clay baths.
- Massage the torso with essential oil of sage, 3 drops to 10 ml almond oil, 3 x per week.
- Infusions of sage tea in the evening 3 x per week (1 teaspoon per cup); alternate with other suitable herbs, chamomile, motherworth or oatstraw.
- Useful herbal tinctures: agnus cactus, wild yam, black cohosh, liquorice, ginseng, life root, or ask your herbalist to advise you.
- The herb maca is useful for hormonal imbalances and also acts as an aphrodisiac.
- Progest is a cream applied topically and widely used as an alternative to HRT; some GPs are able to prescribe it, or contact the Natural Progesterone Information Service, PO Box 131, Etchingham TN19 ZN.
- In the US it is possible to find a choice of wild yam creams in health stores or try Women's International Pharmacy, 5708 Monono Drive, Madison, WI 5316-3152; or Biotanica, Sherwood, Oregon. Tel. 800 -572-4712.

Menstruation

Very few women and young girls experience the monthly cycle without problems. Menstruation can be painful, delayed, scanty, disappear altogether or become more frequent.

- Choose from essential oils of chamomile, 4 drops + anis, 2 drops, or cypress or nutmeg, 2 drops + lavender, 4 drops.
- Sage or tarragon extract or infusion.
- Prepare a poultice on which you spread the drops of essential oil with a wooden spatula; apply to abdomen, cover with a towel and rest in a comfortable position for 1–2 hours, while drinking an infusion of sage and lavender or tarragon; do this once or twice daily until improved.

- The herbs agnus cactus and shepherd's purse have been found to be very useful.
- With associated headaches, take St John's wort herbal capsules, 1–3 x daily while suffering (check with your doctor if you are taking other kinds of medication and you are considering St John's wort as it may interfere with certain drugs, and could increase sensitivity to the sun's rays).
- Drink red clay.
- Reduce your intake of high fatty foods.
- Make sure you eliminate daily as constipation does not help matters.
- Add fibre to your daily regime.
- Reduce stress.
- Eat the foods recommended above under Menopause.
- Liver congestion contributes to menstrual problems.

Mouth ulcers

Aphta often appear when people are run down or stressed. The immune system gets low.

- Rinse the mouth with a glass of lavender water to which you have added a tablespoon of green clay (infuse the flowers or powdered lavender; use 1 teaspoon to a glass).
- Take L Lysine 500mg in the morning.
- Increase your intake of vitamin C.

Multiple sclerosis (MS)

MS is an auto-immune disorder, leading to a deterioration of the myelin sheath surrounding the nerves in the brain and spinal cord, causing an initial inflammation. When the body's immune system attempts to repair the damage, it is actually attacking the body as opposed to protecting it, resulting in the formation of scar-tissue (lesions) which inhibits the conduction of nerve impulses to pass through the newly formed sclerotic tissue. The symptoms experienced depend on the area where the plaque is formed. Symptoms include: blurred vision and other eye problems, poor balance, ringing in the ears, dizziness, speech problems, tiredness, bladder and bowel problems, pins and needles in feet and legs, feeling of numbness in parts of the body, facial neuralgia and numbness.

According to macrobiotic principals, the body starts to deteriorate from a lack of vital chemical elements, particularly those coming from our nutrition and from a high fat diet and too much sugar. From my own experience in dealing with MS cases, this has been certainly true. I also found there to be a high level of metal toxicity in the system.

- Avoid gluten, sugar and milk.
- The diet should be low in fat and cholesterol.

- Avoid getting constipated as this could contribute to the problem.
- Avoid being overheated.
- Reduce stress.
- Take care of the lymph system.
- Remove mercury fillings if it is found to be necessary; check for heavy metal toxicity.
- Aim to maintain a strong immune system; avoid infection which can trigger the problem.
- Stick to the dietary guidelines.
- Digestive enzymes could be needed.
- Take lecithin 3 capsules daily; this helps muscle weakness and aids co-ordination and balance, helps the myelin sheath and the transmission of nerve impulses.
- Also take vitamin B 12, and a strong multi B.
- Essential fatty acids, Omega 3 and Omega 6, i.e. flaxseed oil capsules, 3–6 daily.
- Mega GLA capsules; vitamin E 400 iu.
- Avoid animal fats and meats, yeasted breads and sweets.
- A macrobiotic diet would be the most beneficial, with white fish 2–3 weekly.
- Drink red or green clay.

Obesity: weight problems

Research indicates that in most cases an excessive consumption of foods that are incorrect are the cause of being overweight. There appears to be an unusually large appetite which drives this person to eat more then the normal amount; hunger is not satisfied hence the need to eat more. It could be psychologically induced due to loneliness, bereavement, insecurity or fear and unhappiness. From this point a positive approach to life is important. Counselling may be helpful.

An excess amount of food is difficult to digest and assimilate, it is hard on the stomach, liver, pancreas, kidneys and the heart; food ferments and decays and will settle somewhere in the system. The extra fat is a store for toxins. This overflow creates an ideal environment for parasites, bacteria and germs, causing lethargy and robbing your vitality. There is a higher risk of cardiovascular problems as well as cancer. Life expectancy is shortened and the immune system gets damaged. The digestive system needs to be repaired. The diet should consist of low calories and whole natural foods.

- Avoid carbonated drinks, sugar, 'sugar free' drinks (which have aspartame or other additives added) and salt; follow the advice for hypoglycaemics.
- Include starches in the form of whole grains, such as millet, rye, buckwheat, rice, vegetables and all kinds of beans; all types of fruits, papaya, plums, dates.

- Combine different types of fruits, vegetables and starches; complex carbohydrates are found in all of these; do not combine proteins with carbohydrates.
- Take various small meals throughout the day.
- Slowly reduce the portions you have become accustomed to.
- Drink more water.
- Take chromium picolinate, 200mcg during the day to reduce your craving.
- Contrary to popular belief starches do not make you fat, as long as they are the right starches.
- Chinese and Japanese people whose diet is mainly rice are generally very slim.
- Avoid going on super diets as the effects don't last and they can be dangerous.
- Take psyllium husks from time to time: 1 tablespoon 30 minutes before lunch and dinner, in a glass of water, daily for 2-week periods with a 2 weeks' break, until the weight is more balanced.
- Follow periods of nutritionally supervised fasting and detoxification to include enemas and colonic hydrotherapy.
- Avoid wheat breads and pasta for a while.
- Take digestive enzymes as the digestive system is generally overtaxed.
- The thyroid should always be considered.
- Try the super green foods to increase stamina and energy levels, spirulina, wheat or barley grass.
- Drink superfine green clay from time to time (as described under Constipation) and sea water.
- Take herbs to move the bowel to include cascara sagrada.
- Drink herbal teas.
- Find an enjoyable form of exercising even if it is only walking or swimming.

Parkinsonism, a degenerative neurological disorder

The symptoms of Parkinson's disease are trembling of the limbs, rigidity, slowness and stiffness. The body is slightly stooped forward. The condition gets worse with age. Mostly affects those over the age of 60, but some people are affected earlier. The cause is an inability to maintain a balance of the 2 types of nerve impulses of the autonomic nervous system: while one set involves movement the other inhibits movement. Worsened by a general wastage of the neurons (nerve cells) in the basal ganglia of the brain. The patient is generally under the care of a doctor as it is a serious condition. A lack of dopamine, and an imbalance of dopamine/acetylcholine is responsible for the tremors in the hands, arms and sometimes the legs. Mental function is usually not affected. The problem is associated with depression. People affected get depressed from the disorder.

- The diet should be high in complex carbohydrates, which promote energy.
- Whole grains including spelt, corn, oats, rice; combine with beans and vegetables.

- Low protein, fish is best: 2–3 x weekly, plenty of sea vegetables.
- Herbally, skullcap (sculletaria lateriflora), ginkgo biloba and ladies slipper (cypripedium calceolus) are very useful.
- Fava beans are a plant source of L dopamine; you can sprout them; also take alfalfa sprouts or tablets; eat all kinds of other sprouted grains.
- Minerals and nutrients should be supplemented; vitamin B complex and B12.
- Fish oil, Evening Primrose Oil (high dose), flaxseeds (capsules or ground up), zinc and selenium.
- Vitamins A and D.
- Superfine clay is beneficial.
- Take digestive enzymes as the digestion is usually impaired.
- Constipation is common.
- Regular bowel movement is of utmost importance to avoid stagnation of built up putrefying matter. Take bowel toning herbs and drink more water.
- Scientists have concluded that the disease can be caused by an accumulation of certain pesticides in the system; also the use of certain anti-psychotic drugs when used in high doses can have similar effects.

Prostate congestion

The prostate gland is situated at around the male urethra, just below the bladder; it is about the size of a walnut. The problem of prostate cancer and benign enlargement, BPH, is on the increase, and not solely reserved for elderly gentlemen. Frequently now much younger men are afflicted. The enlargement is due to age, diet and an excess production of the male hormone di-hydrotestosterone, and can reduce the urinary stream, leading to dribble and frequent need to urinate just a few droplets.

- Follow the general dietary outlines in this book; *see also under* Breast lumps; Balding.
- Take saw palmetto the herb which is also highly beneficial as a preventative; about 300 mg daily, tincture or capsules.
- Other nutrients include zinc, B complex to include B6, trace amounts of copper, pumpkin seeds, flaxseeds as an oil, 2 tablespoons, or up to 6 caps daily initially; reduce to 3 after a period of time; always refrigerate flax-oil, can go rancid quickly if left out.
- Take digestive enzymes and vitamin E, 400iu daily.
- Avoid foods that have been contaminated with pesticides and hormones.
- Reduce beer and alcohol intake; cut down on caffeine.
- Ginseng is a tonic.
- Drink carrot juice for up to 3 months (drink within 15 minutes of juicing to ensure all the vitamins are intact) or use tincture of wild carrot (daucus carota).
- Eat organic brown rice as that will assist absorption of the vital elements

obtained from the carrot juice and help carry out the toxins while taking the carrot juice which is quite a powerful treatment.
- Detoxify: take enemas and occasional colonic irrigation; take psyllium husks (1–2 table spoons daily in water) from time to time.
- Drink green clay.

Psoriasis

Psoriasis is mostly seen as a condition caused by an inability to deal with the body's waste products through the normal elimination channels; it manifests itself on areas such as the knees and elbows, but can also appear in the face and other parts of the body. The signs are raised scaly patches of inflamed skin tissue. The raised patches form due to the cells under the skin reproducing 10 x faster than normal; the old skin cells are not being shed and stay underneath forming layers of grey/white flakes. It always gets worse from the wrong diet and when under stress.

- Prepare elderflower infusion, 1 pint; add this to your broken clay pieces; make a poultice and apply to inflamed skin; leave for 30 minutes to 1 hour.
- Use blood cleansing herbs such as; burdock root, dandelion, yellow dock root, sarsaparilla, mountain grape and milk thistle for the liver.
- You can have baths with 300–500g of powdered yellow clay combined with elderflower infusion 3–4 x weekly; add 1 teaspoon of garlic oil (see 'How To's, make your own garlic oil).
- Adjust your diet and also take care of the spleen and kidneys.
- Try the herbs, red clover and golden rod, 1 or 2 cups every other day.
- Apply an ointment made with the herb chickweed.
- Reduce your intake of meat and alcohol and other foods that give a toxic build up.
- Avoid citrus fruits.
- Take seawater or liquid trace minerals.
- Drink yellow clay, eat seaweeds and white fish.
- Black sesame seeds ground up, 1–2 teaspoons daily.
- Take high GLA, flaxseed oil, in capsules or liquid form, keep refrigerated.
- Vitamin A and E 400iu, lecithin 2 or 3 capsules daily.
- Follow the general dietary principals under Candida.
- Have weekly enemas.
- See the sun.
- Take occasional cleansing diets, for 1 or 2 days.
- Start the day with a glass of carrot juice; for lunch have vegetable soup and a salad with all kinds of local vegetables of the season, with plenty of sprouted seeds.
- At dinner have a meal of 50% steamed vegetables and 50% short grain brown rice.

Raynaud's disease

A circulation problem affecting the hands and feet, which can result in gangrene and can sometimes be a symptom of scleroderma. It can be exacerbated by taking certain drugs to reduce blood pressure, including some drugs used to treat asthma.

- Herbal help is taking up to 2 teaspoons of cayenne pepper daily in powder form and infused or sprinkled on food (works faster when infused); garlic and ginkgo biloba.
- Take lecithin granules 1 tablespoon with your 3 meals.
- Take evening primrose or borage oil capsules 1000mg; high GLA oil can also be massaged into the fingers.
- Drink superfine green clay at intervals.
- Magnesium is a needed element.
- *See also* Circulation and Chilblains

Rheumatism

Rheumatic inflammations of the joints gradually worsen due to the erosion of the articular cartilage. The tissues supporting the joints are also damaged and it is very painful. Some benefits may be attained with the use of certain seaweeds in the bath. Dietary involvement is always considered. A diet high in animal foods will rob the system of oxygen in the nerves surrounding the joints and muscles; they also form acids which make the condition worse.

- Avoid dairy products, artificial sweeteners and additives, fats and salt, bananas and orange juice.
- There may be an allergy to certain types of food which can worsen the condition, such as plants of the nightshade family, potatoes, tomatoes, aubergines and peppers; they are very acid forming and not so easy to digest.
- Avoid citrus fruits.
- Try acupuncture and massage.
- Taking specific nutrients and minerals are beneficial such as amino acids containing the polysaccharides, known as glycosaminoglycans and also sufficient amounts of chondroitin sulphate; this is available as a powder or in capsules, taken with a specific mineral formula called (B Alive) which is available by mail order (see B Alive, p. 216) a great improvement can be achieved.
- Add essential fatty acids, high GLA and flax oil.
- Take alfalfa tablets and barley grass.
- Helpful herbs to choose from are: ginger, oregano, burdock root, white willow, garlic, celery seeds or powder and sassafras.
- Drink infusions of star anise or tincture of wild carrot (daucus carota) which is particularly good for the treatment of gout; also try green tea and drink more water.

- Essential oils, birch tar and rosemary; dilute in sweet almond oil, for a massage. (3 drops of each in 15ml).
- Make clay poultices for painful areas with infusions of rosemary and nettles.
- Drink superfine green clay, away from foods (30 minutes before or 2 hours after).

Salmonella

This infection causes severe diarrhoea and vomiting; it is always best to consult your doctor at once. The debilitating effect of ongoing diarrhoea is not good as the potassium levels in the blood get very low. The patient will get very weak and dehydrated quickly. There is usually a need to be given specific antibiotics for about 3–5 days.

- You can supplement with acidophilus as soon as the antibiotic therapy is over.
- Also take the green or white clay while on this treatment; continue for 3 weeks.
- Keep the diet light with plenty of soups and broths, as well as home-made apple-sauce or grated apple until the patient's appetite has been restored.
- Herbs, peppermint, slippery elm and oakbark.

Scleroderma

Local thickening and hardening of skin tissues, hands and fingers. Can also affect internal organs (sclerosis). To treat:

- Immerse feet and hands in a bowl of hot grated celery soup.
- Grate celery bring to boil for 5 minutes and use at body temperature, for 10–15 minutes daily.
- See also Raynaud's Disease.

Shingles

This condition is of viral origin and affects the nerve-endings which can be damaged. The problem can occur when highly stressed or worried (most skin conditions worsen under stress) and when suffering from candida, these factors can cause a weakening of the immune system. Shingles are usually visible as a belt of bubbly burning eruptions around the waist, but can also be present in other parts of the body such as the back, the hairline and eyebrows; it is also known as *herpes zoster*.

- To treat: sprinkle superfine green powder over the eruptions to dry them.
- Apply 'cloister' oil or balm (helps to dry the eruptions faster).
- Take flax and borage oil capsules, 1000 mg each until better (2 of each daily).
- You may need extra calcium and magnesium.
- Aim to alkalise your system; take alfalfa tablets, 6 daily.

- Follow the diet recommended for candida.
- Apply Vita Fons II ointment (see Resources, p. 230), between clay applications and try aloe vera cooling gel.
- L Lysine, 500 mg 2 x daily; take vitamin C 2000mgs and high level B complex.
- Avoid chocolate, peanuts and orange juice.
- Strengthen the immune system to avoid recurrence: take a course of lymph decongestant herbs; drink infusions of golden rod, golden seal and echinacea.

Sinus problems

Sinus problems are very common and often a chronic condition that people learn to live with. They can start at changes of season, worsen from allergies or can be caused by bowel toxins and toxic blood or are of bacterial or parasitic origin. Diet affects the condition, too much fat in the diet, too much protein or too many simple carbohydrates.

- When the condition is acute minimise the above foods and increase your intake of whole grains and vegetables.
- Try inhaling green clay powder, 1 tablespoon dissolved in a glass of water, 3 x daily. (a few drops at the time)
- Apply a clay poultice to the eyebrow area with 1 drop of mint.
- Take herbs to clean the blood and the lymph system, e.g. chaparral, yellow dock, golden seal and sweet sumach.
- Steam inhale eucalyptus and peppermint oils (add 2–3 drops of each to a bowl of hot water; place the head over the bowl and cover with a towel) or apply 1 drop of each to the palms of your hands; rub hands together and place over the nose breathing in.
- Add garlic, cayenne and ginger to your diet and aim to alkalise the body by eating properly.
- Drink Miso soup with chopped up spring onions, garlic and ginger.
- Carrot juice, up to 3 glasses daily with wheatgrass (optional). This is very detoxifying.
- Drink superfine green clay.
- Take care of the bowel: use psyllium husks and bowel herbs.
- Have regular enemas with green clay or lemon.
- Check for parasites (Darkfield test).

Skin problems

These can stem from toxic blood, hormonal problems, congested liver, lymph or overworked kidneys.

- Use burdock root extract, wild pansy extract and wahoo.
- Cleanse problem areas with elderflower tea; apply with cotton wool and allow to dry naturally.

- Prepare a broken clay poultice with the water from the above infused herbs and apply.
- You can use the fine clay powder (yellow or green) for this treatment as well; make an infusion of burdock root and mix with the powder; allow it to become the thickness of honey then it can be painted on the irritated parts.
- This is very good for problems associated with certain skin parasites (adding a few drops of black walnut tincture); drink the herbs as well or use tincture.
- Drink green clay 2 times daily, to help detoxify the blood.
- Infusions of golden rod, yarrow and sarsaparilla can be alternated with the above herbs, every other day; 2 cups daily, until improved.
- You can try 10ml of Safi, a herbal blood-purifier from Indian grocery stores, daily for 1 month, taken in a little juice once daily.
- Use a hard skin brush (not if skin is broken).
- Skin problems can be of emotional origin; try nervine herbs in that case, such as wild cherry and limeblossoms.

Skin, slack

See the recipe under Breasts; use the clay as a mask anywhere it is needed on the body. At home treat one area at a time.

- Try a trip to a clay spa if you get the chance.
- Drink more water.
- Check kidney health.
- There could be weakness with the connective tissues, cross linking of collagen.
- There is a lack of minerals, particularly sodium, calcium fluoride and silica, and there is a need for chondroitin sulphate; take anti-oxidants, vitamins E, C etc.
- Essential fatty acids; digestive enzymes; add sea-foods and seaweeds.
- Exercise and use the treatment under Congestion.
- Stretch swim or walk, try low weight-bearing exercises or pilates.
- See Resources, p. 233 for the book, *Strong Women Stay Young*, with easy exercises to strengthen muscles which will help the skin as well.

Sprains

From accidental falls or to treat swollen limbs from knocks, bruises or pain.

- First, apply a thin layer of arnica cream to the painful area and take homoeopathic arnica 6, 2 tablets every 2 hours, for the first day in 6 doses. Then 3 x daily for 1 or 2 weeks.
- Externally use 2 drops of lavender and 2 of juniperberry, 1 teaspoon of turmeric powder, spread over a clay poultice; add the drops of essential oil, apply to the sprain and secure; leave on for maximum time.
- Or take 2 tablespoons of comfrey powder, 1 tablespoon of slippery elm, 1

tablespoon of chamomile flowers, powdered, and 1 tablespoon of powdered green clay (use less if area to be treated is small); add boiling water to the mixture and stir; mould together until a cake-like dough is formed.
- Wrap the poultice in a strong sheet of paper towelling and apply to the area as warm as possible.
- Secure with strips of sheeting and safety pins; leave on as long as possible; maintain warmth with a warm water bottle; this poultice is reusable and can be reheated 3 or 4 times.
- Alternate with applications of Vita Fons II ointment.
- Be sure it is a sprain you are dealing with by having an X ray if there is any doubt; otherwise the treatment will take an awful long time, and can be complicated.
- *See under* Ankle, broken

Stones, gallbladder

High cholesterol and a pre-disposition is the culprit. The stones can contain calcium deposits and pigments, mostly from animal products. An excess of cholesterol tends to settle in the tissues. This is where they start to cause irritation and inflammation and in the gallbladder they become stones. A small amount of stones are generally asymptomatic and up to 30% of people have them.

- Benefits will be achieved immediately if a low fat diet is implemented.
- On a spiritual level stones are a manifestation of congealed energy; maybe the person is taking too much care over the welfare of others: this obstructs the energy flow; the obligation to others could prevent a normal balance of energy and 'aggression' to flow naturally.
- There is often a need to let off steam, in one way or another; voice classes are a good way or mantric chanting, calming and balancing the relevant chakras.
- A naturopathic practitioner may be able to help you rid yourself of stones with the famous gallbladder flush; this takes place over a 24 hour period and involves the intake of olive oil and lemon or grapefruit juice among other ingredients.
- A diet rich in plant foods is free from cholesterol.
- Beneficial herbs are berberis vulgaris, milkthistle, dandelion, fringe tree bark and wahoo.
- Lecithin reduces the size of the stone; take 3 teaspoons of the granules daily with food.
- Use green clay, externally and internally.
- Homoeopathically use calc carb or nat mur.

Stones, kidneys

Usually caused by a diet of excesses, protein being one of them. Often too much salt is consumed and there is a lack of hydration. The body has a limited ability to store protein, so when we consume too much, the liver and kidneys overwork and enlarge. The kidneys produce more urea which, since it has a diuretic action, puts more stress on the organ, producing more urine and causing a loss of essential trace minerals. The most important mineral lost is calcium. This calcium ends up in the urine and urinary system and contribute to becoming stones after continual abuse. Also aids in the development of osteoporosis as high protein intake causes calcium to be leached from the bones.

- With a reduction of protein intake the recurrence of stones will be reduced.
- Herbs to reduce stone formation, gravelroot, juniperberry, and hydrangia root
- Drink superfine green clay and take seawater twice daily; homoeopathically, see above.

Throats, sore

- Gargle with clay water, prepared with an infusion of 1 teaspoon of thyme to a cup of boiled water.
- Leave to cool, strain and add the teaspoon of clay; or try gargling with H_2O_2, one teaspoon to a glass of water.
- Apply a poultice to the throat area with one drop of eucalyptus and one drop of thyme diluted in 5 ml of base oil (such as grape-seed or almond-oil).
- Alternate clay applications with Vita Fons II ointment.

Thyroid imbalance

The thyroid governs the body's metabolic rate and is part of the endocrine system. It acts to regulate the rate of oxygen consumption in most of our bodily tissues, influences the activities of the nervous system and regulates the way we utilise fats, sugars and carbohydrates. It produces several hormones of which the most important are thyroxin (T4 and T3) and calcitonin (which with the help of the four parathyroid glands helps to maintain calcium balance and bone strength). The gland works together with the hypothalamus and the pituitary gland, from which it receives hormonal messages. A thyroid deficiency causes the level of cholesterol in the blood stream to rise. This can lead to narrowing of the arteries (athero-sclerosis) if not checked.

- Signs of deficiency and lowering function are: drooping eyelids, swollen tongue, swollen features, dry coarse skin, thinning of the outer parts of the eyebrows.
- If the thyroxin levels are low, you may be predisposed to raised blood cholesterol and athero-sclerosis.

- You could be suffering from constipation and might have cold hands and feet.
- You may also experience a tingling sensation in the hands and feet.
- The mind can go fuzzy and you could become irrational.
- You may also suffer from depression and tiredness.
- An under-active function of the gland may result in constant headaches and also leads to an accumulation of nitrogenous wastes, which could result in problems related to respiration such as asthma.
- Low thyroid function in women can affect the menstruation, making the cycle more heavy and of a longer duration, whereas with a hyper thyroid function it is the opposite.
- An imbalance can also be involved in fertility problems.
- For optimum thyroid function keep up your iodine levels through your diet.
- Include kelp supplementation if you do not like eating seaweeds.
- Helpful foods are: apricots, eggs, dates, broccoli and small amounts of radishes.
- Helpful balancing herbs: gentian, melissa, Irish moss and dulse.
- For over-activity try the herb bugleweed.
- Drink superfine green clay.
- Take digestive enzymes.
- Avoid sugar, high protein and excess fluid intake.
- See your doctor; you may need therapeutic doses of thyroxine, which work very well in conjunction with a healthy natural approach to diet, food supplements and exercise. Some of the herbal alternatives are good as an adjunct, check this with your doctor.
- Homoeopathically there are several remedies.
- To check your own thyroid function you can try the 'Barnes' temperature test: as soon as you wake up before getting out of bed take your temperature, under the armpit for 10 minutes, record this for 5 days; normal temperature is between 36.4ºC (97.6ºF) and 36.7ºC (98.2ºF); if your temperature is 97.6ºF or below, the thyroid function is considered to be low; above 98.4ºF its function is hyper and if taking thyroxin you may be taking too much.
- The normal blood tests for thyroid function, do not always show a deficiency, particularly in young women, so the above is a good alternative (Vega, AK, humoral pathology and iridology are other ways of checking; see Resources.

Tonsillitis

Again the problem is caused by a poor dietary intake and a run-down immune system. Removing the tonsils is not recommended, as they are an important part of the immune-lymphatic system, and act to prevent bacteria and germs from entering; this is why they swell up and inflame when compromised. They are just doing their job. When they are taken out germs have a much easier access to the rest of your body, which can lead to general infection, bowel problems and illness.

- Lower all sweet consumption, dairy products and heavy wheat intake.
- Externally, 3 drops of ginger, geranium, sage, lemon and only 1 drop of thyme.
- Apply a clay poultice with a choice of 1 or 2 of the essential oils; wrap the cloth around the neck and secure, leave for 1 hour, twice daily; gargle with 2 drops of myrrh in warm water with a teaspoon of H_2O_2 (see echo, p. 220).
- Avoid constipation; take suitable herbs and drink red or green clay.

Tooth abscess

Short-term treatment: prepare small clay balls; slowly mix together a little water with powdered green clay and a tiny bit of honey, roll them over a board so they are shaped into small balls, you can add a pinch of powdered cloves if desired, bake in an oven for a few minutes. They can be placed in the mouth on the painful area. Alternatively, apply tincture or oil of myrrh directly to the area on a cottonbud. See the dentist.

Tumours

- Apply a thick clay poultice to the affected part, and leave for maximum time; use twice daily.
- Add 2 drops geranium, or coriander if desired; continue until swelling is reduced.
- Drink green clay.
- Detoxify the liver by taking tincture of milkthistle (20 drops 3 x daily) and a course of wormwood capsules (2 capsules 2 x daily).
- Purify the kidneys with marshmallow or uva ursi; drink 2 cups of infusion daily for 2 or 3 weeks.
- Take pancreatic enzymes and flax/linseed oil.
- Take herbs to improve the lymphatic system, such as chaparral.
- Use the parasite programme, drink tea of red clover (read Chapter 5 on Cancer).
- Try Professor Jurasunas' infrared ceramic balls (see Resources, p. 219).
- Drink Zell-oxygen.

Urinary problems

Urinary problems can happen at any time. Cystitis is very common; later on there can be a decline in kidney function due to ageing. The kidneys gradually lose some of their glomeruli (the filters) and the rate of filtrate formation is halved by the age of 70. This can be the result of impaired renal circulation due to arterio-sclerosis which affect the entire circulatory system. Sometimes there is retention of urine, where the urine backs up into the system and can cause an increase of uric acid and gout. Bladder shrinkage is another problem and loss of bladder tone. Older people tend to drink less. One reason is they want to avoid continual visits to the loo and also they forget.

- Useful essential oils are ginger, birch, sage, fennel, cajeput, geranium.
- Apply a poultice to the kidney area, to which you add 2–3 drops of ginger essential oil; leave for 20–30 minutes and repeat daily, changing the oils at intervals.
- Drink infusions of e.g. horsetail, lemonbalm, marshmallow root and golden rod.
- Take celery seeds to reduce uric acid (fluid extract, powder or tincture).
- Drink more pure water.
- Attend to the underlying mineral imbalance (lack of natural sodium, celery juice).
- Drink clay from time to time and take a good mineral formula.
- If stones have been diagnosed, you can use herbal tinctures or infusions of: hydrangia root or gravelroot.
- Homoeopathically there is a very good remedy which, if taken at the onset of cystitis, will help the inflammation to abate quickly; for bacterial infections and cystitis: cantharis 30 and B Coli 30 – take 2 tablets twice daily for 1 week.

Uticaria (hives)

Itchy irritating skin rash which can be caused by certain foods, touching certain plants or by drugs.

- 3 drops of chamomile or oregano essential oil, diluted in 15ml of almond oil or glycerine can be applied.
- Use very fine green clay powder and apply as talcum to affected area.
- Also drink superfine green clay or prepare a paste with very fine green clay and peppermint infusion, making it the thickness of honey; add the drops of essential oil and paint on to the affected area.
- Detoxify the liver with liver purifying herbs: burdock, dandelion and sassafras.
- Purify the blood with yarrow, stinging nettles and ginger.
- In the bath add two handfuls of oatmeal with 2 drops of peppermint essential oil.
- Homoeopathically try rhus tox 6
- Natural treatment can take time.

Varicose veins

Can be hereditary, or caused by liver congestion, digestive problems, weak connective tissues and poor circulation.

- Use 3 drops of cypress essential oil, garlic juice or lemon; apply a poultice to the affected areas.
- Prepare the poultice by dissolving 3 tablespoons of broken clay in 2 cups of horse chestnut infusion, to which has been added 1 tablespoon of cider vinegar; add the drops of cypress oil to the poultice when ready on the cloth and apply.

- You can alternate the cypress oil with lemon, 3 drops or garlic juice or oil ½ teaspoon; leave for about one hour; make sure not to bandage the poultice too tightly and put your feet up.
- Wash off with warm water when ready. (1 hour)
- Drink horse chestnut tea or take a tincture; other useful herbs are butcher's broom, horsetail, bilberry and violet flowers which contain a high level of rutin.
- Rutin is a bio-flavenoid helpful for increasing capillary strength and reducing arterio-sclerosis; it is also found in buckwheat; alternatively rutin can be obtained in tablets from your healthstore.
- Take a minimum of 100mg rutin daily.
- Take vitamin B complex, C, D and E and lecithin.
- Calcium, magnesium, potassium and zinc can be taken as part of a multi-mineral supplement.
- A multi vitamin combination would be helpful.
- If varicose veins are due to a constitutional weakness then taking chondroitin sulphate as a powder is highly recommended as that would partly take care of the collagen deficiency as collagen supports our veins and arteries (collagen weakness can result in 'cross linking' with all its problems of weakening muscles and skin, causing premature ageing etc.; collagen is what gives the cells and tissues structure; it is the stuff that holds us together; at least 40% of the body's protein is collagen).
- Take calcium fluoride and silica from time to time.
- Also address the digestive disturbances and possible constipation.
- Take superfine green clay.

Verrucas

Verrucas are very difficult to get rid of. They are mostly caught in swimming pools and saunas and appear on the soles of the feet.

- Make a paste with thuja extract or tincture, 15 drops; garlic juice or oil, ½ teaspoon; lemon essential oil, 3 drops; and very fine green clay with enough water to make into a paste.
- Apply to the verruca with a cotton-bud (store in a 50ml tub and keep in the refrigerator).
- Have a warm clay foot bath, 3 x weekly by dissolving a handful of broken clay in a bowl of water, add 4 drops of lemon essential oil; place the feet in the bowl and relax.
- Use 1 part clay to 4 parts water.
- Kolorex ointment (contains the herb pseudo winterata and anis) works very well with a little patience; apply at least twice daily; use in combination with the herbal capsules by the same name, 1 or 2 daily (if unable to obtain, find alternative brands that contain these herbs, or ask your herbalist for them).

- The above treatment also works on other types of fungal conditions and warts (order from Noma, or the Nutri centre in the UK).

Whitlows

Acute inflammation to the deep tissues of the fingers, including the nails and bones.

- Apply a warm clay plaster, leave for 1 hour, rest for 1 hour, then continue for several treatments.
- Alternate with cabbage leaves packs.
- Add salt to a warm hand bath.

Wrinkles and ageing

Some of us age more rapidly than others. Most people are obsessed with age and will go to any length to delay this natural process. In California it is a rarity for someone *not* to go under the plastic surgeon's knife, to enhance, cut off or reconstruct body parts. Often they overlook the real culprit which is diet and lifestyle (remember the Hunzas in Chapter 5).

Ageing can be accelerated by a variety of factors, some of which have already been covered. Your physiological age could be much older or younger than the date on your birth certificate. Your liver could be like that of a 65 year old and you may be only 35.

Smoking, drinking, drugs – how do you relax? How do you cope with day to day problems? Are you happy? Do you have children or keep a pet? What are you interested in? Do you love the person you are with or is it just a habit? All of these play an important factor in the ageing process.

- If your bones are starting to ache and you are experiencing stiffness, that can make you feel old; avoid this by using some of the suggestions here.
- Include brown rice in your diet 3 or 4 times per week.
- Cut out the wheat and sugar, eat more green foods, eat less meat.
- Exercise and dance.
- Try B Alive (see Resources, p. 216), an effective mineral combination and healing green clay.
- Take Zell-oxygen, a powerful anti-oxidant.

Ageing and wrinkling is mostly due to the presence of free radicals, in an acidic environment aided by stress. This accelerates the breaking or decaying of tissues, and changes the collagen structure, causing a cross linking of collagen. Collagen when aggregated by cross-linking through the presence of free radicals becomes stiff and the natural elasticity is diminished. A loss of elastin is related to an accumulation of cholesterol and fat in the arteries from the diet. This should be addressed by taking appropriate dietary measures as this can eventually lead to arterio-sclerois.

- To improve skin, muscles and tone in the body, help is at hand in the form of chondroitin sulphate; this substance is an amino sugar containing polysaccharides, a gel-like substance similar to that found in the intercellular material of the cartilaginous structures in the perichondrium. Cartilage is part of the support and framework for various parts of the body; it does not have a direct blood supply, so if an injury occurs it is slow to heal, this is where this substance is invaluable (see Resources, p. 217, for suppliers).
- Stress plays an enormous part as well as diet, lack of exercise and pollution. They destroy your healthy cells, which then become acidic waste products in your body. Certain nutrients are helpful such as vitamins A, B and C and the chemical elements sodium, iron, silica and selenium; also essential fatty acids, vitamin E and digestive enzymes.
- Reduction of all artificially and chemically produced foods will make a difference. An acidic body condition will accelerate ageing.
- Through proper diet, plenty of vegetables, fruits and nutritional therapy, you will be able to withstand certain effects of environmental pollutants as your immune system will work better and you will be able to dispose of toxins and poisons properly and not accumulate them in the tissues where they cause breakdown and havoc.
- BioCeramica supply the Japanese ceramic disk which they call BC (see also Introduction and Chapter 22). This disk can be used to take out the poison in your lipstick for one, but it has so many uses that I recommend one to anyone caring about their health and beauty. The small disk can be easily carried in your pocket. Whatever you eat or drink can be placed upon the disk for 10 seconds where it will reduce all that is harmful in your food, drink or make-up. Remedies or medicines placed upon the disk will be more powerful and work better, essential oils will disperse much easier in your bath water or base oil and they will become stronger so you can use less and they will last longer. When the disk is placed upon an area of pain the pain is lessened.
- Avoid all products containing mineral oil, colour, sugar, salt, saturated fats, flavouring, additives and pesticides.
- Minimise alcohol intake and too much coffee.
- Reduce or stop smoking.
- Avoid over-exposure to the sun; use a good sunscreen; remember though that you do need some sun for vitamin D and general well-being; the sun is beneficial and can make you feel good, but too much will accelerate ageing; find your right amount of exposure; always use an appropriate sunscreen, at least 25–35 SPF for the face or fair skins.
- Take up alkaline activities such as meditation and yoga.
- Try light weight bearing exercises: see the recommended book in Resources (*Strong Women Stay Young*) which gives instructions for easy-to-follow exercises to increase muscle strength at home or in the gym.

- Pilates from New York is getting increasingly popular for obvious rejuvenating reasons (see Resources, p. 228).
- Beauty comes from within; think about that first before spending a fortune on expensive creams and salon treatments; minimise the use of products containing alcohol on the skin or hair.
- A fine beauty treatment – clay facial masks: mix superfine white or green clay with almond or olive oil, a few drops of vitamin E and 3 drops of lemon or 3 drops of carrot essential oil; apply to the affected area, once or twice weekly; clay helps to exfoliate, encouraging new skin cells, refining and firming.
- Regular use of clay helps prevent and diminish wrinkles, toning and activating the surface tissues and muscles and eliminating dead cells which contribute to the ageing look.
- Alternate this mask with a seaweed and clay mixture; you can try adding the tincture of the herb gota kola which is rejuvenating to the skin; mix 10 drops in your mask or add a few drops to your facial oil or cream.
- Apply Rama (a pure essential oil blend to balance body and soul) to your wrists, temples or solar plexus or add to your bath; for a massage blend a few drops with sweet almond oil (see Resources, Nutri Centre and Wholistic Research).
- Have a daily fresh air bath and get plenty of sleep.
- *Skinbrush* your whole body daily (see instructions under 'How To's); this helps remove dead skin cells, makes your skin smooth and soft, helps the skin to breathe and thus helps release toxins; there is a hard bristle brush for the body and a smaller softer complexion brush for the face, neck and décolleté; make sure it is made of natural bristle, not plastic.
- Increase your potassium rich foods for cell health.
- Be positive.
- Try facial acupuncture for wrinkles, available at selected London clinics (or enquire from your acupuncturist).
- Keep the blood clean by regular detoxification and bowel cleansing.
- Internally; take Omega 3 oils, GLA, flaxseeds, lecithin, whey powder, digestive enzymes, vitamin C, B complex and vitamin E.
- Drink superfine clay regularly.
- Helpful herbs: ginseng, damiana, sarsaparilla, gota kola, garlic, wild willow bark, horsetail and milk thistle.
- Oatstraw, rich in silica for skin and hair health; to prepare a tea see under 'How To's.
- Eat 3 almonds and 1 brazil nut daily or every other day, soaked overnight.
- Avoid fashionable diets.
- Drink sufficient water.
- Become conscious of what you put into your body, aim to be pro-organic and anti-genetically modified.
- Pesticides, chemicals, hormones, sugar, salt, too much protein, drugs, smoking,

liquor – all of these destroy natural beauty.
- Follow a naturopathic approach to diet and lifestyle.
- Always learn more about how you can help yourself with natural foods, herbs and living.
- If in doubt consult your local naturopathic physician.

Appendix 1
Rejuvenating cleansing

- Cleanse the face daily with a milk made from white clay to which you have added 10 drops of lime essential oil.
- Prepare the milk by adding 1 cup of water to 2 tablespoons of white clay then add the drops of oil to the mixture.
- You may keep this for up to 3 weeks in the refrigerator; store in a glass bottle (shake before use); prepare a fresh mixture after 3 weeks.
- Use morning and night.

Daytime and evening

- During the day use a mild lotion to which you have added oils of lime and neroli, 10 drops of each to 100ml.
- In the evening use St John's wort oil, this is very rejuvenating and good for the skin; apply the oil to the face and neck, then wait a few minutes and wipe off any excess before going to sleep (Hauschka).
- Alternate with a mixture of almond oil, an equal portion of vegetable glycerine and 10 drops of rose essential oil to 50 ml.
- Give yourself a rejuvenating facial massage with a little of the above oil (and for extra luxury add 2 drops of rose, neroli or frankincense essential oil).
- Using both hands, start at the forehead and massage downwards quite strongly, covering the entire face and neck, then move the hands back up towards the forehead do this 36 times every day. (or a minimum 2–3 x weekly).
- There is an organic very fine facial carrot oil which is a powerful wrinkle repellent and rejuvenator which absorbs into the skin and can be used at night, available from Nutri Centre or Wholistic Research.

Further notes

- You will find it fun to make and do these simple treatments for yourself and your friends, they are inexpensive and effective.

- If pregnant or breast feeding it is always good to consult a herbalist for advice before taking any herbs internally.
- Some of the herbs mentioned may be available only through herbalists.
- Caution on using the herb St John's wort, if you are taking medically prescribed drugs, as the herb is said to prevent medicines from working properly, check with your doctor or pharmacist before using this herb.
- **Vit A.** High levels over 2000i.u. should be avoided during pregnancy, also persons prone to kidney stones should check with their doctor.
- **Vit B.s.** Taking isolated B's for a long time may induce a deficiency in the other B vitamins, always take a B complex with them, if taking L-Dopa check with your Doctor before taking B Complex.
- **Vit C.** High doses can cause diarrhoea and stomach cramps. Check with your Doctor if taking drugs for cancer treatment as high levels may interfere. Always take medical advice before taking large doses of C when on any long-term drug therapy.
- **Vit. E.** avoid high levels over 200i.u., if suffering high BP or taking anti-coagulant drugs.
- **Minerals** should be taken as a multi, chemical elements can cause problems when taken solo.
- **Calcium**, it is best to avoid taking calcium supplementation as an isolated mineral, particularly with renal problems. The same applies to magnesium.
- **High GLA.** Supplementation should be used with caution if taking blood-thinning medicines such as warfarin and heparin.

Appendix 2
'How to's

A. Make an infusion
- Prepare 1–2 teaspoon of your chosen dried herbs per cup of boiled water as a general rule (with fresh herbs use double the amount).
- Infuse in a pot for 5–20 minutes (except when using oatstraw which must be *boiled in water* for 40 minutes to get the valuable silica out which benefits the health of your skin and hair).

B. Prepare an enema
A coffee enema, encourages the liver to release bile to the gallbladder, which can sometimes get sluggish. This helps to detoxify and eliminate waste products.

Bile is a beneficial greenish/golden fluid secreted by the liver which emulsifies and absorb fats.

- Take 2 tablespoons of organic coffee and boil in 1 pint of water for 10 minutes; strain and add 1–1 1/2 pints of previously boiled water.
- Set up the enema kit and make sure the bag is hanging on a hook a good metre above your head.
- Fill the bag with the prepared mixture which should be at body temperature.
- Release any air bubble by running the liquid through the tubing a little bit before insertion.
- Lie down in a comfortable position and allow the fluid to enter your bowel, you can turn your body towards the right to help move the fluid further up the colon.
- Some people new to enemas might prefer to have them while lying in a warm bath; this will help relax the muscles; there is no need to panic – you will have time to reach the toilet.
- You will find that after a few practices it is not hard and you will be able to retain the enema longer.
- Don't worry if at the first time you cannot hold the enema for very long.

- The duration of the enema will also depend on the ingredient used; some can be retained for 20 minutes with ease and practice, some for only 5–10 minutes.
- Before you take your coffee enema it might be advisable to have a clear lukewarm water enema – about 1 pint to have a clear out; this way you can avoid having to evacuate the carefully prepared mixture too soon; ideally one should be able to retain this enema for 20 minutes.

Other suggestions for enemas
- Lemon juice, dilute 1 table spoon in $1^{1}/2$ pint of warm, previously boiled water.
- Chamomile flowers, 1 tablespoon to 1 litre (infuse and strain).
- Peppermint leaves, 1 tablespoon to 1 litre. (infuse and strain)
- Clay, 2 teaspoons to 1 pint.

Colonic hydrotherapy
This is sometimes recommended during a cleansing fast or to help remove accumulated toxins or parasites as part of a programme. It needs to be given by a professional therapist. Contact ARCH (formerly CIA) in England for a list of qualified therapists (see Resources, p. 218).

C. Prepare mullein oil for the ears
- Take 2 handfuls of mullein flowers; put into a wide mouthed jar (from organic herb trading, or freshly picked).
- Add warm, cold pressed olive oil until all flowers are covered over.
- Put the lid or cork on, and shake the contents well.
- Put it in a warm place such as your drying cupboard or near the oven, or in the sun if available.
- Shake the contents from time to time.
- After 2–3 weeks you will have the wonderful remedy for all types of ear problems, ready to use.
- Strain the contents of the jar through a cotton cloth into a jug and bottle (use small dropper bottles).
- Give any spare oil to friends or store in a dark place.
- You can warm the oil before use for added comfort.
- Apply 2–3 drops to the ear twice daily; in some cases immediate relief is noted.
- Another simple ear treatment is using equal amounts of warmed sesame oil and ginger juice or powder; 3 or 4 drops brings relief.

D. Prepare garlic oil
- Peel 6 cloves of raw organic garlic and crush; macerate in a jar the same as for mullein but use 150ml of sweet almond or sesame oil.

- Keep in a warm place for 1 week; press and strain through a muslin cloth.
- Bottle and use.
- For problems with the ears, use 2–3 drops per ear.
- Also use on areas such as psoriasis, swollen glands and the thorax, in cases of asthma and bronchitis.
- You can add 2 teaspoons of garlic oil to a clay poultice and apply to the affected area.
- These oil treatments can also be used on your animals.

Garlic treatment for asthma

- Peel a raw garlic segment, chop up and add to a small glass of hot water.
- Drink twice daily.
- Chew a sprig of parsley afterwards if desired.
- Experiments have shown a reduction in asthma symptoms after 2 weeks of use.

Garlic soup

- Use a whole head of garlic; add to $2^{1/2}$ cups of water; simmer for 10–15 minutes.
- Put the cooked garlic cloves through the blender with a little of the liquid.
- Add 1 tablespoon fresh chopped parsley and 1 tablespoon Miso and serve (Miso is a paste made from fermented barley, rice or soya and is available from the macrobiotic section of your health shop; this soup is very good for the immune and digestive system).
- *Note:* some people are allergic to garlic.

E. Prepare ginger tea

Ginger tea is helpful for coughs.

- Cut 3–4 slices of fresh ginger.
- Add to 1 cup of water, simmer for 5 minutes.
- Add honey if desired.

F. Prepare lemon tea

Lemon tea is cleansing and alkalising.

- Take the juice of half a lemon; boil the peel in water and simmer for 5 minutes.
- Add to the juice; add a tiny bit of honey if desired and drink before breakfast.

G. Prepare a cabbage leaf poultice

- Place raw cabbage leaves on a painful area.
- Secure with cling film and cloth.
- Leave for 1–2 hours.

H. Make your own barley or wheat-grass juice

- Take a handful of whole wheat or barley, place in organic soil in a plant pot or tray in your kitchen.
- Experiment a bit on the size of the container and the amount you need if it is just for 1 or more people.
- Give it plenty of water and in 2–3 days the grass will start to appear.
- Grow until about 6–8 inches and then juice the grass or put it through the blender with your banana smoothie or carrot juice, or you can have it by itself; then start growing them again.

To sprout seeds

- Get some glass jars, rubber bands and muslin cloths to cover the jars.
- Wash the seeds and place in the jar, add enough water to fill half the jar, soak for 8 hours and drain.
- Wash them through a colander and put the seeds back in the jar, filling the whole jar with water this time.
- Then drain again, put the seeds back in the jar and keep upside down at an angle of 45º.
- You will need to rinse the sprouts 2 or 3 x daily to ensure they remain fresh.
- Make sure they remain wet, because if they are allowed to dry out they are useless.
- Continue this for 4–5 days, after which they are ready for use.
- Keep refrigerated and use within 1 week.

I. Test your pH balance

- From your pH test kit, tear off a small strip, and put on the tongue.
- The ideal pH for saliva is 6.5–6.8.
- pH test kits are available from Enzyme Process or the Nutri Centre in the UK (see Resources, pp. 220, 227) or in US health stores.

J. Skin brushing with wood and bristle brush

- Buy a hard vegetable bristle brush, (health store).
- Brush the whole body starting from the feet upwards.
- Always brush towards the heart.

a) skinbrush face.

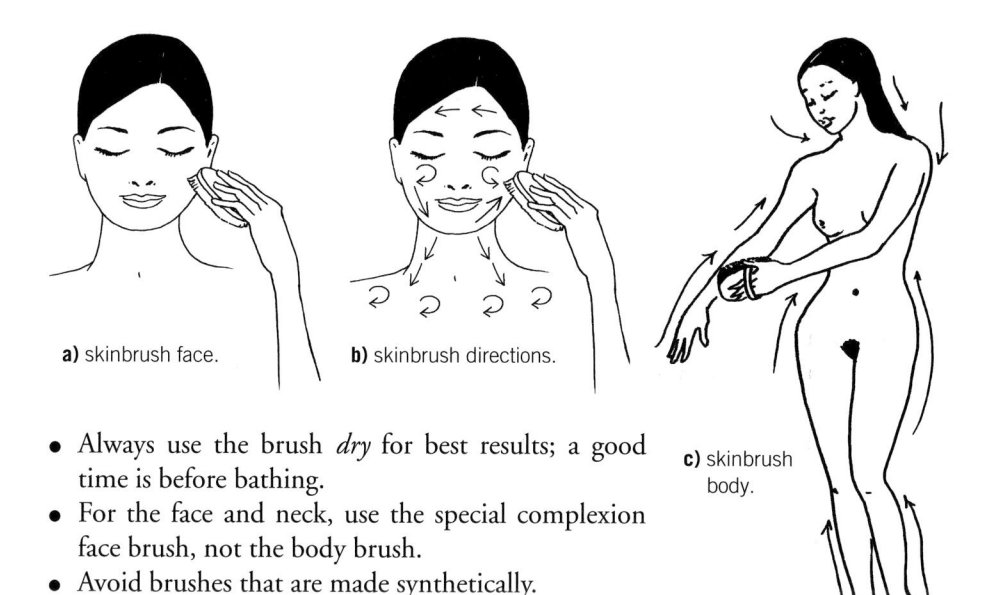

b) skinbrush directions.

c) skinbrush body.

- Always use the brush *dry* for best results; a good time is before bathing.
- For the face and neck, use the special complexion face brush, not the body brush.
- Avoid brushes that are made synthetically.
- See Figures a), b) and c) above: follow the directions of the arrows; always dry brush towards the heart.

Appendix 3
Note on high carbon foods

High carbon foods increase mucous and acidity. They should be reduced in cases of asthma, rheumatism, catarrh and stomach ulcers etc. Some of the highest levels are found in: butter, chocolate, wheat, barley, rice, corn and peas.

Appendix 4
The Elements

Elements	Wood	Fire	Earth	Air/metal	Water
Viscera	Liver	Heart	Spleen/pancreas	Lungs	Kidneys
Bowels	Gallbladder	Small intestine	Stomach	Large intestine	Bladder
Seasons	Spring	Summer	Late summer	Autumn	Winter
Planets	Jupiter	Mars	Saturn	Venus	Mercury
Colours	Green	Red	Yellow	White	Black
Climate	Wind	Heat	Cold	Dryness	Humidity

We are all the elements, created from Heaven and Earth. The five forces of energy, or changes of energy that exist within everything in the universe are all part of yin and yang. Together they can create a harmonious balance. When there is an imbalance the elements can oppose and destroy each other; the same happens in human beings; when we live harmoniously with the universal law we will flourish; when we start to work against this natural law everything will decline including our health.

Resources

1. Suppliers, organisations and therapists

Acupuncture
List of practitioners in the UK:
1. The British Acupuncture Association
34 Alderney Street
London SW1 4EU

2. College of Traditional Chinese
Acupuncture
Tao House
Queensway
Leamington Spa
Warwickshire. CV32 5EZ

In the US:
1. The American Academy of Medical
Acupuncture
Suite 500
5820 Wilshire Boulevard
Los Angeles
California 90036
Tel: 213 937 5514

2. The American Association of
Acupuncture and Oriental Medicine
433 Front Street
Catasauqua
Pa 18032
Tel: 610 433 2448

Ainsworths Homoeopathic Pharmacy
36 New Cavendish Street
London W1 7LH
Tel: 020 7935 5330
Fax: 020 7486 4313

American Academy of Medical Acupuncture
Suite 500
5820 Wilshire Boulevard
Los Angeles
California 90036
Tel: 213 937 5514

American Association of Acupuncture and Oriental Medicine
433 Front Street
Catasauqua
Pa 18032
Tel: 610 433 2448

American Association of Naturopathic Physicians
PO Box 20386
Seattle
WA 98112

American Herbalists Guild
PO Box 1683
Soquel
California 95073
Tel: 408 464 2441

American Institute of Vedic Studies
PO Box 8357
Santa Fe
NM 87504-8357

Ann Wigmore Institute
PO Box 429
Rincon
Costa Rica 00677
Tel: 787 868 6307
Runs courses for people needing special diets and cleansing procedures.

Aromatherapy
List of practitioners from:
The International Federation of
Aromatherapists (IFA)
182 Chiswick High Road
London W4 1PP
Tel: 020 87422605

Association of Research and Enlightenment (ARE)
(Information on Edgar Casey)
Virginia Beach
Virginia
USA

Ayurvedic Institute
PO Box 23445
Albuquerque
NM 87192-1445
Tel: 505 291 9698
Information on Ayurveda and the home study course.

B17 Laetril treatment
B17 treatment can be obtained in several clinics in Mexico and Germany. For an information pack in Britain, contact:
The Cancer Alternative Information Bureau
PO Box 285
405 Kings Road
London SW10 0BB
Fax: 020 7352 2833
The address of the Mexican clinic is:
The Oasis Hospital
Playas de Tijuana
Mexico
www.oasisofhope.com

The address to obtain the B17 tablets and kernels in the States is:
Health World
(G Edward Griffin's Store)
Box 4228
Thousand Oaks
CA 91359
Tel: 800 595 6593
www.health.world.com

or:
Information and kernels from
Alternative Remedies
8 Elm drive
Market Drayton, Shropshire TF9 3HA
Tel: 01630 657922
www.fsmarketplace.co.uk/cancerremedies
www.alternativeremedies.org
see also, **Cancer treatments**

Bach Flower Remedies
6 Suffolk Way
Abingdon
Oxon OX14 5JX
Tel: 01235 550086

B Alive
Available by mail order from:
Hildreth and Cocker
Freepost
London SW12 0BR
Tel: 020 8671 6275
Fax: 020 8673 4659
Email: orders@hildrethcocker.demon.co.uk

Biocare Ltd
Lakeside
180 Lifford Lane
Kings Norton
Birmingham B30 3NU
Tel: 0121 433 3727
For quality nutritional supplements.

Bioceramic clay disk and spoon
Available from **Bioceramica** to improve the taste of water and foods.

Bioceramica Group Ltd
LOE House
159 Broadhurst Gardens
London NW6 3AU
Fax: 020 7624 6384
UK importers of the Japanese Bioceramic disk.

Blessed Herbs
109 Barre Plains Road
Oakham
Massachusetts 01068
Tel: 1 800 489 4372

British Acupuncture Association
34 Alderney Street
London SW1 4EU

British Homoeopathic Association
27a Devonshire Street
London W1N 1RJ

British Naturopathic and Osteopathic Association
Frazer House
6 Netherhall Gardens
London NW3 5RR

British Wheel of Yoga
Hamilton Place
Boston Road
Sleaford
Lincs NG34 7ES

California Institute for Human Science
701 Garden View Court
Encinitas
CA 92024

Cancer Alternative Information Bureau
PO Box 285
405 Kings Road
London SW10 0BB
Fax: 020 7352 2833
Contact for an information pack on B17 and other treatments.

Cancer treatments
Magnetic Energy Therapy is used quite successfully at the CSCT for the treatment of cancer:
The Centre for Cell Specific Cancer Therapy (CSCT)
Avenida Palacio de los Deportes 121
Esq. G. Meja Rocart
El Millon Santo Domingo
Dominican Republic
Tel: 809 534 2090
Fax: 809 534 3089
Email: DRCSCT@codetel.net.do
www.csct.com

The Immuno Augmentative Therapy Centre helps address the basic underlying condition and shows how to keep your immune system in optimum function:

Immuno Augmentative Therapy Centre
PO Box F-42689
Freeport
Grand Bahama
Tel: 242 352 47755
Cancer treatment websites
www.apricotsfromgod.com
www.contrearhospital.com
www.cose.com
www.health-world.com
www.world.without.cancer.net/case.html
See also **B17 Laetril treatment**

Casey *see* **Edgar Casey**

Centre for Cell Specific Cancer Therapy (CSCT) *see under* **Cancer treatments**

Chiropractors
For a list of chiropractors write or telephone:
McTimoney Chiropractor Association,
21 High Street
Eynsham
Oxford OX8 1HE
Tel: 01865 880974

In US:
International Chiropractors Association,
741 Brady Street
Davenport
Iowa 52808

Chondroitin sulphate
Available by mail order from:
Hildreth and Cocker
Freepost
London SW12 OBR
Tel: 020 8671 6275
Fax: 020 8673 4659
Email: orders@hildrethcocker.demon.co.uk

Clay in the UK from
Beewell
Chesterfield
S42 6QQ
Tel: 01246 220130

Natural Remedies
35 Brecknock Road
London
N7 0BT
Tel: 020 7267 3884
Wholistic Research (see under W)
and from selected health stores.

In Australia contact:
Select Botanicals
Upper Level
53 College Street
Gladesville NSW
Sydney
Australia 2111
Tel: 00 612 981 704 00

Clay workshops
Apply for a list of ongoing clay workshops in London and Japan. Seminars by different healers and clay retreats in California or Europe; please send SAE to:
Sunny Seminars
PO Box 3007
London NW3 2UZ
Tel: 020 7586 3412
Fax: 020 7586 7892

College of Traditional Chinese Acupuncture
Tao House
Queensway
Leamington Spa
Warwickshire CV32 5EZ

Colonic hydrotherapy
List of practitioners, UK, from the Association and Register of Colon Hydrotherapists, ARCH formerly the CIA;
Log on to www.colonic-association.org

US:
International Association of Colon Therapists
051 Hilltop Drive

A11
Redding
Ca 96002
Tel: 916 222 1498
See also **Home enema kits**

Credence Publications
PO Box 3
Tonbridge
Kent TN12 9ZY
Tel: 01622 832386
www.credence.org

Crystal Hill Multi Media
137 Biodorne Drive
Waynesville
NC 28786
Email: danwinter@aol.com

Contact Daniel Winter for information on International Earth Emergency Network.

Dance workshops
Given by, among others, Farida Sharan, author, lecturer, natural physician, iridologist, mystic dancer; apply to Sunny Seminars for details on Farida's dances in the UK or contact Farida's website for dances throughout the US:

Email: farida@purehealth.com
www.purehealth.com

Darkfield microscopy or the HLB test (humoral pathological blood test)
Check on the state of your blood which is displayed on a screen. All that is needed are a few drops of your blood from a finger prick. It is possible to observe parasites, what type and how or if they are interfering with your health. Fungus, mercury and cholesterol levels, life-threatening diseases, stress levels, how healthy your blood is etc.
Contact:

In the UK:
Mossley Therapy Centre
Tel: 01457 87342

In Canada contact:
Tel: 001 604 925 8932

In the USA information about training in the above technique or a list of practitioners can be obtained from:
Enderlein Enterprises
PO Box 704
Mount Vernon
Washington 98273
Tel: 360 424 6025

or from:
The Darkfield Microscope Training Institute
Tel 1 888 635 4413
www.enzymeres.com

Prof. Serge Jurasunas
Holiterapias – Terapias Naturais Lda.
Rua de Misericordia 137 –1, 1200-2722
Lisbon
Portugal
Tel: 351 21 347 11 17/8
Fax: 351 21 347 11 11
www.natiris.mail.telepac.pt
See also Part I, Chapter 5: Cancer.
Information about training and sales of the Darkfield Microscope in Britain available from; The Mossley Therapy Centre,
Tel: 01457 873429.

DeFries, Michael *see under* **Holographic devices**

Drill Hall Arts Centre
16 Chenies Street
London WC1E 7EX
Tel: 020 7637 8270
For voice and dance classes.

Dulwich Health Society
130 Gypsy Hill
London SE19
Fax: 020 8766 6616
Provides information on geopathic stress

Earth Changes
For those who want to keep abreast of the winds of change visit:
www.matrixinstitute.com
PO Box 336
Chesterfield
NH03443
Tel: 1 603 363 4164
Fax: 1 603 363 4168

East West
PO Box 712
Santa Cruz
Ca 95061
Tel 1 800 717 5010
www.planetherbs.com

Home study courses in herbology by Michael Tierra:
East West Herbs
Chinese and Western herbal products. They have a wide range of herbs from all over the world. They stock the anti-malaria herb Artemesiae Annuae in powder or capsules (available by mail order):
Langston Priory Mews
Kingham
Oxon OX7 6UP
Tel: 01608 658862
Fax: 01608 658816
Freephone order line: 0800 072 0202

Echo UK
Woodside
Melmerby
Ripon HG4 5EZ
Email: echoH2O2@aol.com
The centre of information on oxygen therapy.

Eclosion testing
Diagnostic technique capable of pinpointing hidden factors that are not always easily detectable through other techniques.
Available in Britain at:
The Hale Clinic
7 Park Crescent
London W1B 1PF
Tel: 020 7631 0156
by Peter Bartlett or contact **Enzyme Process** *for a practitioner in your area.*

Edgar Casey
For newsletter and membership enquiries in Britain also suppliers of Edgar's remedies, contact:
13 Prospect Terrace
New Kyo
Stanley
Co. Durham DH9 7TR
In the US:
Association of Research and Enlightenment (ARE)
Virginia Beach
Virginia
USA

EM (Effective Micro-organisms)
The book, EM: An Earth Changing Revolution *by Dr Teruo Higa, products and information, formerly available from EM Technologies Inc., is now available in the USA from:*
Sustainable Community Development
PO Box 14278
Shawnee Mission
Kansas 66285-4278
Tel: 913 541 9299
Fax: 913 541 0380

Enderlein Enterprises
PO Box 704
Mount Vernon
Washington 98273
Tel: 360 424 6025

Enzyme Process
4 Broadgate House
Westlode Street
Spalding PE11 2AF
Protomorphogens, pancreatic enzymes; homoeopathic remedies, PH testing paper for acid/alkaline saliva test. They offer some products such as pH testing papers to the general public; other than that their products are only available through your health practitioner.

Farida Sharan's School of Natural Medicine
PO BOX 4220
Albuquerque
New Mexico 87196–4220.
Tel: 888 593 6173
Fax: 888 593 6733
www.purehealth.com

Feng Shui
Master Sam Ng, Eastern mystic practitioner
6 The Greenway
Uxbridge
Middlesex UB8 2HP
Tel: 01895 254533

For geomancing, feng shui and personal transformation. This powerful unassuming mystic healer is available worldwide. It is to him that other feng shui experts turn for advice. He is able to deal with negative imprints which we can pick up while in the womb; he returns you to that moment and removes the imprint, balances the chakras and measures your aura; he clears the home or business of unwanted vibrations caused by gridlines or other forces, including those left behind by previous occupants, enabling you to be more healthy, harmonious and prosperous. For more information contact him directly. He runs occasional workshops in Wales and London which are unique and never repeated. For a list of feng shui experts contact:
The Feng Shui Network International
Tel: 07000 336474

Fresh Water Filter Co. Ltd
Gem House, 895 High Road
Chadwell Heath
Essex RMG 4HL
Tel: 020 8597 3223
Fax: 0870 056 7264

Friends of the Earth
26–28 Underwood Street
London N1 7JQ
Tel: 020 7490 1555
www.foe.com

Geomancing see **Feng shui**

General Council and Register of Osteopaths
56 London Street
Reading
Berkshire RG1 4YR
Tel: 01734 576585

Geopathic stress
The Dulwich Health Society
130 Gypsy Hill
London SE19
Fax: 020 8766 6616
Provides information on geopathic stress

Giovanni Hair Care, Inc.
PO Box 39378
Los Angeles
Ca 90039

Greenways Natural Health Centre
180 Baslow Road
Totley
Sheffield S17 4DS
Colonic hydrotherapy and list of practitioners
Tel: 0114 2360890
Fax: 0114 2362142

Guild of Naturopathic Iridologists
94 Grosvenor Road
London SW1V 3LF
Tel/Fax: 020 7834 3579
For information on where to find a naturopathic iridology physician in your area.

Hale Clinic
7 Park Crescent
London W1B 1PF
Tel: 020 7631 0156
Well known complementary health care centre, offers treatments in most therapies.

Hauschka (see natural cosmetics)

Health Systems
PO Box 2211
Barnet
Herts EN5 4QN
Tel: 020 8449 7771

Health World
(G Edward Griffin's Store)
Box 4228
Thousand Oaks
CA 91359
Tel: 800 595 6593
www.healthworld.com
For B17 tablets and kernels.

Healthy House
Cold Harbour
Ruscombe
Stroud
Glos GL6 6DA
Tel: 01453 752216
Email: info@healthy-house.co.uk
www.healthy-house.co.uk
For ECO paints, varnishes and other products related to environmental health for allergy sufferers; also water filters and allergy free bedding.

Helios Homoeopathics
89–95 Camden Road
Tunbridge Wells
Kent TN1 2QB
Tel: 01892 536393 (24 hrs)
Fax: 0800 015 67900

Herbalists and macrobiotics
Most health stores have a special section with macrobiotic foods and a selection of seaweeds.

Resources

Herbal practitioners
List from:
(UK) Unified Register of Herbal Practitioners
(URHP)
58 Fairmantle Street
Truro
Cornwall TR1 2EG
Tel.: 018772 222699

in the US:
(US) American Herbalists Guild
PO Box 1683
Soquel
California 95073
Tel: 408 464 2441

Herbco
www.herbco.com
A good place to find herbal suppliers.

Herb Research Foundation
1007 Pearl Street
Suite 200
Boulder
CO 80302
Tel: 303 449 2265
Fax: 303 449 7849
www.herbs.org
Provides an information service on the benefits and safety of medicinal plants, and resources.

Higher Nature
Burwash Common
E Sussex
TN19 7BR
American supplements, pro-gest, grapefruit seed extract etc.; herbal formulations, skin brushes.

Hildreth and Cocker
Freepost
London SW12 OBR
Tel: 020 8671 6275
Fax: 020 8673 4659
Email: orders@hildrethcocker.demon.co.uk
Suppliers of chondroitin sulphate and B Alive.

Hippocrates Health Institute
1443 Palmdale Court
West Palm Beach
Fl. 33411
Tel: 561 471 8876
Fax: 561 471 9464
www.hippocratesinst.com
For dietary and detoxifying regimes according to Anne Wigmore.

Holistic Health College
94 Grosvenor Road
London SW1V 3LF
Tel: 020 7834 3579
For naturopathic iridology courses.

Holographic devices
Protective holographic devices from renowned homoeopath:
Michael DeFries
19 Wellfield Avenue
Muswell Hill
London N10 2EA
Tel: 020 8883 0767
He produces powerful holographic devices for, personal or home protection at very reasonable rates. Protection against EMFs from TV's or computers. Devices for purifying water supplies and for refrigerators to prolong the freshness of foods naturally.

Home enema kits
Available from:
The John Bell and Croydon Pharmacy
50 Wigmore Street
London W1U 2AU
Tel: 020 7935 5555
Also from:
The Nutri Centre
7 Park Crescent
London W1B 1PF
Tel: 020 7436 5122
Or maybe your local pharmacy could order one for you.

Homoeopathic practitioners
List from:
Society of Homoeopaths
2 Artisan Rd
Northampton NN1 4HU
Tel. 01604 621400

or:
British Homoeopathic Association
27a Devonshire Street
London W1N 1RJ

In the US:
National Centre for Homoeopathy
801 North Fairfax Street
Suite 306
Alexandria
Virginia 22314
Tel: 703 548 7790

Homoeopathic supplies
1. Ainsworths Homoeopathic Pharmacy,
36 New Cavendish Street,
London W1 7LH
Tel: 020 7935 5330
Fax 020 7486 4313

2. Bach Flower Remedies,
6 Suffolk Way
Abingdon
Oxon OX14 5JX
Tel: 01235 550086

3. Helios Homoeopathics
89–95 Camden Road
Tunbridge Wells
Kent TN1 2QB
Tel: 01892 536393 (24 hrs)

4. NOMA, Complex Homoeopathy Ltd
Unit 3
1–16 Hollybrook Road
Upper Shirley
Southampton SO16 6RB
Tel: 01703 770513
Fax: 01703 702459

5. Weleda (UK) Ltd
Leonor Road
Ilkeston
Derbyshire DE7 8DR
Tel: 0602 303151
Homoepatic remedies and Wala products, also stocks 'levisticum' eardrops.

Immuno Augmentative Therapy Centre
PO Box F-42689
Freeport
Grand Bahama
Tel: 242 352 47755
Here they help address the basic underlying condition and show how to keep your immune system in optimum function.

Institute of Complementary Medicine
For a list of complementary practitioners send a SAE to:
PO Box 194
London SE16 1QZ
Tel: 020 7237 5165

Institute of Optimum Nutrition
Blades Court
Deodar Road
London SW15 2NU
Tel: 020 8877 9993
Courses and consultations with nutritionists.

International Association of Colon Therapists
051 Hilltop Drive
A11
Redding
Ca 96002 USA
Tel: 916 222 1498

International Chiropractors Association
741 Brady Street
Davenport
Iowa 52808 USA

International Earth Emergency Network
For more information contact
Daniel Winter
Crystal Hill Multi Media
137 Biodorne Drive
Waynesville
NC 28786
Email: danwinter@aol.com
or:
Dr B.K. Wee
World Research Information Centre
22 White House Park
Singapore 1025
Tel: 65 323 2032
Fax: 65 235 9862

International Federation of Aromatherapists (IFA)
182 Chiswick High Road
London W4 1PP
Tel: 020 8742 2605

International Iridology Research Association (IIRA)
PO Box 1442,
Solona Beach,
Ca 92075-1160 USA
Tel 888 682 2208
www.iridologyassn.org
Dedicated to the raising of iridology awareness in N America, send for details of training courses and membership

International Kundalini Yoga Teachers Association
RT 2, Box 4
Shady Lane
Espanola NM 87532
Tel: 505 753 0423
Fax: 505 753 5982
www.yoghibajan.com

International Macrobiotic Institute
Kientalerhof
CH-3723 Kiental
Switzerland
Information on training, courses and workshops

Iredale Mineral Cosmetics
148 Spencer Road
Austerlitz
NY 12017

Jensen (Dr Bernard Jensen)
Dr Jensen has written many important books and charts on iridology and nutrition; these are used by naturopaths all over the world. He has also developed a wonderful, high-quality range of nutritional supplements. My favourite lecithin supplement comes from him. He has a Liquid Dulse supplying iodine in drops which is good for balancing the function of the thyroid and what is mostly lacking in our diet. There is a product to replenish our much depleted sodium levels, in the form of goat's whey; it's called Capri Mineral Whey and is helpful for pains in the joints, counteracting acidity due to sodium depletion from the stomach wall. It is also good for the kidneys. Order from the address below or check with Sunny Seminars for supplies in Britain. Charts, videos, cassettes and books from:
Dr Bernard Jensen International
24360 Old Wagon Road
Escondido
California 92027
Tel: 760 749 1248
Fax: 760 749 2727

John Bell and Croydon Pharmacy
50 Wigmore Street
London W1U 2AU
Tel: 020 7935 5555

John Maxwell *see under* **Spiritual healing from the Akashic records**

Jurasunas, Professor Serge, *see under* **Darkfield microscopy**
Check with 'Sunny Seminars' for availability of his infrared ceramic balls and also where to obtain his energy sand baths and find out about forthcoming lectures.

Kundalini Yoga *see under* **Yoga**

Kushi Institute of Europe
Programs and workshops
email: kushi.eur@macrobiotics.org

Lamberts
1 Lamberts Road
Tunbridge Wells
Kent TN2 3QE
Offers good range of quality supplements (practitioner supplies).

Macrobiotics Today
(bi-monthly magazine)
George Oshawa Macrobiotic Foundation
Vega Study Centre,
1511 Robinson Street
Oroville
CA 95965
USA
Tel. 916 533 7702
Fax. 916 53 7908

McTimoney Chiropractor Association
21 High Street
Eynsham
Oxfordshire OX8 1HE
Tel: 01865 880974

Manic Depression Fellowship
8-10 High Street
Kingston upon Thames
Surrey KT1 1EY

Master Sam Ng *see* **Feng shui**

Maxwell, John *see under* **Spiritual healing from the Akashic records**

Meningitis
Any questions about meningitis: keep yourself informed. Contact the registered charity founded in 1986:
National Meningitis Trust,
Fern House
Bath Road
Stroud
Gloucestershire.
24 hr support line: 0845 6000 800
Main office Tel: 01453 768000
Fax: 01453 768001

Michael DeFries *see under* **Holographic devices**

Motoyama Institute for Life Physics
Inokashira 4-11-7
Mitak-shi
Tokyo
Japan

National Centre for Homoeopathy
801 North Fairfax Street
Suite 306
Alexandria
Virginia 22314
Tel: 703 548 7790

National Federation of Spiritual Healers (NFSH)
Head office:
Old Manor Farm Studio
Church Street
Sunbury on Thames
Surrey TW16 7RG
Tel: 01932 783164

National Meningitis Trust
Fern House
Bath Road
Stroud
Gloucestershire
24 hr support line: 0845 6000 800
Main office Tel: 01453 768000
Fax: 01453 768001

Natural Books and Products
Art Jensen.
1718 E Valley Parkway, Unit C,
Escondido Ca 92027
US Tel: 888 743 1790
Int. Tel: 001 760 743 1790

Natural cosmetics
1. *To encourage the skin to normalise and balance itself, Dr Hauschka products are available from:*
Elysia Natural Skincare
Haselor
College Road
Bromsgrove
Worcestershire B60 2NF
Tel: 01527 832 863
Also available in selected health shops in the UK and abroad.

2. Jane Iredale
Great range of loose and pressed mineral powders, eye and lip colours, all made with minerals without synthetic dyes.
Iredale Mineral Cosmetics
148 Spencer Road
Austerlitz
NY 12017
Distributed in the USA by
Calleel and Hayden
518 17th Street
Suite 1800
Denver
Co 802002

In the UK call for mail order availability:
0800 328 2467
or:
0122-320 8882

Natural hair care
1. Giovanni Hair Care, Inc.
PO Box 39378
Los Angeles
Ca 90039

2. *Skin-Lyte and Hair-Lyte herbal hair and skin rejuvenators from:*
Nature's Path
PO Box 7862
Venice
FL 34287 USA

Natural pest control
www.gardens-alive.com
www.invisiblegardener.com

Naturopathic iridology
What is naturopathic iridology?
It is a non-invasive, non aggressive approach to natural medicine, covering the analytical science of iridology which is the careful observation of the irises, reading the information conveyed through over 28,000 nerve fibres found in the iris. It is the only science that backs up all spiritual principals. It will show you how you can and must leave pollution out of your life.

The iris is connected to the brain via the iris-stalk to the hypothalamus. We observe the state of tissues and organ function of a person. Each part of the iris is closely connected to a specific organ or system. We can see which traits are inherent or which ones are acquired through our lifestyle or diet We observe the rate of vibration, inflammation and what stage it has reached, where toxins are settling and the integrity of the tissues. The philosophy that goes with iridology is important :

Good cleansing, good diet and good thinking. We aim to stir the patient in the right direction but he/she must want to do what is right and be willing to learn the simple steps back to health. Iridology can take you back to the cause of the problem.

It is a stepping-stone in the analytical field, involving education not medication.

The various colour changes in the iris from chemical dispositions combined with the density of the fibre structure, between the intestinal zone and the periphery, determines the constitutional type.

At a consultation (depending on the training of the practitioner) the patient will be offered appropriate nutritional, dietary, herbal or homoeopathic support and advice on cleansing and restoring good health. These being made easily apparent from the highly individualistic information reflected in the neural reflex information of the individual.

All graduates from the colleges mentioned have received a thorough and comprehensive training.

In Britain:
The Holistic Health College
94 Grosvenor Road
London SW1V 3LF
Tel: 020 7834 3579
In the USA:
Farida Sharan's School of Natural Medicine
PO Box 4220
Albuquerque
New Mexico 87196-4220
Tel: 888 593 6173
Fax: 888 593 6733
www.purehealth.com

Nature's Path Inc.
PO Box 7862
Venice
FL 34287

Naturopathic Research Labs Inc.
PO Box 7594
North port.
Florida 34287 USA
Tel 941 426 3375
Fax 941 426 6871
Information and orders for liquid trace minerals (tracelytes). Also suppliers of a wide range of quality nutritional remedies and books. Protomorphogens, vitamins, lecithin etc. All prepared in a base of liquid tracelytes.

Neals Yard Remedies
Organic or wild crafted herbs, essential oils and clay. Neals Yard shops are found throughout the UK. Call them for a list.
Head office:
26–34 Ingate Place
Battersea
London SW8 3NS
Tel: 020 7498 1686
Fax: 020 7498 2505

NOMA, Complex Homoeopathy Ltd
Unit 3
1–16 Hollybrook Road
Upper Shirley
Southampton SO16 6RB
Tel: 01703 770513
Fax: 01703 702459

Non-toxic products
For ECO paints, varnishes and other products related to environmental health for allergy sufferers; also water filters and allergy free bedding, contact for brochure:
The Healthy House
Cold Harbour
Ruscombe
Stroud
Glos GL6 6DA
Tel: 01453 752216
Email: info@healthy-house.co.uk
www.healthy-house.co.uk

Nutri Centre
7 Park Crescent
London W1B 1PF
Tel: 020 7436 5122
Fax 020 7436 5171
www.nutricentre.co.uk
Most nutritional supplements and clay can be obtained at this relaxed centre, close to the leafy, green, relaxed ambience of Regent's Park where qualified personnel are always on hand to give advice. They can supply almost all remedies or order them for you. They do an excellent speedy mail-order service, world-wide. The Centre includes an amazing Bookstore, carrying most titles on Holistic medicine including Iridology, Nutrition, Meditation, Yoga, many self help books, and a huge choice of alternative health magazines.

Oasis Hospital
Playas de Tijuana
Mexico
www.oasisofhope.com
The Mexican clinic for B17 Laetril treatment.

One Peaceful World
Macrobiotics for Planetary Health and Peace
Kushi Foundation for One Peaceful World.
Box 7m
Becket, MA 01223 USA.
Tel: 413 623 5742
Fax: 413 827 8827
Training, workshops etc.

Organic Herb Trading Co.
(formerly Hambleden Herbs)
Court Farm
Milverton
Somerset TA4 INF
Tel: 01823 401104
Fax: 01823 401001
This company supplies organically grown herbs. They offer a wide range of herbs and tinctures, including the famous Caisse, 'Essiac' either as a tincture or the formula of the 4 herbs for infusion.

Organic produce
For information about organic produce and the latest on GM foods:
Soil Association
Bristol House
40–56 Victoria Street
Bristol BS1 6BY
Tel: 0117 929 0661
Fax: 0117 925 2504

Osteopaths
1. The British Naturopathic and Osteopathic Association
Frazer House
6 Netherhall Gardens
London NW3 5RR

2. General Council and Register of Osteopaths
56 London Street
Reading
Berkshire RG1 4YR
Tel: 01734 576585

Oxygen therapy
The centre of information on oxygen therapy:
Echo UK
Tel: 01765 640440
Email: apandcp@aol.com

Phyto-biophysics
20 Flower formulas, helpful for releasing energy blocks, anti-dotes the vibrations of poisons from 'the earth on which we live', harmonises negative emotions and sadness, which then aids recovery.
The Institute of Phytobiophysics
D&P Ltd, 10 St James Street, St Hellier, Jersey.
Tel: 01534 738737
www.phytobiophysics.co.uk

Pilates
the famous New York method
The Pilates Studio
890 Broadway
New York, NY10019
available in London at
The Studio,
6a Lonsdale Road, London NW6 6RD
Daphne Pena Teacher of the Pilates method.
One to one classes.
Tel: 020 7372 3490 or 0771 878 5870

Progesterone.
Natural Progesterone Information Service
Send SAE to,
Woman to Woman,
PO Box 131,
Etchingham TN19 7ZN

Protomorphogens, pancreatic enzymes
Homoeopathic remedies, pH testing paper for acid/alkaline saliva test; available from:
Enzyme Process
4 Broadgate House
Westlode Street
Spalding PE11 2AF
They offer some products such as pH testing papers to the general public; other than that their products are only available through your health practitioner.

Psychic surgery
From the Philippines, Rev. Alex L. Orbito. *Spiritual healer, President for Life of the Philippine healers. Miraculous healing has been experienced by many.*

For information of retreats, healing sessions(world wide) books and seminars:
Circle Pyramid of Asia,
International Healing Centre,
Cabanbanan, Manaoag,
Pangasinan, Philippines
Tel: +63 75 519 4365
Fax: +63 75 519 2964
Email: orbit@compass.co.ph
www.pyramidofasia.com

Los Angeles contact:
Tel: 310 522 9703
Fax: 310 522 9719

Regenerative Nutrition
Inland seawater supplies: seawater carries the same chemical elements as our blood.
NONI (herbal anti-depressant) anti-oxidant preparations, magnetic therapy, Zell-oxygen.
Mail order products from health researcher/homoeopath Mr John Claydon at:
Les Autelets, Sark
Channel Islands
GY9 0SF
Tel: 08707 446 850

School of Natural Healing
Herbal Education
Founded by Dr John Christopher 1953; for brochure:
PO Box 412, Springville UT 84663
USA Tel: 1 800 372 8255
Email:snh@avpro.com
www.schoolofnaturalhealing.com

Sharan, Farida *see under* **Dance workshop**

Society of Homoeopaths
2 Artisan Road,
Northampton NN1 4 HU
Tel: 01604 621400

Soil Association
For information about organic produce and the latest on GM foods:
Bristol House
40–56 Victoria Street
Bristol BS1 6BY
Tel: 0117 929 0661
Fax: 0117 925 2504

Spiritual healing from the Akashic records
This means 'the record of everything that was, is, and will be, within the one time-space continuum'.

1. National Federation of Spiritual Healers (NFSH)
Head office:
Old Manor Farm Studio
Church Street,
Sunbury on Thames
Surrey TW16 7RG
Tel. 01932 783164

2. Mr John Maxwell
Member of the NFSH
Apartado 5325
Suc.10, 07011
Palma de Mallorca
Spain
Tel. 0034 971 631197

This powerful gifted healer is a 'grab him when you can' phenomenon. Available in New York, London, Berlin and other parts of Europe. Contact Sunny Clay, for dates in London. Or call him in Spain.

3. Rev. Alex L. Orbito (see psychic surgery)

Star West Botanicals
11253 Trade Centre Drive
Rancho Cordova
CA 95742

Tigon Ltd
Eden House
Edward Street
Anstey
Leicester LE7 7DP
Tel: 0116 235 5020
Fax: 0116 236 6841
UK suppliers of Wild Olive leaf extract and 'Eden' extract. Royal Oil and wild oregano.

Trinity Herbs
PO Box 1001
Graton
Ca. 95444
Tel: 707 824 2040
Fax: 707 824 2050 (supplies green clay)

Unified Register of Herbal Practitioners
58 Fairmantle Street
Truro
Cornwall TR1 2EG
Tel: 01872 222699

Vega machine testing
Combining traditional acupuncture theory and the theory of classical homoeopathy, the readings are taken from minute electrical vibrations within the body. There is no use for needles; the readings are taken from a connection on the skin (usually the foot), with a probe, while you hold on to an electrode which puts you on the same circuit as the machine. Specific readings can be done to check allergies,

mercury toxicity etc. Available from Mr John Morley at:
140 Harley Street
London W1N 1AH
Tel: 020 7487 2617
or for a list of practitioners, contact the training centre in Southampton:
NOMA, Complex Homoeopathy Ltd
Unit 3
1–16 Hollybrook Road
Upper Shirley
Southampton SO16 6RB
Tel: 01703 770513
Fax: 01703 702459
Stocks 'Neurapas' and Kolorex cream and capsules.

Vita Fons II ointment and water
These products are created by Elizabeth Bellhouse, they work on body, soul and spirit benefiting all living things, bringing harmony of function and perfection of form to our whole being. The preparations are encoded with a numinous energy which upgrades the interface between the spiritual aspect of the user and the inherent, incorruptible PERFECTION (the Divine Core). The ointments are applied to the relevant chakras, and the drops can be taken internally, when out of balance or unwell, they can be used as an adjunct to speed up healing. Personally, the drops have saved my life, after the birth of one of my sons, 20 years ago, (this story will be covered in a future book). I have used the ointment on a woman who was unable to walk while pregnant and had to remain in bed from the 6th month onwards, as when she stood up the doctors feared the baby would simply drop out. After 10 days of application to the abdomen, Chakras 1, 2 and 7 she could walk around again and was fine.
For information on how to use a Chakra chart and order form write (The old fashioned way, no telephone or email) to:

Vita Fons II Ltd
Combe Castle
Elworthy
Taunton
Somerset TA4 3PX

Voice classes
In London at:
The Drill Hall Arts Centre
16 Chenies Street
London WC1E 7EX
Tel: 020 7637 8270
Elsewhere check your local paper, alternative health magazine or ask at your local library.

Water improvement
To improve the quality of your water:
Fresh Water Filter Co. Ltd
Gem House
895 High Road
Chadwell Heath
Essex RMG 4HL
Tel: 020 8597 3223
Fax: 0870 056 7264

In the US:
Ion & Light Co
2263 1/2 Sacramento Street
San Francisco
Ca 94115.
Tel: 1 800 426-1110
www.ionlight.com
www.waterwise.com
Also try the Bioceramic clay disk and spoon, available from **Bioceramica** *,the Nutri Centre or* **Wholistic Research** *to improve the taste of water and foods.*

Weleda (UK) Ltd
Leonor Road
Ilkeston
Derbyshire DE7 8DR
Tel: 0602 303151
Homoepatic remedies and Wala products; also stocks 'Levisticum' eardrops.

Wholistic Health and Life Extension Books
Whale Books
Kentchurch
Hereford HR2 0BZ
Tel: 01981 240125

Wholistic Research Co.
Unit 1, Enterprise Park
Claggy Road
Kimpton
Hertfordshire SG4 8HP
Tel: 01438 833100 Fax: 01438 833541
Email: info@wholisticresearch.com
www.wholisticresearch.com

Supplies charts, books, juicers, iridology torches and cameras, and all kinds of health equipment, such as aerobic rebounders, they also supply therapeutic clays.

Wolf (Harry Wolf): iridology and training
1278 Glenneyre
153 Laguna Beach
California 92651.
Tel/Fax: 714-362-4959

World Research Information Centre
22 White House Park
Singapore 1025
Tel: 65 323 2032
Fax: 65 235 9862
For information on International Earth Emergency Network, contact Dr B.K. Wee.

Yoga
1. *Kundalini yoga classes and yoga and sahaj sound healing workshops, given by Guru Dharam, Br Ac, C RGHM, at various locations in London. Also for acupuncture. Sound healing is a unique therapy very helpful after sudden shocks, emotional crisis, trauma, etc. For further information send an SAE to:*
PO Box 20631
London NW6 1ZU
Tel: 0958 928252
www.btinternet.com_-landraagon

2. *For a list of yoga teachers:*
The British Wheel of Yoga
Hamilton Place
Boston Road
Sleaford
Lincs NG34 7ES
Internationally write to:
The International Kundalini Yoga Teachers Association
RT 2, Box 4
Shady Lane
Espanola NM 87532
Tel: 505 753 0423
Fax: 505 753 5982
www.yoghibajan.com

Zell-oxygen, available from Wholistic Research, the Nutri Centre or Regenerative Nutrition

Zen Clinic
32 Notting Hill Gate
London W11 3HX
Tel: 0207 229 8666
Fax: 0207 221 6932

2. Recommended reading

Books
Most books are available from the Nutri Centre, in London and in the States from the alternative bookshop found within your local health store.

Aihara, Herman (1986) *Acid and Alkaline.* George Oshawa Macrobiotic Foundation. Oroville, California. 95965
An excellent book explaining and listing in detail which foods are acid forming and which are the best alkalisers. Aihara is well known for his books and teaching on macrobiotic living.

Bach, Dr Edward (1931) *Heal Thyself.* The C.W. Daniel Company Ltd
This booklet is a useful tool for those interested in how emotions affect our health. Dr Bach developed the now famous Bach flower remedies

Blackie, Dr Margery G. (1986) *The Patient, Not the Cure.* New Delhi: B. Jain Publishers Ltd.
A useful introduction to homoeopathy.

Brown, Lynda (1999) *The Shoppers Guide to Organic Foods.* London: Fourth Estate.

Buhler, Walter (1979) *Living with Your Body.* London: Rudolph Steiner Press.
Looks at man as mind, body and spirit, in relation to health and illness. From gaining good health through nutrition, healthy living etc. We must find the answer through understanding the forces within us.

Cayce, Edgar (1986) *The Edgar Cayce Collection,* 4 vols. New York: Wings Books, Random House.
A study of the life and work of this amazing visionary; on dreams, healing, diet and health, and on ESP.

Chancellor, Philip (1994) *The Handbook of the Bach Flower Remedies*. W.P Daniels and Co.
Gives practical information on the prescribing of remedies.

Clark, Hulda R. (1993) *The Cure for All Cancers*. Pro-Motion Publishing
Some of her regimes are a little strong but her formulations are very good. Use as a clearance programme as part of a general protocol when dealing with deficiencies.

Colbin, Anne-Marie (1983) *The Book of Wholemeals*. New York: Ballantine Books.
If you don't know where to start and need ideas for wholesome meals, this is a wonderful book which instructs you on what to stock up for your kitchen; how to plan menus and cook with variety, using the vegetables, grains and fruits of the seasons.

Cousins, Norman (1981) *Anatomy of an Illness*. Bantam Books.
In this best-seller Norman describes how he overcame a crippling illness with the power of his mind, aided by his physician.

D'Adamo, Dr Peter (1998) *The Eat Right Diet*. Century, London.
By knowing your blood type you can eat the right foods to help you attain optimum health. Certain foods should never be eaten by certain blood types whereas others can act as a medicine. Some blood types are prone to certain illnesses, more so than others. The book gives recipes, menus and outlines on all the blood types. Very useful (if you don't know your blood type, your doctor/practitioner can arrange this test for you).

Davis, Patricia (1988) *Aromatherapy an A to Z*. M & P.
Contains an extensive amount of valuable information on the safe use of essential oils.

Day, Philip (1999) *Cancer: Why We Are Still Dying to Know the Truth*. Credence Publications, PO Box 3, Tonbridge, Kent TN12 9ZY. Tel: 01622 832386
Email: admin@credence.freeserve.co.uk

Dethlefsen, Thorwald and Dahlke, Dr Rudiger (1990) *The Healing Power of Illness*. Element.
This book helps one to explore the meaning of one's symptoms and how the patient is involved in the bringing out of his/her illness. How to gain strength and learn from one's illness. For those who wish to be enlightened and look at illness from a less traditional standpoint.

Dextreit, Raymond (1979) *The Healing Power of Clay*, Geneva: Editions Aquarius S.A.
The first comprehensive book written about clay.

Diamond, Harvey and Diamond, Marilyn (1985) *Fit for Life*. Bantam Books.
Provides information on proper food combining ideas.

Dyer, Dr Wayne (1998) *How to Manifest Your Destiny*. Hay House.
A pick-yourself-up book, valuable for times when you feel you are stuck in a rut or cornered by a situation. Just reading one or two pages will restore your faith in humanity.

Edwards, Gill (1991) *Living Magically*. London: Piatkus.
Helpful aid to dealing with negative emotions and how to bring more magic into your life.

Erasmus, Udo (1993) *Fats that Heal, Fats that Kill*. Alive Books.
Very comprehensively explains the dangers of heating oil, what the wrong fats are doing to your health, and which oils are safe and beneficial to take.

Frawley, Dr David and Lad Dr Vasant (1992) *The Yoga of Herbs: An Ayurvedic Guide to Herbal Medicine*, Lotus Press, PO Box 325YH, Twin Lakes, Wi 53181 USA.

Harwood, A.C. (1979) *The Way of a Child*. London: Rudolph Steiner Press,
The book follows the Rudolph Steiner philosophy, exploring the way we have lost track of allowing the child to develop in a more

natural way, allowing them to use their imagination through music, painting, drawing, colouring, singing, dancing etc. which is what they should be allowed to do until about 7 years of age, instead of trying to make them into little Einsteins.

Heyn, Birgit (1987) *Ayurvedic Medicine: The Gentle Strength of Indian Healing*, Thorsons Ltd, Wellingborough, Northamptonshire NN8 2RQ.
Describes how to use the power of nature, to restore a state of balance. Using the heat of the sun, light, air and water, combined with mineral, vegetable and animal substances to achieve balance of mind and body.

Higa, Dr Teruo (1993) 'EM'
An *Earth Changing Revolution*: Sustainable Community Development (for address and contact details, see page 220).

Janov, Dr Arthur (1991) *The New Primal Scream*. Enterprise Publishing Inc. 725 Market Street, Wilmington, DE 19801
Primal therapy 20 years on. Helps one to get to the bottom of heartfelt inner feelings, showing the way to relieve much suffering from past trauma. Topics include: origins of manic depression, and obsessive compulsive behaviour; the nature of stress tension and anxiety; the immune system and catastrophic disease; illness as a silent scream and the lifelong effects of birth.

Jensen, Dr Bernard (1981) *Tissue Cleansing through Bowel Management*. Dr Bernard Jensen International.
A must for your bedside table.

Jensen, Dr Bernard (1988) *Foods that Heal*. Avery publishing Group.
Excellent guide to the benefits of using fresh, natural and unadulterated foods for prevention and healing of illnesses.

Khalsa, Dr Dharma Singh (1998) *The Mind Miracle*. London: Arrow Books Ltd.
This very good book covers the many aspects of brain health; it also has a section on some of the Yoga techniques mentioned in Chapter 9 on Asthma.

Kneipp, Father Sebastian (1972) *Mein Wasser Kur* (*My Water Cure*). William Blackwood & Sons.

La Tourelle, Maggie (1992) *Applied Kinesiology: An Introduction*. Thorson.
Useful and simple self-testing techniques for food allergies, supplements etc.

Lindlahr, Dr Henry (1975) *Philosophy of Natural Therapeutics*. Saffron Walden, Essex: C.W. Daniel Co. Ltd.
For the serious student; Dr Lindlahr was one of the greatest pioneers of the natural health movement of his time; here he covers the general principals of natural cures; there are three other volumes in this series.

Morningstar, Amadea with Desai, Urmila (1990) *The Ayurvedic Cook Book*. Lotus Press, PO Box 2, Wilmot, WI 53192.
Personalised nutrition for your constitution (vata, pitta, kapha).

Motoyama, Dr Hiroshi (2000) *Karma and Reincarnation*. London: Piatkus.
Motoyama is a Shinto priest, psychic and healer; this is a helpful book for understanding our own karma, the law of cause and effect.
More information, journals etc. from:
The Motoyama Institute, for Life Physics (see p. 225); Health Systems (p. 221), or The California Institute for Human Science (see p. 217).

Nelson, Dr Miriam E. (1997) *Strong Women Stay Young*. Bantam Books.
www.strongwomen.com
How to strengthen your muscles and stay young and supple

Oshawa, George (1986) *The Order of the Universe*, George Oshawa Macrobiotic Foundation, 1511 Robinson Street, Oroville, California 95965.
The founder of macrobiotics.

Oshawa, George (1967) *The Macro-biotic Guide Book for Living*.
Translated by Herman Aihara.
George Oshawa Macrobiotic Foundation,

1511 Robinson Street, Oroville, California 95965.
Contains the wisdom of the Far East, essays on love, marriage, childcare, ageing and more.

Paulson, Genevieve Lewis (1997) *Kundalini and the Chakras.* Llewellyn Publications.
Comprehensive information on how to release the power of the force of kundalini safely and on how to cleanse and develop the chakras and their energies.

Perry, Foster (1993) , When Lighting Strikes a Hummingbird, Bear & Company
Describes the awakening of a healer. When he was struck by lightning in a wheat field his world was transformed, he was taken on a journey of initiation, transformation and experienced a rapid expansion of consciousness. This book tells the story of his evolution. His CD, 1994 'Other Worldly' Triloka Records 'We Dye The Wheat Fields Gold', takes you on a spiritual journey and is very powerful.

Pfeiffer, Dr Carl and Holford, Patrick (1996) *Mental Health and Illness.* Ion Press, 34 Wadham Road, London SW15 2LR.
Brain health through nutrition.

Richards, Dr B. (1999) *The Good News on Cancer.* The Press on the Lake, Sandwich Kent. CT13 9RT
Available from Wholistic Health and Life Extension Books, see p. 230.

Sachs, Robert (1993) *Rebirth into Pure Land.* Zivah Publishers.
A true story of birth, death and transformation, that can help heal your loss.

Schroeder, Dr Henry A. (1973) *The Trace Elements and Man.* Old Greenwich, Connecticut: Devin-Adair Co.
Schroeder is a leading authority on the little known field of trace elements in relation to living organisms. He has concluded his findings after years of experimenting, at the unique Dartmouth Medical School, Trace Element Lab. in Vermont. Well worth a read and for reference, for those interested in the minerals from our earth.

Scovel Shinn. Florence (1925) *The Game of Life and How to Play It*, De Vors publications, Box 550, Marina del Rey CA 902994

Shivanada Yoga Centre (1999) *The Yoga Cook Book.* Fireside Books.
Very useful for healthy alternative cooking.

Stanchich, Lino (1989) *Power Eating Programme: You Are How You Eat.* Healthy Products Inc.
Explains in detail the importance of a good long chew, how it will affect your health and longevity.

Svoboda, Roberto E. (1988) *Prakuti, Your Ayurvedic Constitution,* Geocom Ltd.
Helps you discover your constitutional type in Ayurvedic terms and which foods agree with you most.

Valnet, Dr Jean (1982) *The Practice of Aromatherapy.* Saffron Walden, Essex: C.W. Daniel Co. Ltd.
A must for the serious student. Covers nearly 50 essential oils, their history, properties and uses.

Vithoulkas, George (1979) *Homeopathy: Medicine of the New Man.* New York: Simon & Schuster, Fireside Books.
This Greek master and teacher of homoeopathy has written a number of books on the subject; he shows how like cures like in homeopathic treatment. Even though it appears simple it takes years of intensive study and experience to comprehend fully and apply successfully. He goes back over the last 200 years in history, to the founder of homoeopathy, Samuel Hahnemann (1755) Dresden, Germany, who began his experiments on himself with Peruvian bark for the treatment of malaria. This book takes you through the exciting discoveries, which have led to this effective healing system where the correct remedy stimulates man's own innate power to heal himself.

Wigmore, Ann (1984) *The Hippocrates Diet and Health Program.* Avery Publishing Group.
A diet mainly consisting of fresh fruits, vegetables and grains and the advantages of sprouted seeds, wheat-grass juices and other super-foods,

which are mostly eaten or drunk in their raw form. Gives various cleansing procedures and easy-to-follow recipes, which allow the body to become balanced, healthy and younger and maintain a normal weight (see also The Hippocrates Institute, p. 222).

Wilde, Stuart (1998) *Silent Power.* Hay House Inc., PO Box 5100, Carlsbad, CA 92018-5100.
Available from The Nutri Centre in London and in most bookstores throughout the USA.
www.powersource.com
The inspirational Stuart Wilde is a mega personality of the Conscious Awareness, Human Potential Movement. His books help you to understand the need to embrace a more warrior like energy, following the path of self-responsibility and the journey of the warrior sage, combining the softness of the feminine spirit and the strength of the warrior.

Wilde, Stuart (2000) *The 6th Sense.* Hay House Inc., PO Box 5100, Carlsbad, CA 92018-5100. Available from The Nutri Centre in London and in most bookstores throughout the USA.
www.powersource.com

Wilde, Stuart (1998) *Weight Loss for the Mind.* Hay House Inc., PO Box 5100, Carlsbad, CA 92018-5100. Available from The Nutri Centre in London and in most bookstores throughout the USA.
www.powersource.com

Wimala, Bhante Y. (1997) *Lessons of the Lotus.* London: Piatkus,
A travelling Buddhist monk gives an insight to his spiritual wisdom with practical steps and exercises to calm the restless mind.

Ypma, Rosemary (1993) *Aroma and Clay Therapy.* Ogham, Almere (Holland). Available at the Nutri Centre or from Wholistic Research.
Covers a variety of uses of clay and essential oils, with a section on animals.

Subscriptions

Alternative Medicine
Bimonthly magazine, full of useful informative articles.
PO Box 1056
Escondido
CA 92033-9871
www.alternativemedicine.com

Kindred Spirit
A quarterly guide for mind, body and spirit; excellent articles on a variety of health and transformational topics.
Foxhole
Dartington
Totnes
Devon TQ9 6EB
Tel: 01803 866686
Fax: 01803 866591
www.kindredspiritco.uk

Macrobiotics Today
Bimonthly magazine.
George Oshawa Macrobiotic Foundation.
Vega Study Centre,
1511 Robinson Street
Oroville
CA 95965
USA
Tel: 916 533 7702
Fax: 916 533 7908

Natural Health
Good magazine with articles on the latest developments on natural medicines.
PO Box 7440
Red Oak
IA 51591-4440
www.naturalhealthmag.com

The Townsend Letter for Doctors and Patients
For those who need to keep up with the latest discoveries in the natural health field. Published in the US, 10 issues per year.
91 Tyler Street
Pt Townsend
WA 98368-6541
Tel: 360 385 6021
Fax: 360 385 0699
www.tldp.com

WDDTY (*What Doctors Don't Tell You*)
A monthly newsletter produced in Britain, updating and informing the public about the effects of drugs, vaccinations etc. and the alternatives. Generally invaluable information which is hard to get anywhere else.
Write to WDDTY.
The Subscriptions Dept is:
WDDTY
Satellite House,
2 Salisbury Road
London SW19 4EZ
Tel: 0800-146054
Tel: 020 8944 5555
Fax: 020 8944 9888
www.wddty.co.uk

Index

Note: References to illustrations are in bold type

A

abattoirs 14
abdomen 81, 166, 187
    lower 135
    swollen 71
abdominal pain 53, 57, 168, 182
abscesses 123, 133, 151
    tooth 200
absorbent 104, 105, 107
absorption 109, 121, 125, 135, 136, 153, 165, 184, 185
Abzug, Bella 45
accidental falls 196
acetaldehyde 18
acetate 60
acetylcholine 31, 190
aches and pains 59, 104, 203
    severe 64
Acid and Alkaline (Aihara) 137, 231
acid(s) 19, 48, 51, 104, 110, 124, 137, 145, 155, 193
    alkaline balance 169
    forming foods 10, 158, 163, 168
    rain 3, 125
acidification 104
acidity 18, 71, 104, 113, 119, 133, 145, 155, 157, 167, 183, 203, 204, 214
    and asthma 77
acidophilus 20, 41, 58, 163, 168, 169, 170, 174, 186, 194
acidosis 23
acne 121, 129, 151–2
actinium 110
activity 77
    lack of 70
acupuncture 22, 174, 193, 205, 215
Adam 69
additives, food 34, 47, 75, 87, 102, 152, 184, 189, 193, 204
adenoids 71, 185
adolescence 151
adolescents 153
adrenal(s) 169, 174, 183
    exhaustion 71
    function 118, 186, 187
    weak 152
    glands 152
    support 155, 179

adrenaline 181
adsorbent 107
adzuki beans 183
aerobic
    bouncing 167
    re-bounder 185
Aesculus 154
aflatoxin 18
Africa 18, 33, 62, 63
aftercare 86
age 191
ageing 104, 118, 124, 145, 146, 171, 182
    anti 43
    effects of 6, 71
    over-preoccupation with 89
    premature 32, 116, 202
    wrinkles 203–6
agitation 85
aggression 29, 115, 197
agnus cactus 187, 188
agriculture 4
agrimony 169
AIDS 18, 62
    alternative cures for 2
Aihara, Herman 231
Ainsworths Homoeopathic Pharmacy 215, 223
air 103, 125
    as element 77, 108, 132
    filtration systems 3
    sickness 23
    traffic 38, 72
    travel 172, 183
AK tests 186, 199
alchemists 120
alcohol(s) 18, 19, 45, 60, 75, 91, 103, 104, 120, 122, 151, 153, 156, 157, 158, 159, 161, 168, 172, 177, 178, 179, 183, 186, 191, 192, 203, 204, 205, 206
Alexander technique 23
alfalfa 76, 157, 158, 159, 169, 176, 193, 194
    sprouted 47, 191
algae 119
alkali 48, 137, 146
alkaline activities 204
alkalisers/alkalising 75, 76, 77, 104, 130, 158, 194, 195

alkaloids 62
alkalosis 152
allergens 153, 171
allergies 17, 31, 51, 53, 56, 57, 72, 85, 152, 153, 154, 167, 177, 181, 182, 193, 195, 211
    food 26, 71
allopathic
    drugs 104
    treatment 42
almond(s) 90, 155, 157, 166, 186, 205
    bitter 41
    milk 12
    oil 67, 154, 160, 161, 165, 166, 167, 169 173, 174, 176, 181, 187, 198, 201, 205, 207
aloe vera 48, 151, 166
    gel 162, 195
    juice 20, 58
ALS (amyotrophic lateral sclerosis) 38
alterative 107
Alternative Medicine 234
Alternative Remedies 216
aluminium 112, 122–3, 127
    functions, benefits and tips 122–3
    hydroxide 109, 125
    plant food 123
    smelting factories 31
    sulphate 122
    utensils 122, 125
Alvarado, Donna 45
Alzheimer's disease 32, 122, 123, 152–3
amalgam fillings 129
Amazon jungle 63
American Academy of Medical Acupuncture 215
American Association for the Advance of Science 45
American Association of Acupuncture and Oriental Medicine 215
American Association of Naturopathic Physicians 215
American Herbalists Guild 215, 222
American Indian 65
American Institute of Vedic Studies 215
amino acids 34, 59–60, 114, 115, 136, 160, 162, 168, 186, 193, 204

Index

ammonia 60, 137
amoebas 54, 105
amphibians 37
amylase 136
anabolic processes 110
anaemia 10, 51, 53, 55, 57, 58, 121, 124, 128, 129, 153
anaesthetics 23
analgesics 64, 107
anaphylactic shock 181
Anatomy of an Illness (Cousins) 232
Andes/Andeans 98, 179, 186
anger 83, 85, 89, 115, 184
angina 153–4
animal(s) 33
   and clay 96–101
   diseases 37
   fat(s) 45, 90, 152, 156, 157, 165, 189
   low 20
   migration changes 37
   products 168, 193, 197
   proteins 157
   rights 29
   wild 61, 96, 97
   zoo 97–8
anions 110
anis 187, 202
aniseed 153
ankle(s) 166
   broken 154
   swollen 119
   weak 71
Ann Wigmore Institute 46, 215
anodyne 107
anorexia 129, 168
antacid 107, 133
anthelmintic herbs 24, 61, 107
anti-ageing 123
anti-anaemia 107, 128
anti-arthritic 123
anti-bacterial 107
antibiotics 3, 11, 14, 18, 19, 28, 49, 100, 104, 147, 152, 170, 174, 194
anti-bilious 107
antibodies 185
anti-catarrhal 162
anti-coagulant 208
anti-depressants 29, 31, 84, 87
anti-diarrhoea 107
anti-emetic 107
anti-histamine 181
anti-infectious 107, 128
anti-inflammatory 107, 170
anti-malaria 181
anti-mycosis 107
anti-oxidant 4, 5, 6, 38, 107, 120, 124, 152, 162, 196
anti-parasitic 61, 107
anti-perspirants 42, 46, 152, 161, 167
anti-psychotics 191
antiseptic 107, 152, 154
anti-social tendencies 70
anti-spasmodic 170, 186
anti-toxic 107

anus 55
   itching of 53, 55
   scratching of 53
anxiety 70, 103, 118, 153, 182
aphrodisiacs 200, 122, 179, 187
aphta 188
appendicitis 56, 57, 116
appendix 56, 57, 185
appetite 129, 194
   increased/decreased 55, 57, 64
   uncontrolled 52, 189
apple(s) 49, 156, 157, 178, 179, 186
   grated 169, 194
   juice 152, 158
   pectin powder 24, 178
   sauce 194
applied kinesiology 61, 153, 178
Applied Kinesiology: An Introduction (La Tourelle) 233
apricot(s) 47, 90, 171, 199
   kernels, B17 from 41, 42, 43
aqua amigdalorum 41
Arabia, ancient 41
ARCH (Association and Register of Colon Hydrotherapists) 210, 218
argileceous materials 126
arginine 114
argument 84
arms, tremors in 190
Armstrong, John 43
arnica cream 196
Aroma and Clay Therapy (Ypma) 235
aromatherapy 145, 216
Aromatherapy: an A to Z (Davis) 232
arrhythmias 118
arrogance 50
artemesiae annuae (aka Qing Hao) 181
arteries 119, 164, 202, 203
   congestion 145
   elasticity of 123
   hardening of 125, 156
   narrowing of 198
arteriosclerosis 114, 119, 120, 123,200, 202, 203
arthritis 24, 54, 113, 114, 157
artichokes 90, 166
artificial foods 31, 152
artificial sweeteners 31–3, 58, 152, 160, 193
asbestos 111
ascarides 54
   in large bowel 52
ash 113
Asia 77, 96
asparagus 121, 123, 158
aspartic acid 31
aspartame 31–3, 87, 189
   and MS 32–3
Aspergillus flavus 18
aspirin 99, 104, 152
assimilation 77, 135, 175
   problems 71, 189
Association for Meningitis 30

Association of Research and Enlightenment (ARE) 216, 220
asthma 17, 34, 53, 66, 69–82, 120, 154–6, 199, 211, 214
   and acidity 77
   drugs 31, 193
   and elements 77–8
   garlic treatment for 211
   herbs for 84
   mental effects of 69–70
   and miasms 73–4
   physical effects of 70–3
   positive thoughts for 76–7
   and skin 74–6
   and yoga 78–82
   ancient philosophy on 82
   Kapalabathi 81–2
   Kundalini yoga: Breath of Fire 80
   relaxation posture 80–1
   sun salutations 78–9
   your voice 81
astringent 151
astrology and medicine 132
atherosclerosis 114, 153, 156, 158, 198
athlete's foot 17, 20
atmosphere 145
atomic density 33
atoms 110
attention deficit disorder (ADD) 34
aubergines 193
Aum cult 38
aura, weakening of 76
Australia 11, 103
Austria 6
autism 27
auto-immune disorders 157, 188
autonomic nervous system 190
autumn 156
Avicenna 41, 132
avocados 31, 115, 157, 178
Avon Cosmetics 63
awareness, increase your 88
Ayurveda
   constitutions 78
   herbal tincture 159
   remedy for hangover 177
Ayurvedic Cook Book, The (Morningstar and Desai) 233
Ayurvedic Institute 216
Ayurvedic Medicine: The Gentle Strength of Indian Healing (Heyn) 233

B

babies 28, 35, 36, 117
   excessive crying 36
   feeding problems and asthma 70
baby
   bottle 35, 70
   food(s) 49
   organic 168
BA ceramic ball application 43
Bach, Dr Edward 231
Bach Flower Remedies 171, 216, 223, 231
back 154, 194

Index

lower 161
bacon 13
bacteria 14, 15, 17, 28, 29, 51, 82, 83, 104, 108, 136, 145, 169, 170, 171, 184, 185, 189, 195, 199
    air-borne 71
    friendly 17, 52, 104
    infection 38, 180
bad company 45
Baghdad 132
baked goods 11
balance 189
    poor 188
balancing 103, 104, 129
baldness 158
B Alive 193, 203, 216
balm of gilead 48, 65, 162, 163, 173
bananas 49, 115, 122, 123, 157, 170, 193, 212
Bancha tea 171, 179
Barings Bank 52
barley 75, 90, 115, 161, 211, 214
    grass 48, 190, 193
    juice 47
    how to make 212
    sprouted 178
Barnes temperature test 199
Bartlett Peter 23
basaltic ashes 111
basil 153, 168
bass 76
bath(s) 164, 183, 193, 203, 205
    clay 95, 171, 187, 192
    Epsom salt 75, 157
    hot and cold 27
    hot/warm foot 162, 166, 182
    clay 202
    steam 74
    of warm milk 53
BAV (Bovine Aids Virus) 12
BC ceramic disk 204
B cells 185
BCG vaccination 27
beans 90, 123, 182, 189, 190
bears 97, 98
beauty 205, 206
bed 36
beef 13, 55
    tapeworm (*Taeniasis saginata*) 55, **55**
beer 14, 158, 191
bee(s) 102
    pollen 152, 179
    stings 180–1
    wax 165
beet(s) 90, 114, 157, 178
    greens 157
    juice 47
beetroot 75, 115, 184
    juice 170
behavioural disorders 31
Beijing 1
belching 53
Belgium 12
belief in what you do 76

benomyl 49
bentonite 134
benzene 38
benzoin 64
berberis vulgaris 21, 65, 171, 174, 197
bereavement 189
bergamot 168, 176
berries 97–8
beta hydrochloric acid 176
BGH/BST: bovine growth hormone 11–12
Bible 69, 95
bifidobacterium 20
bilberry 173, 202
bile 184, 209
    acids 165
    salts 137, 184
biliary duct 54
biocatalyst 120
BioCeramica 146–7, 204, 216
bioelectric research 105
bio-flavenoids 202
biological activity 112
Bio-salt 91
birch 159, 201
    tar oil 157, 194
birds 97–9
birth defects 49
bites 71, 95, 180–1
    see also mosquitoes
blackberries 154
blackcurrant 184
black bile (melancholic) 25, 132
black cohosh 187
Blackie, Dr Margery G. 231
black sounds 81
bladder 129, 136, 172, 191
    infections 53
    problems 188, 200
    stones 100, 116
bladderwrack 164
Blair, Tony 4
Blake, William 82
blastocystis hominus 54
Blessed Herbs 216
blessed thistle 153
blisters in mouth 18, 53
bloated stomach 17, 53
blood 33, 54, 57, 58, 112, 118, 121, 134, 161, 166, 167, 183, 184, 194
    cells 55, 114, 145
    clean 74, 105, 195, 205
    clots 54
    disorders 73
    flow 130, 158, 161
    fungus in 34
    as humour (sanguine) 132
    pressure 72, 119
    high 109, 118, 153, 154, 155, 158–9
    increase in 34
    low 71, 159, 172
    reduction of 193
    purification 159, 171, 172, 192, 196, 201

    quality affected 71
    red cells 106
    red corpuscles 111
    stream 26, 184, 198
    toxic 116
    sugar 145
    imbalance 56, 115
    levels 129
    low (hypoglycaemia) 58, 71, 85, 178–9
    tests 63, 85, 128, 137, 153, 185
    thinning 156
    toxins 173, 195
    vessels 158
    white cell count, reduced 121
blood root 173
blueberries 47, 179
blue flag 161, 185
blurred vision 188
boars 98
body
    movement 49, 89
    temperature
    see temperature (body)
boils 123, 173
bone(s) 73, 112, 118, 120, 137, 198
    aching 203
    broken 154
    deficiencies/problems 90
    hardening of 123
    marrow 121
    red 185
    pains in 65
    strength 186, 198
boneset (*Eupatorium perfoliatum*) 64, 65, 180
Book of Wholemeals, The (Colbin) 231
borage 123, 173
    oil 152, 193, 194
bottom, spots on 53
bouncer 161
bovine aids virus (BAV) 12
bovine growth hormone 11–12
bovine papilloma virus 12
bowel 115, 116, 134, 136, 170, 195
    ascarides in large **52**
    cancer 52
    cleansing 205
    flora 168
    friendly bacteria 174
    herbs 195
    movements, regular 58, 65, 74, 86, 151, 164, 166, 190, 191
    natural function 101
    pockets (diverticulitis) 170, **170**
    problems 17, 31, 109, 188, 199
    toxins 195
Benign Prostate Hyperplasia 191
Bradford 34
brain 19, 34, 52, 84, 88, 115, 119, 123, 152, 153, 157, 188
    cancer 35
    chemistry 32
    degeneration 145
    disturbances 71, 181

exercise 89
fog 34
health 90, 159–60
inflammation 152
affecting membranes 27
tumours 32
brainwashing 35
bran 182
brandy 64
bras, under-wired 161
Brassica vegetables 20
Brazil 20, 21
brazil nuts 205
bread 18, 19, 75, 90, 102, 177
rye 90
wheat 90, 114, 190
yeasted 189
yeast free 90
breast(s) 160
cancer 11, 43
and mammograms 40, 45
and pesticides 45–6
feeding 161, 208
fibrocystic breast lumps 46
lack of tone after childbirth 160
lumps 161–2
mask 160
sore nipples 161
tumour 40
breath 69, 77, 80, 81, 130
bad 53
and mind 70
Breath of Fire 80, **80**
breathing
deep 78–81, 182
exercises *see under* exercises
problems 32, 55, 59, 69–82, 154–6
shallow 78, 82
see also asthma; respiration problems
brewer's yeast 125
BRGM laboratories 126
Britain 2, 6, 12, 13, 14, 15, 43, 46, 47, 48, 95, 103, 135, 203, 212, 215, 221, 225, 226
British Acupuncture Association 215, 217
British Columbia 46
British Homoeopathic Association 217, 223
British Naturopathic and Osteopathic Association 216, 227
British Wheel of Yoga 216, 230
broccoli 20, 125, 168, 199
bromelain 48, 157
bronchi 54
bronchial
catarrh 71
congestion 57, 72, 162
bronchioles 162
bronchitis 19, 162, 211
broncho-dilators 81
Brown, Lynda 231
brown rice 16, 20, 47, 75, 99, 115, 169, 186, 203

organic 169, 191–2
bruises 196
brushing skin 75, 151, 164, 167, 196, 205
with wood and bristle brush 212–13, **213**
brussels 123
BSE 9–10, 13, 14
BST (Bovine somatropin) 11
buckwheat 20, 47, 183, 186, 189, 202
bugleweed 199
Buhler, Walter 231
builder's dust 73, 167
buildings causing illness 36
burdock root 48, 171, 173, 192, 193, 195, 196, 201
burns 162, 180
buses 38, 72
Bush, George W. 4
butcher's broom 153, 202
butter 156, 214
butternut bark 61

C

cabbage 20, 203
juice 180
leaf poultice, how to prepare 212
organic 161
cadmium 124
caffeine 87, 156, 157, 168, 191
cajeput 201
calc carb 163, 197
calc fluor 162
calcification 118, 163
calcitonin 198
calcium 10, 112, 114, 117, 118–19, 120, 123, 125, 127, 137, 186, 187, 194, 198, 202
carbonate 118
deficiency 54, 58, 90, 175
deposits 123, 197
fluoride 160, 164, 196, 202
functions, benefits and tips 118–19
metabolism disturbances 73
pump 113
supplements 76, 118
calc phos 154
calendula 161, 173
California 49, 128, 203
California Institute for Human Science 217
calories 33, 88, 115
calves 10, 12
campylo 14, 15
Can-1 20
Can-2 20
Canada 65, 218
cancer(s) 17, 33, 34, 35, 36, 40–50, 53, 73, 77, 97, 125, 189
alternative cures for 2
B17 (laetrile) 41–2
magnetic energy therapy 43
Tenko Seki ceramic 43–4, **44**
bowel 52

brain 35
breast 11, 43
and mammograms 40, 45
and pesticides 45–6
and candida 46
cervical 12
and chemotherapy 18, 40
in chickens 14
colon 11, 116
and diet 47–8
and Essiac 48
factors involving development of 44–5
home therapy 46
liver 18
and organic food 47
personalities 49–50
positive approaches to 49–50
prostate 191
research 40
screening for 40, 45
and toxic foods 49
treatments 217
uterine 186
Cancer Alternative Information Bureau 216, 217
Cancer: Why We Are Still Dying to Know the Truth (Day) 41, 231
candida 17–18, 22, 29, 52, 85, 90, 151, 152, 186, 192, 194
and cancer 46
tips 20
canker sores 163
canned produce 47, 102
Cannon of Medicine (Avicenna) 132
Capri Mineral Whey 224
capsicium 61
caraway 153, 169
carbohydrates 18, 25, 112, 113, 136, 137, 145, 190, 195, 198
high complex 168, 178, 190
refined 116, 164
carbon 110, 113, 115
acid 33
dioxide 60, 184
absorption 5
foods 154
note on 214
carbonated drinks *see under* drinks
carbonic acid 145
carbonic gas 33
carcinogenics 18, 31–2, 34, 38, 39, 47, 160
cardamon 179
cardiovascular system 159
problems 189
care, lack of proper 86
carelessness 69
carnitine 160
carrot(s) 47, 75, 90, 99, 115, 157, 168, 170, 171, 178, 186, 205
juice 47, 170, 177, 184, 191, 192, 195, 212
oil 207

tincture of wild (daucus carota) 191, 193
cars 38–9
cartilage 204
cascara sagrada 48, 109, 166, 190
Cassia herb tea 181
catabolic processes 110
catalyst 107, 135, 136, 169
catalytic converters 38–9
cataracts 123, 172
catarrh 65, 104, 173, 214
catarrhal conditions 163
catheter feeding 18
cats 58, 61, 100, **100**
cat's claw *see* Una de Gato
cattle, infected 9, 12, 55
cauliflower 20
Cayce, Edgar 72, 157, 219, 231
    Association of Research and Enlightenment (ARE) 216
cayenne pepper 20, 74, 155, 156, 158, 159, 161, 164, 172, 193, 195
cecum 56, 57
celery 20, 47, 75, 90, 123, 157, 158, 168
    juice 201
    seeds 163, 193, 201
    soup 159, 194
    tablets/tincture 157, 163
cell(s) 74, 78, 81, 105, 110, 111, 118, 120, 121, 123, 134, 136, 153, 204
    B 185
    membranes 38
    T 25, 185
cellulite 103, 163–4
cement
    dust 73, 167
    reinforcement 5
Central America 6
central nervous system 62, 120, 152
Centre for Cell Specific Cancer Therapy (CSCT) 43, 46, 217
Centre for Immuno Augmentation in the Bahamas 46, 217
centrifugal process 33
ceramic(s) 111
    bowl 139, **140**
    clay balls 43, 200
cereals 18, 182
cerebo-spinal fluid 146
cerebral palsy 17
cervical cancer 12
chakra(s) 197
cleansing 80
chalk 33
chamomile 131, 165, 168, 169, 170, 171, 172, 173, 175, 182, 187, 197, 201, 210
    oil 151, 157
Chancellor, Philip 232
channel of sound 81
chaparral 159, 161, 163, 185, 195, 200
charcoal 33
cheese 19, 90, 115, 156, 177
cheddar, organic hard 90

cow's 75
    goat's 31, 75, 90
    non-organic 48
    organic 48, 90
Chemical Dictionary, The 18
chemical fertilisers 2
chemicals 45, 77, 205
chemical sprays and paints, strong-smelling 45, 167
chemical structure 110
chemotherapy 18, 40, 42, 108
cherries 47
    sugarless sour 157
chest 27, 154, 167
    infection 155
chestnuts 90, 155, 183
chewing
    clay 96
    food 76
    gum 32
    and gums 24–6
chi 77
chicken 'flu 15
chicken(s) 13–16
    farms 3
    organic 48
chickweed 192
chi-kung 89
chilblains 164
childbirth 160, 161
childhood vaccinations 27–8, 155
children 15, 31, 34, 45, 47, 51, 59, 66, 72, 89, 117, 170, 203
    early maturing of 117
chin, double or fatty 165
China 36, 37, 190
Chinese medicine 26, 95, 104
'Chinese restaurant syndrome', MSG 34
chiropractors 217
chlorella 48, 119
chloride compounds 38
chlorine 18, 110
chlorophyll 33
chloroquine 62, 63
chlorpyrifos 49
chocolate 11, 75, 152, 168, 177, 195, 214
cholera 96
cholesterol 75, 120, 121, 156, 159, 165, 184, 188, 197, 198, 203
    LDL (bad) 153
    testing 165
choline 153
chondroitin sulphate 193, 196, 202, 204, 217
Chondrus Crispus (Irish moss), tincture of 176
CHONPS 113–15
Christian Church 96
chromium 114
    picolinate 178, 190
chronic fatigue syndrome 24
chrysotile 111
cicatrising 107, 138

cider vinegar 201
cinchona tree 62
cinnamon 179
Circle Pyramid of Asia 228
circulation system 90, 200
    problems 59, 71, 153, 164, 172, 177, 179, 193, 201
CJD *see* vCJD
citronella 64, 180
citrus fruit 76, 157, 163, 192, 193
Clark, Hulda R. 53, 59, 231
clary sage 179, 182
clay 6, 38, 42, **106**, 122, 124, 149, 153, 164, 171, 217–18
    action of mineral elements found in 117–25
    and bacteria 136
    bath 95, 171, 187, 192, 200
    beneficial for intestinal flora 145
    and bentonite 134
    Bernard Jensen's use of xiii
    and BioCeramica 146–7
    black mud hair pack 176
    broken 109, 151
    ceramic balls 43
    and chemical structure 110
    cleansing 207
    colours of 127, **127**, 133
    as curative medium 95–6
    enema 210
    and enzymes 136
    activation of (body catalysts) 136
    and Father Kneipp 96
    fibrous 109, 111
    foot bath 202
    green 14, 20, 24, 31, 95, 109–10, 111, 112, 127, 134, 136, 151, 152, 153, 154, 155, 157, 158, 159, 160, 162, 163, 164, 166, 167, 169, 170, 171, 174, 175,176, 177, 178, 180, 184, 186, 188, 189, 192, 194, 197, 200, 203
    composition 127–8
    trace elements 127
    grey 111
    hair care with 175–6
    hair pack 176
    importance of particle size 133–4
    importance of quality 126
    inhaling 195
    licks 98
    mask **140**, **141**, 149, 151, 152, 165, 171, 172, 175, 196, 205
    milk 151
    packs 27
    paste 180, 181, 201
    phyllitous 109
    points to consider when using for first time 133–4
    poultice 27, 74, 109, 149, 151, 153, 154, 155, 157, 161–2, 163, 167, 170, 172, 173, 174, 177, 180, 183, 184, 187, 192, 194, 195, 196–7, 198, 200, 201–2, 211
    for breast lumps 161–2

how to make and apply 139–43, **140, 141**
utensils needed to prepare 142
preparing 142–3
power of 135–8
practicalities and chemical structure 109
quality and colours 126–9
and radioactivity 110–11
red 26, 98, 109, 128, **128**, 153, 160, 175, 177, 178, 186, 187, 188, 189, 200
spa (California) 128
shampoo 67, 175
spa 196
storing 109
superfine 191, 205
superfine green 24, 47, 109, 127, 160, 162, 165, 167, 168, 170, 171, 172, 173, 174, 177, 179, 182, 185, 187, 190, 193, 194, 195, 198, 199, 202, 205
superfine red 128, 179
superfine white 24, 129, 205
therapeutic action of healing 107–8
therapy 93–147
tube 180
twelve things you should know 103–4
very fine green 24, 60, 109, 127, 165, 169, 172, 196, 201, 202
very fine yellow 129, 196
other benefits 129
and vinegar mask 96
warm plaster 203
water (drinking clay) 42, 52, 58, 76, 88, 99, 100, 105, 108, 119, 129, 134, 138, 145–6, 149, 152, 153, 155, 156, 158, 159, 160, 162, 163, 164, 166, 167, 169, 170, 172, 173, 174, 175, 176, 177, 178, 180, 182, 183, 184, 185, 187, 188, 189, 190, 192, 193, 195, 196, 198, 199, 200, 201, 205
how to prepare for drinking 144–7
stage I 144
stage II 144
importance of good water 145–6
what should it look like? 109–10
when to avoid using it 109
when used externally 105–6
when used internally 104–5
white 109–10, 129, 133, 151, 169, 175, 178, 194, 207
yellow 88, 109, 129, 151, 152, 158, 164, 169, 170, 171, 174, 176, 178, 183, 186, 192
cleansing 105, 128, 129
diets 192
programmes 46, 66, 132, 134
rejuvenation 207–8
climate(s) 72
unstable 37

warm 56, 57
moist, tropical 57
climb hills or stairs, unable to 71
cloister oil 194, 217
cloves 20, 59, 60, 61, 63, 181, 200
CNRS (National Centre for Scientific Research) 126
cobalt 112, 124, 127, 128
functions, benefits and tips 124
cocoa butter 165
coconuts 90
cod 76
coeliac disease 165
co-enzymes 120
Q-10 160
coffee 120, 123, 204
enema 184, 209–10
organic 76
cola 14, 85, 137, 146
cola vera 164
Colbin, Anne-Marie 231
cold-pressed vegetable oils 158
cold-water washing (Father Kneipp method) 27
colds 36, 81–2, 122, 155, 180
collagen 145, 196, 202, 203
College of Traditional Chinese Acupuncture 215, 218
colloidal
aluminium 122, 123
particles 105, 110, 134
Colombia 6
colon 30, 56, 75, 89, 166–7, 168, 186
cancer 11, 116
problems 24, 159, 182
transverse 52
colonic hydrotherapy 134, 167, 190, 210, 218
colonic irrigation 53, 77, 170, 192
colostrums 1227
colour preservatives 47, 204
coltsfoot 74
tincture 154
combining food 177
comfrey 154, 196
compassion 89, 131
complacency 89
complaining, avoid excessive 76
compresses 27
compulsive behaviour 85
computers 35–6, 177
concentration 117
aid to 24
lack/loss of 31, 69
confidence, lack of 69
conflict 84
confusion 86, 87
congealed energy 197
congestion 139, 162, 166, 172
leading to sluggishness 166
congestive heart failure 118
connective tissues 118, 120, 123, 145, 164, 196
weak 103, 201
constipation 29, 46, 48, 53, 55, 58, 86,

87, 88, 101, 108, 116, 121, 134, 138, 144, 151, 157, 161, 166–7, 170, 176, 182, 184, 188, 189, 191, 199, 200, 202
constitutions, Ayurvedic 78
constriction, feeling of 153
contamination 49, 108
contraceptive pill 18
control 184
convenience foods 34
cooking
and enzymes 136
microwave 34–5, 48
with quality stainless steel pots 152
co-ordination 189
copper 112, 122, 124, 127, 128, 191
coil 36
functions, benefits and tips 124
coriander 67, 179, 200
corn 20, 49, 90, 123, 154, 190, 214
corrective 107
corium 163
cosmetic(s)
natural 225
surgery 203
toxins 45
cot death 36
coughs and coughing 28, 53, 59, 104, 162, 211
accompanied by a cold 167
chronic 71
counselling 86, 89, 189
Cousins, Norman 232
cows 9–11, **11**, 12, **29**, 122
BGH/BST: bovine growth hormone 11–12
cheese 75
milk 9, 10, 11–12, 35, 75, 90, 125, 157, 165
cramps 58, 60, 118, 119, 166, 168, 170
cranberry 21, 179
juice 61
cranial osteopath 22
creativity 34
Credence Publications 41, 43, 218
crime 2
criticism of other people, avoid 76
Crohn's disease 121, 168
cross-linking 145, 196, 202, 203
crying, excessive (of babies) 36
Crystal Hill Multi Media 37, 218, 223
crystallisation 33
cucumbers 123, 158
Culpepper 132
curcumin 157
cumin 169, 185
cured foods 48
Cure for All Cancers, The (Clark) 59, 232
curved spine 22, 23
cut flowers 73
cycling 89
cypress 160, 179, 187, 201, 202

cystitis 116, 200, 201
cysts 54

D

D'Adamo, Dr Peter 232
Dahlke, Dr Rudiger 231
dairy products 90, 156, 193, 200
　infected 11
Dalai Lama 147
damiana 179, 205
damp conditions, living in 18, 19
dance workshops 218
dancing 49, 89, 167, 203
dandelion 48, 151, 158, 161, 165, 166, 179, 184, 192, 197, 201
　tea 187
dandruff 158, 176
Darkfield microscope (or HLB) test 33–4, 53, 61, 195, 218
Darkfield Microscope Training Institute 219
dates 90, 189, 199
Davis, Dr Devra Lee 45
Davis, Patricia 232
Day, Philip 41, 231
dead, preserving 96
deaths 15, 29, 38, 41, 42, 85
debility 145, 168–9, 174
decongestant 107
deep breathing 78–9, 182
Deet 63
defence system *see* immune system
defensive posturing 23
DeFries, Michael 35, 219, 222, 224
degeneration 114
dehydration 166, 172, 183, 194, 198
demulcent herbs 168, 170
dengue 64, 181
Denmark 6
dental care, lack of 176
dental problems 116
　carries 124
dentists 22, 23–4, 30–1, 129, 200
dentures 25
deodorising 107, 108
depression 10, 17, 24, 29, 31, 38, 69, 80, 83–9, 116, 118, 123, 174, 179, 180, 181, 182, 186, 190, 199
　factors that worsen conditions 85–8
　and histamine 85
　and importance of good mind 83
　and importance of thyroid 84
　manic depression and lithium therapy 84
　rules for body and soul 88–9
dermatophytes 19
Derry, Dr David 46
Desai, Urmila 233
desensitisation 35
despair 70, 85
desperation 87
destructive tendencies 73
Dethlefsen, Thorwald 232
detergent 107
detoxification 43, 58, 77, 88, 95, 96, 104, 107, 113, 127, 129, 134, 135, 138, 151, 157, 171, 172, 176, 184, 190, 192, 195, 196, 200, 201, 205, 209
Dextreit, Raymond 232
Dharam, Guru 80, 81, 230
DHT (DiHydroTestosterone) 158
diabetes 18, 113, 120, 121, 145
Diamond, Harvey and Marilyn 232
diaphoretic 132
diaphragm 81
diarrhoea 14, 17, 25, 53, 55, 57, 58, 120, 129, 161, 168, 169, 170, 182, 194
diesel 38
diet 77, 132
　avoid crash/fashionable diets 88, 205
　bad 45, 103, 151, 191, 192, 193, 199, 203, 204
　cleansing 192
　of excesses 198
　improving 72, 88, 104, 165, 169, 185, 187, 192, 193
　natural whole food 125
　unbalanced 153
dietary fibre 116, 161, 165, 170, 182, 188
Diet Coke 32
digestion 97, 136, 145, 155, 175, 184, 191
　problems 10, 22, 25, 29, 52, 54, 58, 61, 71, 119, 125, 129, 151, 169, 176, 177, 182, 189, 201, 202
digestive enzymes 51, 58, 61, 104, 125, 152, 153, 155, 169, 175, 176, 178, 184, 189, 190, 191, 196, 199, 204, 205
digestive system 75, 77, 83, 91, 190, 211
digestive tract 108, 121
di-hydrotestosterone
dioxin 48
disabled people 3
disease, learn from your 88
disinfectant 107
distension 57
diuretics 120, 198
diverticulitis (bowel pockets) 170, **170**
dizziness 26, 32, 34, 55, 71, 96, 120, 121, 145, 178, 188
doctors 104, 123
dogs 61, 99, **99**
Dominican Republic 43
dopamine 32, 190
doshas 77
Dowling, Dorit Itzhaki 219, 227
dowsers 36
doxycycline 181
Drill Hall Arts Centre 219, 230
drinking water 18, 30, 36
drinks 35
　canned 47, 102
　carbonated 120, 168, 189
　fizzy 10, 32, 120, 170
　soft 137, 172
　sugar-free 189
drowning, nightmare of 70
drug(s)
　abuse 2, 45
　long-term use 51
　medical 18, 27, 29, 31
　recreational 18, 203
　reduction 89
　toxic side effects of 27, 29, 42, 76, 81, 85, 86, 99, 101, 131, 152, 153, 157, 172, 177, 179, 184, 201, 205
dulse 75, 152, 157, 199
Dulwich Health Society 36, 219, 220
duodenum 54, 58
dust 73, 167, 171
Dutch Consumer Federation 14
dwarf tapeworm (*Hymenolepisis nana*) 56, **56**
Dyer, Dr Wayne 232
dysentery 57, 96, 105

E

ear(s)
　aches (otitis media) 105, 170
　candles 170
　how to prepare mullein oil for 210
　imbalance of inner 120
　lobe, crease in 154
　problems 211
　ringing in 120, 188
　wax, excessive 170
earth 108, 130
　damage/pollution to 2, 10
　as element 132
　in Ayurvedic medicine 77
　in feng shui 37
　evolution of 4
　magnetic grid disturbances 37
　replenishing 116–17
Earth Changes 219
earthquakes 37
East West 219
East West Herbs 219
Eat Right Diet, The (D'Adamo) 232
EBV 185
EC (Edgar Cayce) Centre 72, 219–20
echinacea 21, 30, 103, 161, 173, 195
　organic herbal tincture 180
Echo UK 220, 227
E. coli 14
eclosion testing 220
ecology 37, 38
ectomorph 77
Ecuador 6
eczema 17, 66, 129, 131, 170–2
Eden extract 156
Edgar Cayce Collection, The (Cayce) 220, 231
Edwards, Gill 232
EFAs 90
egg(s) 13, 115, 125, 156, 199
　avoid raw 15

free range 909
organic 48, 90
yolks 20, 31, 90, 121, 153
Egypt, ancient 41, 95
elasticity 115, 123, 124, 203
elastin 145, 203
elbows, scaly skin on (psoriasis) 192
elderberry flowers 30, 151, 173
elderflower 180, 192, 195
elderly people 30, 89, 124, 129, 137
electrical equipment 35
electric currents 110
electricity 110
electrodes 110
electrolytes 51, 52, 169
electromagnetic frequencies *see* EMFs
electromagnetic radiation 135
electro-micro-diffraction 126
electrons
    discharge of 110
    exchange of 110–11
elements 108, 113, 115, 132, 155
    in Ayurvedic medicine 77–8
    on earth's crust 105
    in feng shui 37
    trace 33, 52, 112, 127, 191
elimination 97, 155, 161, 164, 167, 188, 192, 209
Elysia Natural Skincare 225
'EM': An Earth Changing Revolution (Higa) 220, 232
EM (Effective Micro-organism) technology 3–6, 220, 233
embalming 96
EMFs (electromagnetic frequencies) 35–6, 177
emotional disorders 18, 34. 37, 154, 170, 196
    upset 18, 69, 73, 170
emotions 83, 84
    purifying 131–2
employment, loss of 85, 87
EMX 6
Enderlein Enterprises 219, 220
endocrine system 198
    balance 186
endolimax nana 54
endomorph 77
endurance 77
energy 37, 60, 77, 81, 83, 120, 136
    congealed 197
    lack of 53, 69, 174, 186, 190
    sand bath (ESB) 43–4, **44**
enema(s) 74, 77, 167, 170, 190, 192, 195
    coffee 184, 209–10
    colonic hydrotherapy 210
    how to prepare 209–10
    other suggestions for 210
    water 210
entamoeba coli 54
entamoeba histolytica 54
environment
    acidic 203
    issues 88

problems 4, 154
repair of 5, 23
toxins 43, 45
Environmental Working Group (EWG) 49
enzyme(s) 10, 22, 24, 25, 31, 42, 47, 48, 97, 100, 111, 113, 117, 118, 120, 121, 124, 129, 145, 146, 164
    activation of (body catalysts) 136
    and clay 136
    lack of 71, 169
    therapy 52
Enzyme Process 212, 219, 220, 228
ephedra 74
epidermic tissue 119
epilepsy 123
epithelial tissues 118
Epsom salt baths 75, 157
Epstein, Dr Samuel 45
Epstein Bar 174
equilibrium 104
Erasmus, Udo 160, 232
essential fatty acids 20, 153, 163, 164, 171, 176, 178, 184, 186, 189, 193, 196, 204
essential oils 64, 146, 151, 152, 154, 155, 157, 160, 168, 172, 176, 180, 184, 187, 194, 200, 201, 204
Essiac 48
ether 77, 132
ethyl alcohol 64
eucalyptus 173, 174, 198
    honey 76
    oil 67, 154, 162, 195
    tea 76
euphrasia 171
Europe 1, 11, 13, 15, 56, 72, 73, 95, 96, 135
evening primrose oil 160, 171, 186, 191, 193
excitement 158
exercise(s) 23, 45, 70, 89, 121, 158, 159, 161, 165, 182, 185, 190, 196, 199, 203, 204
    Breath of Fire 80, **80**
    breathing 78–9, 162, 182
    Kapalabathi 78, 81–2
    lack of 204
    light weight bearing 204
    relaxation posture 80–1, **80**
    Sun Salutations (*Surya Namaskara*) 78–9, **79**, 182
    for voice 81
exfoliation 205
exhalations 78–81, 162
exhaustion 38, 69, 85, 129, 168, 172, 174, 185
expiration 146
extra-cellular fluids 119
EWG *see* Environmental Working Group
eye(s) 54, 131, 171–2
    bags 172
    bath 171
    blue rings around 53

brows 194, 195, 198
cataracts in 123

F

face, scaly skin on (psoriasis) 192
facial mask, clay **140**, 149, 151, 152, 165, 171, 172, 175, 196, 205, 207
facial massage 207
facial neuralgia 188
faeces 57, 58, 136
see also stools
failing eyesight 123
    health of 123, 171
    irritation 171
    itchy 53, 171
    lids, drooping 198
    problems 188
    strain 177
    wash 95, 171
    see also vision
fainting 71, 178
Far East 33, 54
Farida Sharan's School of Natural Medicine 220, 226
'far infra red rays' 43
farmers 10, 12, 15, 46, 47, 116
farming methods
    intensive 52
    natural 10
fast foods 10, 11, 103
fasting 157, 170, 172, 173, 176, 190, 210
fatigue 54, 122, 138, 178
    chronic 52
fat(s) 103, 112, 113, 114, 120, 125, 136, 137, 156, 159, 161, 165,184, 185, 189–90, 193, 198, 203, 209
    cells 163–4
    low 44
Fats that Heal, Fats that Kill (Erasmus) 160, 232
fatty acids 120, 156
fava beans 191
FDA 2, 49, 99
fear 70, 76, 83, 85, 118, 183, 189
feet 54, 57, 188, 193, 202
    bath 173
    care 173
    cold 199
    soles of 166
    swollen 119
    tingling 199
    verrucas on 202
feng shui 37, 220
Feng Shui Network International 220
fennel 74, 169, 201
    essential oil of 161
    tea 176
    infusions 161
fenugreek 74
fermentation 169
ferrous iron, transformation into ferric iron 110
fertilisers 31, 116
fertility problems 121, 199

fever(s) 14, 27, **28**, 30, 63, 64, 65, 168, 172, 174, 180, 181
feverfew 26
fibre *see* dietary fibre
fibrin 145
fibrocystic breast lumps 46
fibromatosis 42
fight/flight response 23
figs 58
filarial elephantiasis (*Wuchereria bancrofti*) 63
filtering drinking water 31, 64, 152
financial problems 85
fingernails
    brittle 119, 123
    hardening of 123
    white spots on 71, 122
fingers 194
Finland 123
fire
    breath 80, **80**
    as element 77, 108, 132, 154
first-aid kit 180
First World War 38
fish 18, 54, 191
    deepwater 20, 47, 48, 76, 90
    flukes 55
    freshwater 56
    migration changes 37
    oil 156, 191
    tapeworm (*Diphyllobothrium latum*) 55, 56
    undercooked or raw 55
    white 20, 76, 90, 168, 189, 192
fissures 73
Fit for Life (Diamond and Diamond) 232
fizzy drinks *see under* drinks
flatulence 108, 168, 169
flavouring 204
flax 90
    seed 158, 161, 163, 168, 179, 189, 191, 205
    oil 58, 153, 192, 193, 194, 200
flies 56
flour
    refined 151, 157
    white 48, 114, 178
flowers 96
flu *see* influenza
fluid(s), body 137, 184
    retention 119
flukes (*trematodes*) 54–5, **55**, 61
fluoride 30–1
fluorine 31, 110, 112
fly killer sprays 167
FMD (foot and Mouth Disease) 16
foetus 58, 120
folic acid 56, 121, 153
food(s) 35
    additives 34, 47, 75, 87, 102, 152, 184, 189, 193, 204
    allergies 26, 71
    combining 177
    contaminated 56

    fatty 188
    fresh 46
    fried 153, 172, 178
    GM 1—2, 46, 100, 102, 205
    greasy 168, 177
    green 48, 203
    low sugar 168
    organic 2, 12, 10, 15, 31, 32, 46–7, 49, 52, 99, 100, 182
    poisoning 14, 15, 29, 95–6, 169
    pre-cooked 102, 172
    processed 120, 152, 169, 178
    raw 157
    refined 19, 172
    rich 165
    spicy 168, 182
    super green 180
    sweetened 180
Foods that Heal 233
forehead 167
forgiveness 77
formaldehyde 31
fox *see* wild fox
fractures 123
    clay for healing 95, 105
    susceptibility to 118
France 6, 111, 126
frankincense oil 207
Frawley, Dr David 232
free radicals 35, 111, 118, 203
free-range 15
French Clay Study Group 126
fresh foods and drinks 46
Fresh Water Filter Co. Ltd 220, 230
fried foods 153, 172, 178
Friends of the Earth 102, 220
fringe tree bark 197
frozen foods/drinks 47
fruit(s) 3, 4, 21, 32, 42, 45, 47, 49, 76, 90, 97, 104, 117, 119, 125, 138, 152, 156, 161, 171, 179, 182, 183, 184, 186, 189, 190, 204
    juices 19, 42, 47, 90, 157
    concentrated 178
    steamed 76
    unwaxed 34
    very sweet 178
    waxed 34
frying in oil 160
fuel efficiency 5
fumitory 151
fungicides 34, 47
fungus 14, 82, 152, 170, 203
    in blood 34
    candida 17–18
    tips 20
    as hidden cause of many ailments 17–21
    mycotoxins 18–19
furuncle 133, 173

G

Galen, Claudius van 41, 132
gallbladder 52, 89, 90, 136, 182, 209
    flush 197

    stones 197
Game of Life and How to Play It, The (Scovel Shinn) 233
gangrene 193
garbage, recycling of 3
gargling 174, 198, 200
garlic 20, 21, 47 48, 58, 59, 61, 74, 75, 154, 155, 156, 157, 158, 159, 167, 173, 180, 185, 192, 193, 195, 205, 210–11
    juice 58, 201, 202
    kyolic 168
    oil 20
    how to prepare 210–11
    soup 211
    treatment for asthma 211
gas, excess 153
gastro-intestinal disorder 176
Gates, Bill 63
General Council and Register of Osteopaths 220, 227
genes 4, 5
Genesis 95
genetic causes 170
genetic damage 31
gentian 199
geomancers 36
Geomancing in Britain 37
geopathic stress 36, 220
George Oshawa Macrobiotic Foundation 224
geranium 176, 200, 201
Germany 13, 19, 27, 35, 43, 96
germs 51, 82, 104, 105, 189, 199
Ghana 63
giardia lamblia 54
Gibran, Kahlil 70
ginger 74, 104, 155, 159, 165, 173, 182, 183, 193, 195, 200, 201
    juice 210
    and lemon hot drink 173
    root 168
    tea, how to prepare 211
    water compresses 183
ginkgo biloba extract 23, 103, 153, 158, 160, 179, 193
ginseng 159, 160, 187, 191, 205
Giovanni Hair Care 221, 226
GI tract 17, 168, 185
GLA 192, 193, 205
    capsules 189
    fatty acids 20, 76, 153, 156
glands
    enlargement of 70
    regulation of 120
    swollen 143
glandular
    fever (mononucleosis) 129, 174
    rejuvenation 169
glass test 30
GM food 1–2, 46, 100, 102, 205
global warming 4
globe artichoke 158, 159, 184
glomeruli 200
glucose 137, 145

Index

gluten 165, 186, 188
glutinous waste 17
glycerine 161, 201
    vegetable 64, 177, 207
glyco-proteins 168
glycosaminoglycans 193
goat(s)
    cheese 31, 75, 90
    milk 12, 13, 31, 75, 90, 119, 125, 157
    yoghurt, live 20, 42
goitre 114
golden rod 131, 172, 175, 183, 192, 195, 196, 201
golden seal 21, 74, 159, 165, 168, 173, 180, 195
    powdered 163
    tincture 155, 163
Goldstone 30
Gomasio 91
gonorrhoea 73
Good News on Cancer, The (Richards) 234
gossip 83
    avoid 76
gota kola 164, 205
gout 14, 90, 114, 115, 193, 200
grains, whole 10, 13, 14, 15, 41, 49, 75, 90, 115, 123, 125, 152, 156, 183, 184, 189, 190, 195
granulomas 53
grapefruit 179
    oil 176
    seed extract 20, 58
grape(s) 49, 157
    juice 197
    red 156
    seed 169, 198
gravelroot 198, 201
greasy food 168, 177
Greece, ancient 41, 95, 132
green clay *see under* clay
green drink 115
green foods *see under* foods
green tea 193
Greenways Natural Health Centre 216, 221
grey sounds 81
grieving 156
gridlines 36
grinding teeth 23, 53
groundwater, poisoning of 47
growth accelerators 2
Guild of Naturopathic Iridologists 221
gum(s) 58, 120, 171
    and chewing 24—6
    disease 174–5
gut 105
gynaecological disorders 71

H

haemoglobin 121, 124
haemolysis 111
haemorrhage 71, 129
haemorrhoids 116
haemostatic 107
Hahnemann, Samuel 63, 66, 73
hair(s)
    animal 73
    baldness 158
    care: with clay 175–6
    colour loss 122
    dandruff 158, 176
    dry, brittle 53, 71, 119, 122, 175
    falling/loss 53, 119, 122, 158, 175
    greasy 176
    and head lice 66–8
    effective treatment 67–8
    and kidneys 183
    line 194
    shiny 176
    spray 167
    strong/healthy 60, 68, 123, 175
Hair-Lyte 225
Haitan 34
Hale Clinic, London 23, 220, 221
halitosis 176–7
ham 13
Handbook of the Bach Flower Remedies, The (Chancellor) 232
hand(s) 193, 194
    care 177
    clay bath **140**
    cold 199
    mask 177
    tingling 199
    tremors in 190
hangover 177
harmonisers 35
Harwood, A.C. 232
Hauschka, Dr 207, 225
    sage footbath 166, 173
hawthorn berry 131, 153, 158
    infusion/tincture 156
    tea 153
hay fever 17, 152
HDL (good cholesterol) 156
headaches 22, 25, 26, 27, 30, 32, 34, 52, 55, 58, 64, 121, 128, 177–8, 181, 188, 199
head
    circulation to 23
    fuzzy 32
    lice 66–8
    effective treatment for 67–8
    injuries 22–3
    pains in 24
healing 107, 122
    crisis 66
    process 103
see also clay
Healing Power of Illness (Dethlefsen and Dahlke) 232
health
    restoring 103
    tips and general guidelines 90–1
Health Systems 227
Health World 216, 221
Healthy House 221
Heal Thyself (Bach) 231

heart 57, 62, 83, 89, 90, 91, 118, 131, 136, 153, 156, 166, 189
    attack 118, 119
    beat 119, 120, 130
    broken 131
    conditions 53, 97, 154, 186
    disease 34, 113, 118, 165
    muscle improvement 118
    palpitations 121
    protection of 120
    rate 72
    strain on 71, 179
heat imaging lasers 45
heavy metal 38, 122, 129
    poisoning through amalgam fillings 178
Helios Homoeopathics 223
helping others 76
hepatic drainage 128
hepatitis A 42
herbalists 22, 27, 159, 164, 179, 187, 202, 208, 221–222
herbal remedies 59
    for parasites
    intensive treatment 59–60
    more treatments 60–1
    teas 75, 138, 173, 190
Herbamere 91
Herbco 222
herbicides 47
Herb Research Foundation 221
herbs 21, 23, 24, 26, 27, 48, 59–60, 76, 88, 96, 125, 131, 132, 153, 169, 173, 197
hereditary factors 168, 172, 201
herpes 17, 174, 185
    zoster (shingles) 194–5
Heyn, Birgit 233
hidden factors of illness 7–91
    miscellaneous 27–39
hiding of condition 70
Higa, Dr Teruo 2, 233
Higher Nature 222
higher self 88
high fat diet 171, 188
high fibre
    breakfast 178
    diet 20
high protein
    to be avoided 199
    diets 137, 168
Hildreth and Cocker 216, 217, 222
Himalayas 41
hippocampus 152
Hippocrates 70, 132
Hippocrates Diet and Health Program, The (Wigmore) 234
Hippocrates Health Institute 222
hips, aches and pains in 121
histamine and depression 85
HIV 17
hives (uticaria) 66, 201
HLB (Humoral Pathological Blood) test 33–4, 43, 44, 171
Holford, Patrick 233–234

Holistic Health College 222, 226
Holland *see* Netherlands, the
holographic materials 35, 222
'Holy Water' 96
homeostasis 91
home enema kits 222
home therapy for cancer 46
homocystine levels 156
Homoeopathic Pharmacies 28
homoeopathic supplies 223
homoeopathic treatments 23, 28, 33, 59, 73, 163, 181
  for malaria 63–4
homoeopaths 35, 59, 73–4, 181, 222
homoeopathy 63, 66, 145, 155, 197, 199, 201
Homoeopathy: Medicine of the New Man (Vithoulkas) 234
honey 13, 65, 91, 104, 200, 211
  eucalyptus 76
Hong Kong 15
hope
  of recovery, living in 70
hopelessness 85, 87
hops 182
hormone(s) 14, 25, 26, 49, 102, 117, 120, 182, 184, 186, 191, 198, 205
  imbalance 103, 187
  problems 195
  therapy 45
horse chestnut 164, 201, 202
horseradish 184
horsetail 123, 157, 158, 201, 202, 205
hospital(s)/hospitalisation 100, 101, 174
  treatment 108
hot and cold baths 27
hot flushes 186
hot liquids 165
hot tubs, chlorinated 59
household
  dust 73
  toxins 45
'how to's 209–13
  make infusion 209
  make your own barley or wheatgrass juice 212
  prepare cabbage leaf poultice 212
  prepare enema 209–10
  prepare garlic oil 210–11
  prepare ginger tea 211
  prepare lemon tea 211
  prepare mullein oil for ears 210
  skin brushing with wood and bristle brush 212–13
  test your pH balance 212
How to Manifest Your Destiny (Dyer) 232
HRT (hormone replacement therapy) 186, 187
humic acid 116
humidifier 154, 162
humoral pathology 132
  blood testing (HLB)24, 61, 199, 218

humours, in body 130
Hunza 41, 125, 203
hydrangia 198, 201
hydration 107, 135, 146
hydrochloric acid 52, 136, 153, 155, 175
hydrogen 110, 111, 113, 115
  fuel cells, cars powered by 38
hydrogenated fats 159
hydrotherapy 27
hydroxyl 110
hygiene 58
  lack of 19
hyperacid stomach 125
hyperactivity 29, 31, 34, 71, 72, 85, 118, 121
hyper-peristalsis 58
hypertension 118, 156
hyperthyroidism 32
hypoglycaemia (low blood sugar) 58, 71, 85, 178–9, 186, 189
hypothalamus 198
hypothyroidism 71

I

ice cream 19, 91
iced drinks 91
IGF (insulin-like growth factors) 11
Illite 126, 128
illness 4
  hidden factors of 7–91
immune system 5, 10, 51, 121, 135, 165, 184
  deficiencies/problems 18, 24, 28–9, 30, 31, 34, 35, 40, 44, 53, 71, 73, 77, 100, 145, 152, 163, 168, 185, 188, 189, 194, 199, 204
  protection of 25, 28, 46. 47, 58, 180, 189, 195, 211
  restoring 41, 42, 115, 118, 130
  see also AIDS
immunisation 63
Immuno Augmentative Therapy Centre 217, 223
immuno-globin A deficiency 18
immunologists 43
impotence 122, 124, 163, 179
inability to cope 17, 85
in-breath 78
Inca 179
incurable diseases 5
indathrene blue 33
India 15, 29, 91
  philosophy 69, 82
indifference to suffering 69
indigestion 54, 55
Indonesia 64, 181
industrial waste 31
infancy 18
infants 27, 35
infections 23, 25, 121, 122, 189, 199
  chronic/frequent 71, 185
  viral 38, 174, 185
  or bacterial 180
Infectoclear 20

inferiority, feelings of 70
inflammation 56, 77, 157, 165, 168, 188, 197, 199, 203
influenza ('flu) 15, 65, 104, 122, 145, 155, 173, 180
injections 30
  like symptoms 29, 30, 64
information 36
infusions, herbal 30
  how to make 209
inhalants 77
inhalation(s) 78–81, 154, 162
  clay 195
inherited (endogenous) features 84
inhalers 72
injections 42
injuries 95, 204
  head or neck 23
injustice, feelings of 86
inland seawater 119
inner child 89
inner ear imbalance 120
inner fire 77
inoculations 185
  see also vaccinations
insecticides 47, 62
insect(s) 56, 63, 102
  bites 71, 169, 180–1
  see also mosquitoes
insecurity 87, 189
insomnia 57, 70, 86, 87, 118, 182
  see also sleep(ing)
inspiration 77
instability, emotional 57
Institute for Naturopathy and Metabolic Medicine 219
Institute of Complementary Medicine 223
Institute of Optimum Nutrition 223
Institute of Phytobiophysics 227
Institute of Radio Technology 35
intelligence 34
intensive care 29
interferon 47
International Association of Colon Therapists 218, 223
International Chiropractors Association 217, 223
International Earth Emergency Network 37, 223
International Federation of Aromatherapists (IFA) 216, 224
International Healing Centre, Philippines 228
International Iridology Research Association (IIRA) 224
International Kundalini Yoga Teachers Association 224, 230
International Macrobiotic Institute 224
International Society for Orthomolecular Medicine 44
Internet 35, 50
intestinal flora 17
intestinal mucosa 57, 58
intestinal mycosis 19

intestinal parasites 20, 52
intestinal regulator 107
intestines 52, 54, 56, 57, 58, 113, 118, 161, 165
  obstruction of 55
  problems 55, 176
intoxication 177
intracellular fluids 119
intravenous drug treatment 100
iodine 46, 110, 112, 114, 152, 199
iodised salt 114
ion 110, 113, 135
  exchange 107
Ion & Light Co. 230
ionisation 110, 126
ioniser 23, 111
Iredale, Jane 225–226
Iredale Mineral Cosmetics 224
iridology 43, 44, 53, 74, 100, 199, 225–6, 230
iris 53
Irish moss 162, 163, 176, 199
IRM 77 microbiological laboratory, France 126
iron 109, 110, 112, 114, 120, 121, 124, 127, 129, 158, 204
  functions, benefits and tips 121
  oxide 128
  supplements 121
irrationality 199
irritability 55, 57, 72, 118
irritable bowel syndrome (IBS, aka spastic colitis) 104, 170, 182
isolation 69, 115
iseoleucine 114
itching 57, 66, 95, 129, 171, 201
  of anus 53
ivy, extract of 165
Iyashiro chi 5

J

jacuzzi 59
jaguars 98
Janov, Dr Arthur 233
Japan 2, 5, 15, 43, 48, 56, 75, 84, 146, 147, 190, 204, 218
jasmine 179
  essential oil 161
jaundice 63
jaw 22–3, 25
jealousy 76
Jensen, Dr Bernard xiii, 10, 44, 77, 83, 166, 219, 224, 233
jetlag 129, 183
job, loss of 85
John Bell and Croydon Pharmacy 222, 224
joints
  aches and pains of 53, 57, 121, 157
  rheumatic inflammation of 193
joy 83, 131, 154, 156
juices
  body 104
  fruit *see* fruit juices

jungle 97–8
juniper berry 167, 180, 183, 196, 198
junk food 104

Jurasunas, Prof. Serge 42, 43, 44, 50, 200, 219

K

kale 20, 90, 168
kaoline 128
kaolinite 126, 129
Kapalabathi 78, 81–2
Kapha 77
karma 82
Karma and Reincarnation (Motoyama) 82, 233
Kava Kava 102–3
kelp 46, 75, 152, 157, 165, 179, 187, 199
Kent, J.T. 155
Kenya 63
Khalsa, Dr Dharma Singh 233
Khella 153
kidney(s) 48, 62, 83, 89, 90, 100, 113, 129, 131, 135, 136, 169, 170, 171, 172, 175, 178, 189, 192, 196, 198, 200, 201
  problems 145, 158, 175, 183, 195
  purifying emotions 131–2
  stones 90, 115, 116, 118, 198
  weakness of 71, 119, 159
kindness 76, 89
Kindred Spirit 235
kinesiology 26
kissing 28, 174
kiwis 32, 49, 179
knees
  aches and pains in 121
  scaly skin (psoriasis) 192
Kneipcure 96
Kneipp, Father Sebastian 27, 96, 233
Kneippiannum 96
knocks 196
Kolorex 20, 202
Krebs, Ernst 41
Kundalini and the Chakras (Paulson) 233–234
Kundalini yoga: Breath of Fire 80, 230
Kushi Foundation for One Peaceful World 227
Kyushu Island, Japan 43

L

Lacey, Dr Richard 10
lactation 121, 161
lactate 137
lacteals 185
lactic acid 137
Lad, Dr Vasant 232
ladies slipper (cypripedium calceolus) 191
laetrile (vitamin B17) 41–2, 216
lagoon sentiment 111

L. arginine 20, 59, 60
Lamberts 167, 224
lamb(s) 10
  organic 90
Lapacho 21
  tea 20
larch pine 154
large intestine 54, 57, 161, **170**
  vermiform appendix of **52**
Larium 181
larvae 54, 57, 58
laser therapy 99
La Tourelle, Maggie 233
lavender 151, 154, 157, 162, 163, 170, 174, 176, 177, 180, 182, 183, 184, 187, 188, 196
  flowers 173, 188
  oil 181
laxative(s) 1257
  herb 59
LDL cholesterol (bad cholesterol) 153, 156
L dopamine 191
leaf crops 123
learning ability 117
lecithin 88, 90, 153, 156, 158, 160, 162, 164, 171, 177, 184, 189, 193, 197, 202, 205
Lee, Dr John 186
leeks 184
Leeson, Nick 52
Legarde 34
Legionnaire's disease 59
legs 188
  tremors in 190
lemonade 19
lemon(s) 32, 157, 168, 195, 200, 201, 202, 205
  balm infusion 154, 177, 182, 201
  essential oil 177, 202
  and ginger hot drink 173
  juice 156, 177, 197, 210
  tea, how to prepare 211
lentils 47, 90, 115, 183
lesions (scar-tissue) 188
Lessons of the Lotus (Wimala) 234–235
lethargy 17, 116, 189
lettuce 122
leucine 114
leucorrhoea 57
Levisticum eardrops 170
libido, low 186
lice *see* head: lice
lies 83
life 110
  expectancy 189
life root 187
lifestyle 203, 206
lifeyeast, benficial, Zell oxygen155
ligaments 137
light 120, 130
Lightning Strikes a Hummingbird (Perry) 233–234
Lima 1
lime

blossoms 196
essential oil 207
flowers 131, 156
infusion 154
juice 155
Lindlarh, Dr Henry 66, 233
linseed 76, 161
oil 20
lipase 136
lipotropic 153
lips, dry and cracked 123
liquid Tracelytes 27
liquorice 21, 74, 173, 179, 180, 187
tincture 155, 163, 167
lithium 127, 128
therapy and manic depression 84
liver 31, 42, 48, 52, 54, 59, 60, 61, 62, 83, 89, 119, 121, 122, 124, 125, 135, 136, 153, 155, 156, 165, 169, 170, 171, 172, 174, 179, 182, 187, 189, 192, 198, 200, 201, 209
cancer 18
problems 55, 90, 158, 183–4, 188, 195, 201
Living Magically (Edwards) 232
Living with Your Body (Buhler) 231
lobelia 74
London 28, 38, 39, 62, 168, 218, 227
loneliness 87, 115, 189
longevity 75
L. ornithine 59, 60
lorries 38
Los Angeles 11, 41
loss of loved ones 85
love 82, 89, 116
and marriage 77
low-calorie/whole food diet 189
low-cost farming 3
low fat, low protein diet 44, 137, 156, 158, 188, 190, 197
low-weight-bearing exercises 196
Lucy (cat) 100
lumps 105
lung(s) 19, 54, 55, 57, 58, 65, 69, 72, 76, 82, 83, 136, 156
problems 30, 38, 69, 71, 74, 145
see also asthma
lungwort 123
lupus 32
Luvos mud xiii
Lymphdiarral ointment 154
lymphocytes 123, 184, 185
lymph 161, 164
congestion 184–5, 195
fluid 146
system 118, 155, 189, 195, 200
problems 23, 46, 63, 174
lymphatic drainage massage 185
lysine 114, 163, 188, 195

M

maca **106**, 153, 169, 179, 186, 187
macaw 97–8, **97**, **98**
Machu Picchu **127**

macrobiotic diet 25–6, 147, 186, 188, 189, 221
Macro-biotic Guide Book for Living, The (Oshawa) 233

Macrobiotics for Planetary Health and Peace 227
Macrobiotics Today 224, 235
macrophages 145
McVeigh, Tracey 36
mad cow's disease 9
magnesium 20, 112, 117–18, 120, 127, 137, 186, 187, 193, 194, 202
functions, benefits and tips 118
supplements076
magnetic energy therapy 43, 46
magnetic grid disruption 37
magnetic resonance imaging 45
magnetism 108, 121, 124
magnets 35
maize 18, 19
malaria 62–5, 181
homoeopathic treatments 63–4
male fern 61
mammogram 40, 45
manganese 112, 120, 124, 127, 155
functions, benefits and tips 120
mangoes 47, 90
mania 29
manic depression 32, 87
and lithium therapy 84
Manic Depression Fellowship 224
mantras 80
mantric chanting 197
maple syrup 91
Marcellus Empiricus 41
Marks & Spencer 14
marshmallow 163, 166, 168, 170, 200
root 201
mask, clay 140, 141, 149, 151, 152, 165, 171, 172, 175, 196, 205
massage 72, 154, 157, 160, 161, 164, 166, 168, 173, 178, 187, 193, 194, 205
oil 169
Maxwell, John 225, 229
McTimoney Chiropractic Association 217, 225
McTimoney chiropractic treatment 23, 162
ME (myalgic encephalomyelitis) 17, 31, 174, 185–6
meals, small (little and often) 75, 190
measles 27
meat 4, 20, 45, 115, 117, 170, 189, 192, 203
derivatives 97
infected 10, 13–15
red 48, 75, 90, 138, 156
undercooked 58
medication 95, 101, 208
wrong 86
medicine 70
and astrology 32
meditation 77, 78, 80, 88, 204

medulla 71, 72
mefloquine 63
Mein Wasser Kur (*My Water Cure*) (Kneipp) 233
melatonin 182, 183
melissa 131, 173, 176, 199
melons 123
memory
aids 24
loss 17, 31, 85, 118, 120, 152
meningitis 27, 28–30, 225
B 28–30
C 28, 30
Nosode 28
menopause 45
cessation of female cycle 186–7
symptoms of 124
menstrual problems 17, 71, 123
menstruation 187–8, 199
heavy 153
problems 187–8
mental
disorders 34, 124
effects of asthma 69–70
effects on physical 83
pollution 2
strength 77
Mental Health and Illness (Pfeiffer and Holford) 233–234
mercury 124
(amalgam) fillings 24, 189
mesomorph 77
metabolic enzymes 136
metabolic rate 198
metabolism 84, 120, 121, 129, 155, 184
metabolites 136
Metahalloysite 126
metal(s) 113
as element in feng shui 37
fillings 51, 58, 88
heavy 38, 122, 129
poisoning through amalgam fillings 178, 189
toxic 125, 188
methanol 31
methione 114, 162
Mexico 42, 43, 216
miasmic traits 66
miasms 66, 73–4, 125, 154
Michael 83, 87–8
microbes 104
microorganisms 4
Microsoft 63
microwave 43
cooking 34–5, 48
migraines 25, 26
milk 3, 48, 49, 53, 71, 115, 156, 182, 188
allergy and asthma 70
almond 12
cow's 9, 10, 11–12, 35, 90, 125, 157, 165
goat's 12, 13, 31, 75, 90, 119, 125, 157

lactose free 21
  products 71
  rice 12, 21, 75, 90, 157
  sheep's 21
  warm, bath of 53
milk thistle 171, 174, 184, 187, 192, 197, 200, 205
millet 20, 47, 90, 154, 178, 186, 189
mind 78, 130, 136
  and breath 70
  fuzzy 199
  importance of good mind, and depression 83
Mind Miracle, The (Khalsa) 232–233
mineral(s) 33, 42, 58, 72, 85, 88, 90, 105, 109, 112, 136, 137, 146, 155, 158, 168, 182, 186, 191, 193, 196
  action of mineral elements found in clay 117–25
  CHONPS 113–15
  complex 74, 118, 178
  deficiency 163, 165, 175
  imbalance 152, 169, 176, 201
  lack of in soil, and parasites 52–3
  metabolism 125
  micro- 114
  oil 204
  problems with our ability to metabolise 125, 153
  salts 111, 119
  supplements 38, 60, 152, 185, 201, 202, 203
  therapy 27
  trace 112–15, 198
mint 153, 195
miscellaneous hidden factors 27–39
misery 185
Miso soup 75, 91, 115, 195, 211
mistletoe 48
  leaf extract 186
MMR vaccine 27
mobile telephones 35, 177
molasses 114, 121
molecules 110
molybdenum 112, 124, 127, 128
  functions, benefits and tips 124
monkeys 97
monosodium glutamate (MSG) 34
montmorillonites 109
mood(s)
  stabilising 84
  swings 10, 29, 88, 115
moon 130, 132
  solar and lunar energy 130–1
  waxing, and hair cutting 175
Morley, John Vega Machine practitioner 230
Morningstar, Amadea 233
Mosley therapy cente 218
mosquito bites 62–5, **62**, 181
  citronella 64
  Dengue 64
  homoeopathic treatments 63–4
MOT 39

mothers 35
motherworth 187
motivation 174
Motoyama, Dr Hiroshi 233
Motoyama Institute for Life Physics 225
moulds 18
mountain grape 192
mouth 55
  blisters 18, 53
  breathing through 82
  infection 28
  lips, dry and cracked 123
  pains in 25
  rinse 58, 60, 163, 172, 176
  ulcers 17, 25, 188
movement 49, 77, 89
mucin 168
muco-proteins 17
mucosal irritation 168
mucous 17, 69, 70, 75, 77, 82, 85, 90, 104, 119, 155, 157, 182, 214
  colitis 14
  membranes 34, 69
muesli 178
mullein 61, 74, 162, 163, 167, 170, 210
  infusion/tincture 154
  oil for ears, how to prepare 210
multiple sclerosis (MS) 17, 24, 36
  and aspartame 32–3, 188–9
mummification 95
mung beans 47, 157
Munich 96
muscle(s) 118, 119, 137, 145, 189, 193, 196, 204
  activity 118
  contraction 112
  pains 119
  slack 123
  spasms 118, 119
  strength 204
  waste 70
  weakening 202
mushrooms 19
music 49, 89
mustard 20
mycoses 19
mycotoxins 14, 18–19
Mycropyl 20
myelin sheath 188, 189
myrrh 160, 174, 200
myke 18

N

nails *see* fingernails
National Academy of Sciences 33
National Books and Products 225
National Centre for Homoeopathy 223, 225
National Federation of Spiritual Healers (NFSH) 225, 229
National Health Service 40, 87
National Institute of Cancer 42
National Lottery Fund 40

National Meningitis Trust 225
nat mur 197
natrium bicarbonate 33
natural clay *see* clay
natural cosmetics 225
Natural Health 235
Natural History, The (Pliny the Elder) 95
natural pest control 226
Natural Progesterone Information Service 187, 228
nature, back to 102–6
Nature's Path 226
Naturopathic Iridology 226
Naturopathic Research Labs Inc. 226
naturopaths/naturopathic diet 40–1, 43, 60, 65, 66, 72, 86, 99, 152, 157, 184, 197, 206
nausea 55, 58, 181
Neals Yard Remedies 227
neck 153
  injuries 23
  aches and pains 27, 30
nectarine 49
negative
  charge 105, 110, 111, 114, 134
  emotion 76
  energy 37, 89, 219
  thoughts 33
negativity 76, 83, 89
neglect 86
Nelson, Dr Miriam E. 233
nematodes 54
neroli essential oil 183, 207
nerve(s) 119, 122, 188, 193
  activity 118
  cells 38, 114, 190
  endings 194
  impulses 153
  tonic 74
nervine herbs 171, 183, 196
nervousness 53, 179
nervous system 32, 72, 105, 120, 123, 155, 198
  autonomic 190
  disorders of 38, 55, 56, 71, 72, 74, 154, 155, 179, 186
Netherlands, the 6, 12, 13, 15, 59, 61
nettle 123, 131, 158, 194, 201
neuralgia, facial 188
neurological disorders 181
neurologists 22
neurons 31, 190
Neuropas 177
neurosurgery 32
neuro-toxins 31, 49
neurotransmitters 31, 86, 152
neutralising 104, 107
New Capital University of Integrative Medicine 44
New Primal Scream, The (Janov) 233
New York 14, 28, 62, 205
New York Academy of Sciences 44
New Zealand 11, 76, 90
Ng, Master Sam 220

niacin 179
niaouli 151, 154, 162, 166
nightmare of drowning 70
nightshade plants 193
night-time vision problems 122
nipples, sore 161
nitriloside 41
nitrogen 113, 115, 137
Niwa, Dr Y. 43
NOMA, Complex Homoeopathy Ltd
    20, 154, 177, 203, 223, 227, 230
Noni 48, 228
non-toxic products 227
nori 75
normalisation 105
North America 56, 65, 73, 135
nose 28
    picking 53
    red vessels on tip of 153–4
    swollen 153
nourishment 89
nuclear
    industry 45
    power stations 111
nucleus 110
numbness 188
nursery schools 3
nutmeg 187
Nutri Centre 20, 168, 203, 212, 222,
    227, 231, 235
nutrient(s) 114, 121, 124, 169, 184,
    186, 191, 193
    assimilation 24
    destruction 34, 35
    malabsorption of 17
Nutriscene 20
nutrition 157, 188
    good 27, 42
    poor 18, 44, 51, 179
nutritional programme 58
nutritional therapy 204
nuts 19, 20, 90, 115, 152, 155, 178
    ground 115

O
oakbark 194
Oasis Hospital, Mexico 216, 227,
oat(s) 19, 90, 178, 190
    bran 20
oatmeal 121
    scrubs 75
oatstraw 187, 205, 209
obesity 116, 123, 189–90
oceans, changes in currents 37
oedema 119, 131
oestrogen 45, 152, 161, 186
Ohsawa, George 147
oil 90
    frying in 160
old age 18, 118, 146
Oligocene elements 136
olive(s)
    green 157
    leaf extract 21, 30, 155, 169, 181

oil 90, 158, 166, 172, 197, 205,
    210
Omega-3 oils 158, 168, 189, 205
Omega-6 189
One Peaceful World 227
onions 47, 58
open-heart surgery 99
optimism, unrealistic 70
Oracle of Medicine 41
oral thrush 18
orange(s) 34
    blossom 153
    juice 19, 193, 195
Orbito, Rev. Alex L. 228, 229
Order of the Universe, The (Oshawa)
    233
oregano 21, 61, 74, 193, 201
organic foods 2, 12, 10, 15, 31, 32,
    46–7, 49, 52, 99, 100, 182, 205,
    227
Organic Herb Trading Co. 48, 210,
    227
organochlorines 45
organophosphates 9, 49
organ(s) 78, 119, 136, 137
    transplants 99
orthodox medicine 19
orthophenylphenol 34
Oshawa, George 233
osteopathic manipulation 72
osteopaths 22, 23, 227
osteoporosis 90, 137, 186, 198
Oswald 34
out-breath 78, 81
ovaries, problems with 130
oven 43
overeating 75, 88
overheating 189
over the counter (OTC) medicines 152
Ovex 59
ovulation problems 17
oysters 122
oxidation 4, 113, 137
oxygen 1, 74, 110, 113, 115, 121, 122,
    130, 145, 193, 198
    increasing levels of 80
    lack of 70, 73, 77, 146, 172
    therapy 220, 228
oxygenation 77, 160, 167, 172
Oxypro 20
ozone layer 1, 37

P
pacemaker 109, 153
pain 138, 139, 168, 196
    killers, natural 99, 105
paints
    non-toxic 73
    strong-smelling 45
    toxic 72–3, 125, 167
Pakistan 41
pallor 70, 121
palm oil 123
palpitations 32

pancreas 10, 42, 52, 90, 121, 124, 136,
    178, 179, 189
pancreatic enzymes 20, 42, 47, 179,
    200, 227
panic attacks 32, 70
Pao d'Arco 21
papain 48
papaya(s) 47, 48, 61, 156, 170, 184,
    189
    juice 42
paralysis, partial 32
parasite(s) 17, 22, 24, 26, 46, 51–61,
    54, 55, 62–4, 66, 71, 82, 85, 95,
    153, 170, 171, 172, 178, 181,
    189, 195, 196, 210
    herbal treatment 59–60
    how do you know if someone has
        them? 53
    how to get rid of them and
        prevent them from returning 58–9
    and lack of minerals in soil 52–3
    more herbal treatments 69–1
    programme 24, 53, 200
    toxoplasmosis 58
    types of 53–8
    wild fox and 61
parasitic bowel invasion **52**
parasitic infections 104
parathyroid glands 198
parents 35
    suffering bereavement/loss 28
Parkinsonism (Parkinsons's disease) 32
    degenerative neurological disorder
        190
parotid gland 25
parrots 98
parsley 20, 75, 157, 159, 178, 184,
    211
parsnips 158
Pasco 154
passion flowers 177, 182
pasta 19, 177, 190
pathogens 104, 185
Patient, Not the Cure, The (Blackie)
    231
pau d'arco 185
Paulson, Genevieve Lewis 233–234
peaches 41, 49
peanut(s) 18, 19, 123, 195
    oil 157
peas 123, 214
pelvis
    imbalance in 23
    misalignment 154
pendants 35
peppercorns 177
peppermint 30, 166, 168, 169, 173,
    177, 180, 182, 184, 194, 195, 201
    leaves, infusion of 173, 210
    tea 129, 169, 176
pepper(s) 123, 156, 168, 193
perception, doors of 83
perfumes, strong-smelling chemical 45,
    161
perichondrium 204

periods, heavy 71
Perry, Foster 233–234
perspiration 53, 65, 120, 136
Peru 6, 15, 21, 63, 97–8, **97**, **127**, 179, 186
Peruvian Indians 62
pest control, natural 225
pesticides 2, 18, 45, 47, 49, 102, 107, 116, 117, 122, 125, 152, 161, 182, 191, 204, 205
  and breast cancer 45–6
petrol 38
pets 56, 89, 203
Pezerat, Prof. 126
Pfeiffer, Dr Carl 233–234
pH balance 18, 19, 51, 52, 77, 104, 119, 120, 130, 152, 155, 167
  how to test 212
  changes 137
  imbalance 23, 146
pharynx 57
phenylalanine 31, 114
Philadelphia 15
Philippines 228
Philosophy of Natural Therapeutics (Lindlahr) 66, 233
phlegm (phlegmatic) 119, 132
phobias 84
phosgene 38
phosphate(s) 125
  fertilisers 31
phosphorus 112, 113, 114, 118, 119, 120, 127
  functions, benefits and tips 120
photographing 'thought forms' 33
photo-phobia 70
phyllitic structure 128, 129
phyllitous clay 109
physical strength, lack of 70
Physicians for Responsible Medicine 12
Phyto-biophysics 228
pickled foods 48
pickles 19, 91
pigs 3, **12**, 12–13
pigs pest 12
Pilates 23, 159, 196, 205, 228
Pilates Studio 228
Pill, The 117
pine, oil of 162
pineal gland 182
pineapple(s) 48, 123
  juice 157
pins and needles 188
pinworm (*Oxyuris vermicularis*) 51, 54, 57, **57**, 59
Pita 77
pituitary gland 26, 118, 120, 130, 198
pizza 11
plague 10
planets 132
plant(s) 54, 61, 77, 96, 122
  foods 45, 197
  withering 237
plaque 165, 171, 176, 188
plasma 146

Plasmodium falciparum 63
plaster dust 73
plastic surgery 203
platinum 38
Pliny the Elder 41, 95
plums 47, 184, 189
  umebushi 48, 160, 180
PMS (pre-menstrual syndrome) 52
PMT (pre-menstrual tension) 122
pneumonia 19, 59
poisoning 63
  food *see* food poisoning
  mercury 24
poison(s) 31, 33, 45, 98, 184, 204
  gas 38
poke root 21, 161, 168
politicians 35
politics 37
pollen 167
pollution 1, 3, 4, 10, 38, 145, 184, 204
  environmental 45, 72, 145, 204
  traffic 38–9, 72
  water 3, 47, 48, 145
polysaccharides 193, 204
pomegranate 61
poppy extract 162
population 4
pork 55
  tapeworm (*Taeniasis solium*) 55, **55**
porridge 47, 169, 186
portal vein 5
Portugal 43, 219
positive
  approaches
    in cancer treatment 49–50
    and obesity 180
  charge 105, 110, 111, 114, 134
  energy 37, 89
  thoughts 33, 76, 205
postmenopausal women 118
posture(s) 79, 80, 82
  bad 23, 70
  defensive 23
  relaxation 80–1, **80**
potassium 110, 112, 114, 118, 119–20, 127, 137, 157, 194, 202, 205
  functions, benefits and tips 119–20
phosphate 119
potatoes 90, 98, 114, 122, 123, 157, 193
pottery 111, 126
poultice
  cabbage leaf, how to prepare 212
  clay 27, 74, 75, 109, 139–43, 151, 153, 154, 155, 157, 161–2, 163, 167, 170, 172, 173, 174, 177, 180, 183, 184, 187, 192, 194, 195, 196–7, 198, 200, 201–2, 211
  for breast lumps 161–2
poultry 14
poverty 46
Power Eating Programme: You Are How

You Eat (Stanchich) 234

Practice of Aromatherapy, The (Valnet) 234
Prakuti, Your Ayurvedic Constitution (Svoboda) 234
pre-cooked food 102, 172
pregnancy 18, 45, 58, 59, 121, 181, 208
  unwanted 117
premature ageing 32, 116, 202
preservatives 102, 114, 126
preserves 91
preventative 135
primary schools 66
prion 9–10
processed foods 120, 152, 169, 178
Progest 187
progesterone 228
proglottids 55, **56**
prolapses 119
Propolis 20, 167, 174
prostaglandin levels 168
prostate gland 121
  cancer 191
  congestion 191–2
  enlargement 158
prostatitis 52
protease 136
protein(s) 10, 15, 77, 90, 112, 113, 114–15, 120, 121, 136, 145, 158, 163, 176, 178, 190, 198, 205
  low 44, 191
protomorphogens 169, 174, 179, 228
protons 110
protozea 58
Prozac 29
pruritis ani 55, 57
pseudo winterata 202
psora 66, 73
psoriasis 73, 121, 124, 129, 192, 211
psychiatrists 86–7
psychic healing and removing of negative energy 228
psychic surgery 228
psychological problems 182
psychosis 157
psyllium husks 20, 60, 76, 134, 157, 166, 168, 170, 182, 190, 192, 195
ptyalin 25
puberty 117, 185
public transport 38–9, 72
pulmonary
  area 155, 162
  disturbances 59
  fibrosis 111
pulses 10, 75, 90, 138, 183
  dried 47
pumas 98
pumpkin seeds 61, 90, 122, 158, 191
  roasted 58
purification 105, 107, 134
  of emotions 131–2
purines 90
putrefaction 145, 169

Index

puy lentils 115
PVFS (post viral fatigue syndrome) 185
pyruvate 60

Q

qi 37
Qing Hao (aka artemesiae annuae) 181
quartz 111
quassia herb 59, 61, 64
quinine 62–3

R

radiation 18, 35, 36, 45, 47, 111
radical 110
radishes 20, 199
radioactive rays 15
radioactivity 110–11
radio waves 35
radium 110
rage 32
raisins 49, 157, 178
Rama 205
rash 30, 57, 58, 131, 201
rats, experiments on 11
raw foods 157
Raynaud's syndrome 193
Rebirth into Pure Land (Sachs) 28, 234
recuperation 180
recycling waste 3, 5
red clay *see under* clay
red clover 48, 161, 192, 200
red wine 91
re-energising 103
refined foods 19, 172
reflexologists 129
regeneration 105, 111, 134
Regenerative Nutrition 20, 36, 228–229
regret 84
rejection in childhood 72
rejuvenation 146, 169, 186, 205
　cleansing 207–8
relationship problems 85, 87, 131
relaxants 105
relaxation 156
　posture 80–1, **80**
religious ceremonies 82
renal circulation, impaired 200
replenishing our Earth 116–17
reproduction 120
　changes in 45
reptiles 37
resentment 84
resistance to illness 77
respiration problems 72, 81, 180, 185, 199
see also asthma; breathing problems
rest 132, 159, 185
restless leg syndrome 118
restlessness 53, 57, 69
reticulin 145
retirement 89
reverse osmosis 146, 152
revitalising 107, 128
Reynolds, Michael 43

Rheishi mushrooms 47
rheumatism 118, 124, 129, 193–4, 214
rheumatoid arthritis 17, 120
rhus tox-6 201
rice 5, 18, 49, 90, 156, 178, 183, 189, 190, 211
　brown 16, 20, 47, 75, 99, 115, 186, 190, 203, 214
　organic 169, 191
　short grain 192
　milk 12, 21, 75, 90, 157
Rice-dream 21, 75, 90, 157
Richards, Dr B. 233–234
rigidity 190
ringing in the ears 120, 188
rodents 97
Rome, ancient 41, 95
root crops 123
Rosa, Luciana Martinez de la 28–9, **29**
rose essential oil 207
rose geranium 67, 164, 166, 185
rosemary 151, 157, 158, 164, 166, 173, 176, 180, 185, 194
Roth, Gabrielle 49
rough sports 22
rounded shoulders 23
round or hookworm (*Necator americanus*) 54, **54**, 57, **57**, 59
routine 85
royal jelly 187
run down, being 18, 36, 180
Russia 35
rust prevention technology 5
rutin 202
rye 90, 178, 189
　flour 90

S

saccharine 31, 33
Sachs, Robert 28, 233–234
sacred stone 127
sadness 83, 156
Safeway 14
Safi 159, 196
sage 21, 48, 61, 151, 157, 160, 164, 166, 168, 174, 175, 179, 187, 200, 201
　tea 21, 187
St John's wort 26, 177, 188, 207, 208
salad 115, 184, 192
　leaves 115
salicin 99
saliva pH 104, 167, 212
salivary glands 25
salmonella 13–14, 15, 129, 194
S. enteritidis 14
salmon fishing 18
salt(s) 91, 153, 154, 156, 157, 159, 164, 172, 173, 183, 189, 193, 198, 203, 204, 205
　added 47
　Bio- 91
　in body 184
　natural 44
　sea 173

table 91, 120, 125, 158
scaly skin (psoriasis) 192
sandalwood 179
Sardinia 29
Sarin 38
sarsaparilla 171, 172, 192, 196, 205
sassafras 61, 154, 184, 193, 201
saturated fats 48, 153, 155, 156, 158, 159, 161, 164, 170, 204
saunas 74, 202
sausages 102
saw palmetto 158, 179, 191
scabies 66
scar-tissue (lesions) 188
schizophrenia 17, 115, 121
School of Natural Healing 229
Schroeder, Dr Henry A. 233–234
Schweitzer, Dr David 33–4, 171, 218
science 33
scleroderma 193, 194
sclerosis 104, 119, 194
sclerotic processes 6, 32, 97, 115, 124, 171, 188
scolex 55, **56**
Scovel Shinn, Florence 233
scratching of anus 53
screening for cancer 40, 45
seafoods 125, 155, 186, 196
season, changes of 195
sea-vegetables 161
seawater 84, 157, 158, 178, 192, 198
seaweed(s) 31, 46, 47, 75, 84, 88, 152, 158, 164, 171, 192, 193, 196, 199, 205
Sebastianeum 96
sebum 158
security 85
sedatives 87, 102, 105
seeds 20, 47, 90, 97–8, 115, 152, 158
　how to sprout 212
　sprouted 20, 115, 192
seepage, preventing 107
selenium 20, 112, 124–5, 127, 128, 158, 162, 178, 191, 204
　functions, benefits and tips 124–5
self-confidence 85
self-esteem, lack of 70
selfishness 83
semen 124
senna 166
sepiolite 111
septicaemia 29
seratonin 31, 32, 86
sesame 90, 166
　oil 210
　seeds 157, 158, 186
　black 192
setbacks 85
sex 35, 89
sexual
　desire 89
　dysfunction 85
　excesses 172, 179
　organs 183
　system 123

shallow breathing 71, 82
shampoo, clay 67
Sharan, Farida 218, 226
School of Natural Medicine 220
sheep 30
   infected brain of 9
   milk 21
sorrel 48
shellfish 75, 90
shepherd's purse 188
Shiitake mushrooms 47
shingles 194–5
Shivanada Yoga Centre 233
shock 18, 69, 180
Shoppers Guide to Organic Foods, The (Brown) 231
short leg syndrome 23
shoulders, rounded 23
Siberia 56
Siberian ginseng 159
SID (sudden infant death) syndrome 27
Silent Power (Wilde) 235
silica 123, 127, 155, 158, 160, 162, 164, 196, 202, 204, 205, 209
   functions, benefits and tips 123
silico-aluminous sedimentary rocks 109
silicon 122, 155
   dioxide 111, 112
Singapore 52
sinus(es) 34, 82, 171
   problems 195
6th Sense, The (Wilde) 235
skin 54, 57, 58, 74–6, 151, 163
   and asthma 74–6
   and insect bites/stings 180
   brushing 75, 151, 164, 167, 196, 205
   with wood and bristle brush 212–3, **213**
   clear 60
   conditions 124, 131
   damaged 95
   diseases 32, 66
   dry 53, 119, 171, 198
   elasticity 115, 123, 124, 203
   hardening of tissues 194
   improvement 204
   itching 57, 66, 95, 129, 171, 201
   poor texture 53
   problems 53, 55, 129, 195–6
   rash 30, 57, 58, 131, 201
   scaly (psoriasis) 192
   slack 196
   specialists 19
   swelling from mosquito bite 63
   tonic 151
   wrinkling 123
Skin-Lyte 226
skullcap 191 (sculutaria lateriflora) 191
sleep(ing) 103, 117, 122, 130, 205
   adjusting arrangements 23, 35, 36, 60
   problems 31, 53, 71, 73, 85, 172, 182

see also insomnia
slippery elm 48, 163, 165, 167, 168, 170, 177, 182, 194, 196
slowness 190
sluggishness 176
   congestion leading to 166
small intestine 10, 54, 55, 57, 58, 165, 168, 185
smectite series 109
smell, sense of 121
smoked salmon 90
smoking 75, 104, 121, 146, 172, 179, 186, 203, 204, 205
snails 54
snoring 53
soap operas 35
social life, poor 70
social order in upheaval 37
Society of Homoeopaths 222, 229
sodium 100, 119, 120, 123, 127, 137, 163, 169, 196, 201, 204
   potassium imbalance 103, 113
   pump 38, 113, 118
soft drinks *see under* drinks
soft tissues 73
Soil Association 47, 227, 229
soil(s)
   acidic 125
   infected/contaminated 56, 58
   lack of minerals in, and parasites 52–3
   lifeless/deficient 37, 114, 116
   rich 124
solar and lunar energy 130–1
solar plexus 81
Solgar 168
sound 80
   healing 81, 160, 230
soups and broths 47, 194
   garlic 211
   Miso 75, 91, 115, 195, 211
   organic vegetable 75
South America 15, 46, 56, 62, 63, 104, 135
South-East Asia 181
soya beans 75, 123, 186, 211
   paste 115
Spain 6, 111, 126
Spanish Flu 15
spasm 139
see also muscle(s): spasm
spastis colitis (IBS) 182
speech
   blurred 32
   problems 188
spelt 20, 47, 90, 178, 190
sperm motility 121
spices 91
spicy food 168, 182
spinach 168
spinal cord 188
   misalignment (or curved spine) 22, 23
spine 81
spirit 72, 78, 83

spiritual healing from Akashic records 229
spiritual sciences 33
spirulina 47, 48, 115, 152, 160, 169, 170, 179, 182, 183, 186, 190
spleen 83, 89, 91, 121, 161, 170, 171, 172, 178, 185, 192
Spock, Dr Benjamin 12
sports 22
   unable to participate in 70
spots on bottom 53
sprains 105, 196–7
   wrist **140**
spring 184
   onions 75, 195
sprouted seeds 20
sprouting your own seeds 161, 212
SSS 63
stainless steel pots 152
Stanchich, Lino 234
staphylococcus 129
star anise 193
starches 17, 53, 59, 120, 125, 189, 190
stars 132
Star West Botanicals 229
steam baths 74
Steiner, Rudolph 232
sterility 17
steroid(s) 18, 100, 120
   hormones 165
stiffness 97, 104, 190, 203
stimulants 19, 107, 135
stinging nettles 201
stings, bee/wasp 180–1
'stinking thinking' 83
stomach 136, 189
   acids 119, 153
   cramps 14
   hyperacid 125
   problems 22, 31, 95, 152
   ulcers 214
stones
   gallbladder 197
   kidney 198
stools 146, 166
see also faeces
storing clay 109
strawberries 3, 49, 158
strength 76, 82
   lack of 70
   mental 77
stress 18, 22, 26, 45, 66, 69, 73, 80, 85, 87, 100, 103, 122, 125, 131, 153, 155, 157, 158, 163, 172, 177, 179, 180, 182, 185, 188, 189, 192, 194, 203, 204
   geopathic 36
   reduction techniques 88, 146, 160
stretch marks 122
string-beans 3
Strong Women Stay Young (Nelson) 196, 204, 233
strontium hydroxide 33
Studio Daphne 228
Stumpf, Prof. 96

suffering, indifference to 69
suffocation, feeling of 153
sugar 10, 19, 21, 32, 33–4, 44, 53, 58, 59, 71, 85, 87, 91, 114, 115, 117, 120, 125, 151, 152, 153, 156, 157, 158, 159, 164, 168, 170, 172, 173, 178, 188, 189, 198, 199, 203, 204, 205
    substitutes *see* artificial sweeteners
    white 47
sugars, body 17, 18, 25
suicide/suicidal tendencies 29, 84, 85, 86, 87
sulphur 113
    dioxide 33
sulphuric acid 33
summer 154
sun 70, 103, 108, 192
    over-exposure to 204
    Salutations (*Surya Namaskara*) 78–9, **79**, 182
    screen 204
    solar and lunar energy 130–1
sunflower seeds 157
Sunny Seminars 128, 218
supermarkets 102, 114
surgery 18, 29, 40, 42, 52, 100, 179
    cosmetic 203
    psychic 228
Surinam 64
Surya Namaskara (Sun Salutations) 78–9, **79**
sushi 55
suspicion 73
Sustainable Community Development 220
Svoboda, Roberto E. 234
sweats 64, 146
sweet almond oil 154, 160, 169, 177, 194, 205, 210
sweets 75, 178, 180, 189, 200
sweet sumach 195
swelling 63, 105, 132, 157, 171, 174, 182, 196, 211
swimming 89, 167, 170, 182, 190, 196
    pools 202
swollen glands 211
sycosis 73
sympathy, rejection of 70
Symphytum 154
synovial fluid 146
syphilis 73

T

table salt 91, 120, 125, 158
tai-chi 89
Taiwan 15
Tamari 91
tannin 121
tansy 61
    flowers, infusion of 59
Tao 77
tapeworm (*cestodes*) 54, 55, 61

adult 56
tap water laden with pesticides or high levels of chlorine 18
tarragon 187
taste, sense of 121
taxis 38
T cells 25, 185
tea(s) 91, 121
    bags 21
    Bancha 171, 179
    Cassia 181
    dandelion 187
    elderflower 195
    eucalyptus 76
    fennel 161
    and peppermint 176
    ginger 211
    golden rod 175
    green 193
    hawthorn berry 153
    herbal 75, 173, 190
    horse chestnut 202
    Lapacho 20
    lemon 211
    peppermint 129, 169
    red clover 200
    sage 21, 187
    Yogi 52
teenagers 35, 174
teeth 22–6, 30, 112, 118, 120, 171
    abscesses 200
    amalgam fillings 129
    broken and rotten 119
    cavities 30
    charge 114
    crowns 174
    dental care, lack of 176
    dental carries 124
    extraction 24–5
    fillings 51, 58, 88, 129, 171
    flossing 175
    grinding 23, 53, 118
    gums 58, 120, 171
    and chewing 24–6
    hardening of 123
    mercury 24, 189
    metal fillings 51, 58, 88, 175, 189
    poisoning through 178, 189
    problem 177
    TMJ (Temporal Mandular disorder) 22–4
    wisdom teeth 24, 26
television *see* TV
temperature (body) 77
    high 59
    keep warm 164
    increase in 138
    reduction of 27
Tenko Seki ceramics 43–4, **44**
termite infestation 5
testicles 124
Thames Water 31
thighs 163–4, 166
thinking 83

Third World 1, 15
thirst 34
thoracic duct 184
thorax 211
thorium 110
'thought forms', photographing 33
threadworm (*Anguillulu intestinalis*) 57
threonine 114
throat 28, 34, 81, 167
    irritated 71
    sore 105, 174, 198
thrush 17, 54
    oral 18
thuja 155, 202
thunder storms 70
thyme 61, 67, 151, 153, 154, 167, 172, 174, 180, 198, 200
thymus 25, 185
thyroid 83, 130, 152, 155, 164, 169, 186, 190
    and depression 84
    imbalance 198–9
    dysfunction 29, 31, 121
    importance of 84
    therapy 32
thyroxin 84, 120, 198, 199
tides 130
Tigon Ltd 229
Tigon's Eden extract 181, 229
time 37
tinned food/drink *see* canned produce
tiredness 34, 96, 121, 188, 199
    chronic 53, 69
Tissue Cleansing through Bowel Management (Jensen) 166, 233
tissue(s) 78, 90, 111, 119, 121, 123, 124, 136, 146, 165, 197, 202
    dead 119
    soft 73
titanium 112
TMJ (Temporal Mandular disorder) 22–4
tobacco 157, 168
toes 166
tofu 90, 186
Tokyo 38
tolerance 76
tomatoes 122, 123, 177, 193
tongue, swollen 198
tonics 65, 91, 100, 119, 128, 156, 159, 179, 185, 187
tonsillitis 199–200
tonsils 185
    swollen 71
toothpaste 30, 31
Townsend Letter for Doctors and Patients, The 235–236
toxins/toxicity 3, 38–9, 46, 55, 58, 62, 71, 72, 74, 75, 77, 78, 86, 88, 105, 111, 113, 119, 123, 125, 129, 134, 138, 145, 151, 157, 158, 159, 161, 164, 171, 172, 173, 176, 177, 184, 188, 189, 192, 204, 210
    environmental 43

fumes 167
non-toxic products 226
toxoplasmosis 58
trace elements 33, 52, 112, 127, 192

Trace Elements and Man, The (Schroeder) 233–234
tracelytes 27, 46, 146, 156, 226
traffic
    calming schemes 38
    congestion 1, 38
tranquilliser 118, 122
Transformational Dance 49
Transformational Feng Shui 37
transmission of nerve impulses 88, 189
transverse colon 52
trauma 22, 73, 163, 177
travel, long-distance 172, 183
trembling limbs 190
tri-calcic phosphate 120
Tri-doshas 77
Trinity Herbs 229
tryptophan 114
tuberculosis (TB) 73
tumble dryers 39
tumours 42, 43, 119, 123, 200
    brain 32
    breast 40
turkey(s) 14
turmeric 48, 185, 196
turnips 20, 168, 178
TV 35–6, 89

U

Ubiera, Dr Ariel Antonio Perez 43
ulcers 73
    stomach 214
ultramarine 33
ultra-violet rays 111
Umebushi plums 48, 167
Una de Gato (cat's claw) 21, 48
under-active thyroid 84
under-developed countries 54
underground streams 36
unexpressed emotions 131
unhappiness 189
Unified Register of Herbal Practitioners (URHP) 222, 229
United Kingdom *see* Britain
United States 6, 11, 12, 14, 15, 27, 29, 33, 44, 46, 95, 99, 146, 183, 187, 215, 217, 218, 219, 221, 222, 225, 230
University of Illinois 45
unleaded petrol 38
unsaturated fatty acids 125
unwaxed fruits 34
uplifting words 76
urea 184, 198
urethra 191
uric acid 90, 114, 115, 123, 137, 166, 200, 201
urinary problems 200–1
urinate, frequent need to 191
urination 120

urine 136, 137, 146, 198
    retention 200
USDA 12
utensils, aluminium 122, 125
uterus
    cancer of 186
    problems with 130
uticaria (hives) 66, 201
uva ursi 183, 200

V

vaccinations 30, 63, 74
    childhood 27–8, 155
vaginal itching 17
vaginitis 57
vagus nerve 23, 72
valerian 177, 182
valine 114
Valnet, Dr Jean 234
value your life 89
varicose veins 116, 123, 201–2
vascular system 90
Vata 77
vCJD (variant Creutzfeldt-Jacob Disease) 9
Vega machine 23
    practitioners 24
    testing 26, 53, 153, 178, 199, 229
veins 118, 164
vegetable(s) 4, 10, 20, 41, 45, 47, 76, 99, 104, 117, 119, 123, 125, 133, 138, 152, 161, 168, 171, 179, 182, 184, 186, 189, 190, 195, 204
    glycerine 64, 177, 207
    green 156, 158, 183, 186
    juices 20, 90, 157
    leafy 186
    organic 90, 179
    raw 20, 56
    sea 191
    soups 173, 192
        organic 75
    steamed 20, 76, 192
vegetarians 124
veins 202
venous congestion 155
vermiform appendix of large intestine 52
vermifuge herbal 52, 61
verrucas 202–3
veterinary surgeons 97, 100
vetiver 179
Viagra 179
vinegars 19, 91, 172
    cider 201
violence 29, 32, 34
violet 48, 202
viruses 4, 15, 27, 28, 29, 124, 136, 145, 170, 173, 184–5, 194
    infection 38, 174, 180, 185
vision
    blurred 188
    problems with 32
    see also eyes

Vita Fons II ointment 154, 195, 197, 198, 230
vitality 82
    decrease in 70, 115, 178, 189
vitamin(s) 33, 47, 99, 100, 114, 120, 136, 186
    A 162, 172, 191, 192, 204
    emulsified 58
    B2 172, 178
    B3 160, 178
    B5 152, 155, 168
    B6 99, 121, 160, 191
    B12 56, 124, 152, 153, 155, 189, 191
    B17 (laetrile) 41–2, 97, 216
    B complex 63, 74, 121, 152, 155, 158, 160, 168, 170, 172, 178, 179, 181, 182, 188, 189, 191, 195, 202, 204, 205
    C 20, 48, 60, 118, 121, 152, 155, 162, 163, 167, 168, 172, 173, 175, 178, 180, 185, 195, 196, 202, 204, 205
    D 120, 165, 172, 187, 191, 202, 204
    E 162, 168, 172, 175, 178, 189, 191, 192, 196, 202, 204, 205, 208
    deficiency 163, 165
    multi-complex 157, 172
    supplements 60, 168, 185, 187
vital meningitis 27
Vithoulkas, George 234
vodka 64
Vogel, Dr 91
voice
    classes 197, 230
    disorders 81
    exercise for 81
vomiting 14, 25, 30, 42, 65, 120, 125, 194
vortex energiser 36
vulvitis 57

W

wahoo 65, 195, 197
Wala 170, 223
walk(ing)
    as exercise 89, 167, 185, 190, 196
    unable to go for long 71
walnut(s) 90, 155
    leaves 171
    tincture 173
    black 58, 59, 60, 61, 163, 172, 174, 176, 181, 196
    green 58, 59
wars 35
warts 73, 203
    on cows 12
waste products 78, 145–6, 192, 204, 209
water 1, 75, 103, 110, 119, 125, 130, 132, 170, 177, 184, 185, 190, 191, 193, 196 205
    authority 31

clay (drinking clay) 42, 52, 58, 76, 88, 99, 100, 105, 108, 119, 129, 134, 138, 145–6, 149, 153, 155, 156, 158, 160, 162, 163, 164, 166, 167, 169, 172, 173, 174, 175, 176, 177, 178, 180, 182, 183, 184, 185, 187, 188, 189, 190, 192, 193, 195, 196, 198, 199, 200, 201, 205
   how to prepare for drinking 144–7
   stage I 144
   stage II 144
   importance of good water 145–6
   clusters 33
   cold-water washing (Father Kneipp method) 27
   contaminated 49
   drinking 30, 36, 52, 54, 90, 151
   as element 108
   in Ayurvedic medicine 77 in feng shui 37
   enema 210
   filtered 31, 64, 152
   gargling 198
   ground-, poisoning of 47, 49
   health tips and general guidelines 90–1
   hydrotherapy 27
   improvement 230
   polluted 3, 145
   pure 48, 58, 90, 201
   retention 113, 119
   reverse osmosis 146, 152
   sea 84, 157, 158, 178, 190, 198
   inland 119, 174
   still 183
   supplies 117, 122
   tap water laden with pesticides or chlorine 18
   therapies 27, 96
   waxed fruits 34
Way of a Child, The (Harwood) 232
WDDTY (What Doctors Don't Tell You) 236
weakness 60, 70, 73, 76
weather
   extreme conditions 37
   reacting to any change in 70, 154
We Dye The Wheatfields Gold (Perry) 234
weeping 156
weight
   control 153, 159
   inability to gain 52, 53
   loss 32, 64
   obesity 189–90
   problems 189–90
Weight Loss for the Mind (Wilde) 235
Weleda (UK) Ltd 223, 230
well-being, emotional 132
wheat 19, 71, 115, 122, 125, 152, 168, 182, 200, 203, 214
   bread 90, 114, 190
   germ 114, 171

grass 48, 115, 157, 158, 177, 190, 195
   juice 161
   how to make 212
When Lightning Strikes a Hummingbird (Perry) 234
whole 90, 184
wheezing 154–6
whey powder 205
Whey to Go 168
whipworm (Trichuriasis) 56, **56**
white fish 20
white sounds 81
white willow 193
whitlow 133, 203
Wholistic Health and Life Extension Books 230
Wholistic Research Co. 230–231
Wigmore, Ann 234
wild animals 61
wild cherry 196
Wilde, Stuart 234–235
wild fox 61
wild pansy extract 195
wild willow bark 99, 205
Wimala, Bhante Y. 234
wind 37
wine 177
   organic 156
   red 90, 156, 159
wisdom teeth 24, 26
witch hazel 151, 154, 187
Wolf, Harry 231
women 17, 45, 58, 152, 153, 163, 199
   menopause 186–7
   postmenopausal 118
Women's International Pharmacy 187
wood
   dust 73, 167
   as element in feng shui 37, 184
wood betony 61
wooden spoon/spatula 142, 144, 172, 187
work 132
World Conference on Breast Cancer 45
World Health Organisation 62
World Research Information Centre 37, 223, 231
World Resources Institute 45
worms 51, 136, 169
wormseed levant (*Artemisia cina*) 59
wormwood 20, 59, 60, 61, 63, 172, 181, 200
worry 83, 172, 177, 182
wounds 138
   healing of 121
wrinkles and ageing 203–6
wrist(s)
   sprained **140**
   weak 71

X

X-ray(s) 25, 45, 99, 100, 154, 197
   diffraction 126

Y

Yakult 168
yams 90
   wild 186, 187
yarrow 158, 196, 201
yeast 18, 19, 34, 189
   brewer's 125
   free bread 90
   fungus/moulds 19, 34
yellow bile (choleric) 132
yellow dock root 192, 195
yellow fever 63
Yin and Yang 77, 116, 169
   exercise (Sun Salutations) 78–9
ylang-ylang 179
yoga 23, 78–2, 88, 89, 159, 160, 167, 182, 204, 231
   ancient philosophy on 82
   and asthma 78–82
   Kapalabathi 81–2
   Kundalini yoga: Breath of Fire 80, **80**
   relaxation posture 80–1
   Sun Salutations (*Surya Namaskara*) 78–9, **79**, 182
your voice 81
Yoga Cook Book, The (Shivanada Yoga Centre) 233
Yoga of Herbs (The): An Ayurvedic Guide to Herbal Medicine (Frawley and Lad) 232
yoghurt, live goat's 20, 42
Yogi tea 52
young girls 118
yoyo diets 103
Ypma, Rosemary 234–235

Z

Zapper 59
Zell-oxygen 20, 47, 76, 145, 155, 160, 169, 200, 203, 231
Zen Clinic 219, 231
zinc 20, 88, 112, 121–2, 124, 137, 152, 158, 160, 165, 167, 168, 174, 180, 186, 191, 202
   functions, benefits and tips 121–2